Robbie McEwen is a professional road cyclist and the winner of three Tour de France green jerseys. Born in Brisbane, he lives in Belgium with his wife and children and rides for RadioShack. This is his first book.

Edward Pickering is a cycling writer and deputy editor of *Cycle Sport Magazine*. He has reported extensively on the international road-cycling scene, including eight Tours de France. He is also the author of *The Complete Practical Encyclopedia of Cycling*.

ONE WAY ROAD

THE AUTOBIOGRAPHY OF
THREE TIME TOUR DE FRANCE GREEN JERSEY WINNER

ROBBIE MCEWEN

ROBBIE MCEWEN AND EDWARD PICKERING

EBURY
PRESS

An Ebury Press book
Published by Random House Australia Pty Ltd
Level 3, 100 Pacific Highway, North Sydney NSW 2060
www.randomhouse.com.au

First published by Ebury Press in 2011

Addresses for companies within the Random House Group can be found at
www.randomhouse.com.au/offices

National Library of Australia
Cataloguing-in-Publication Entry

McEwen, Robbie.
One way road: the autobiography of Robbie McEwen/Robbie McEwen &
Edward Pickering.

ISBN 978 1 86471 258 2 (pbk)

McEwen, Robbie.
Cyclists – Australia – Biography.
Bicycle racing.

Other authors/contributors:
Pickering, Edward.

796.62092

Cover design by Blue Cork
Front-cover image by Timm Kölln, from 'The Peloton'
Back-cover image by Graham Watson
Unless otherwise indicated, all internal professional-cycling images © Tim De Waele/
www.tdwsport.com

Internal design by Xou, Australia
Typeset in Bembo by Xou, Australia
Printed and bound by Griffin Press, an accredited ISO/NZS 14001:2004 Environmental
Management System printer

To friends who have lost their lives
in pursuit of their dreams

Contents

1   A Canterbury Tale   1

2   The Eight-Year-Old Pro   9

3   Darren   19

4   Charlie   29

5   You're Wrong, I'm Right   35

6   Pros and Cons   44

7   Sprinting (I)   52

8   A First for Everything   61

9   Angélique   70

10 Bank Withdrawal   76

11 Feeling Average   91

12 All Trained Up and Nowhere to Go   101

13 The Best Job in the World   110

14 It's Not that Easy Being Green   121

15 Sprinting (II)   135

16 How Much Is a Green Jersey Worth?   143

17 Why I Am the Way I Am   158

18 The Most Important Man in Cycling   166

19 Victor   176

20 Aussie Rules   186

21 Surfing the Peloton   196

22 Stuey   206

23 My Boys   215

24 My Best Victory (Salute) Ever   228

25 Mini-Me   244

26 Cadel   252

27 Katusha   261

28 Rehab   269

29 Tour Down Under   278

30 The Hardest Sport in the World   285

31 My Last Ever Win   299

32 One Way Road   310

Major Professional Results   317

Acknowledgements   323

Index   325

1

A Canterbury Tale

MY EYES OPEN. *I'm on the ground.*

The last thing I remember is sitting nice and easy mid-bunch in the peloton, surrounded on both sides by fast-moving riders. The speedo is reading somewhere north of 50 kilometres per hour. I'm not really aware of it, but my mind is subconsciously running through and making my body execute a checklist of things to do. My team are with me. I feel comfortable. I'm right where I should be – surfing the bunch, using the energy of the riders in front of me to pull me along, near the front but without the wind in my face. One more energy gel, Robbie. Drink. Sit tight. Wait.

I look over. Freddie's safe – Fred Rodriguez, my American leadout man, the rider who will launch me into a sprint I've been so intent on winning that I've recently started dreaming about it.

Twenty-one kilometres to go. I'm going to win. I'm the fastest man here. I have prepared. I am ready. Everything is going according to plan.

Then the road narrows. I hear shouts. Riders touch their brakes, then pull hard as they realise their combined width adds up to more than that of the road. I have to go pretty heavy on the anchors to make sure I don't run into the guys in front, just slowing in time not to hit the rider ahead of me.

And because I'm pulling so hard on the brakes, there's a lot of weight on the front wheel, and whoever is behind me – who isn't paying attention, or just doesn't slow in time – runs straight into me, disturbs the very delicate equilibrium that is keeping my bike on the ground and sends me arse over head, flipping right over the handlebars. The last thing I see is the ground rushing up to hit me, hard.

An intense sting of pain forces my whole body into a tight knot. I've bashed my knee. Shit. That wasn't in the plan.

I realise where I am. I've crashed. The stage win is disappearing down the road at over 50 kilometres per hour. I'm on the ground, I'm hurt and my bike is screwed. It's over.

I've been thinking about this stage – the first of the 2007 Tour de France – for a long time, which is unusual for me. I don't normally fixate on a particular stage. I want to win every single sprint, so prioritising one would be like taking the others less seriously, and I take sprinting *extremely* seriously. But oddly, ever since it was announced that the Tour would host a stage finish in Canterbury in its short visit to England, that name resonated with me.

I read somewhere that somebody had gone and scouted out the finish. I didn't see the pictures, but from the description it sounded right up my street. Slight downhill over a couple of k, into a dip, snake through a roundabout, then come around the left and uphill. More than a false flat. Then another bend to the left – the crux of the sprint – and false flat, almost flat for a couple of hundred metres, maybe 250, all the way to the line. My kind of sprint. You beauty.

From the moment I read that, I knew it was a finish for me. It had my name all over it. I had decided I was going to win in Canterbury.

You're not going to win.

The first thing I do is jump up and shout every swear word I know, which is standard in these situations. Then I conduct a quick audit of the situation. Knee: fucked. My wrist is really hurting, and my first thought is that it's broken. I can't move my hand – it is in agony.

But worse than the damage to my body is the damage to my morale. I've already given up. I'm absolutely filthy that I've crashed and hurt myself. No stage win for me today. Probably not this week, judging by the way my knee and wrist are feeling.

One of my teammates, the Belgian Johan Vansummeren, has stopped. 'Robbie, come on,' he says, urgently.

'Fuck it. It's over. Forget it,' I reply.

But he's already picked up my bike and has put the chain back on while I am hobbling around swearing. I don't want to, but I climb back on and we slowly start to ride. It feels like I've got broken glass in my knee every time I turn the pedals, and I can't stand up to push because I can't support the weight of my upper body on my wrist. The only real hope is to ride in to the finish, get some physio, recover, hope the damage isn't as bad as it feels and come back again another day. So much for Canterbury.

I'm riding behind Summie, and we've sped up, just enough to loosen up my injuries a bit. Summie, six foot five and just about the only rider in the peloton who's thinner than his bike, has got this rhythmic bobbing style when he rides. He's all elbows and knees, but, bloody hell, he's a diesel. You can put Summie on the front of the bunch and he'll still be there 100 kilometres later, bobbing away and making the riders behind him wish he'd slow down.

We're going a little faster again, and I'm in his wheel, thinking, *You are dreaming; it's you and me against a thundering bunch.* But Summie's bobbing along, going so hard that we are passing other people held up by the crash, and they can't keep up with us.

Of course, the news has gone through the race radio that I've crashed, and the Lampre and Quick Step teams, working for their sprinters, my rivals, the Italian Daniele Bennati and Tom Boonen from Belgium, have gone to the front of the bunch. They're drilling it. Bennati and Boonen know I'm faster than them, so they're taking this opportunity to put me out of the race.

This is why I'm in trouble: the bunch, swapping riders at the front, each taking a short turn to set a high pace before the next takes his place, will be covering the last 20 kilometres of this stage at an average of around 55 kilometres per hour. Summie's not going to be able to match that on his own. He could probably hold them for a few kilometres, maybe five, but he'll get no rest, while the riders on the front of the bunch will do a few hundred metres before dropping back and recovering. It's cold, hard logic versus futile hope. Cold, hard logic is the favourite at this point in time.

It must be making good television – two teams riding their arses off on the front of the bunch, and here's me with one teammate, looking extremely pissed off.

You're joking. We're never coming back. Don't worry about it, Summie. You can't do it on your own. I need more help.

We come around a corner, and suddenly the cavalry arrives. Dario Cioni, from Italy, and the Belgians Wim Vansevenant, Leif Hoste and Mario Aerts – four of my Predictor-Lotto team-mates – freewheeling along, looking back for me, have waited. You beauty.

From my team, only Freddie, Cadel Evans and Chris Horner, from the USA, have stayed in the bunch. Evans is a good chance for the top five in the overall race, so he needs to stay up there. Freddie has been told to stay in case I don't make it back so that he can do the sprint.

And as I join the train, I realise that the tiniest chance has flickered into life. Five riders against the bunch – improbable but not impossible. And like a switch being flicked in my head, the rage and anger I have been feeling since crashing is channelled into a determination so focused that you could shout in my ear and I wouldn't hear you. I am angry at the teams who are riding to put us out of it. Angry at being hurt. Angry at having crashed. Angry that my ambitions for this stage – my stage – are in ruins. And each time I turn the pedals, I gather the anger in my mind, moulding it into the willpower I need to get back to the bunch.

The boys are flying. They've been told about Lampre and Quick Step, and it's really pissed them off, making them ride harder. We're going at a constant 60 kilometres per hour, and, little by little, we're coming back towards the convoy of team cars that follows the peloton. Luckily, the commissaires haven't imposed a *barrage*, a mandatory gap between the back of the bunch and the convoy. If we can reach the convoy, we can use the slipstream of the cars to catapult ourselves right back into the race.

Seventy kilometres per hour now, and we are in the shelter of the cars. It's put me into trouble – while the boys are closer to the backs of the cars and benefiting from the slipstream, I am at the back of the line and getting less help. Fifteen kilometres to go. Twelve to go. Ten to go. Bit by bit, we're coming back.

At eight kilometres to go, we're close. With six or seven to go, we finally arrive at the back of the bunch. Hoste wants to take me right up to the front immediately, but I just need a quick breather. Trouble is, as well, the back of the bunch is a strung-out line of suffering riders. Guys are beginning to get popped – dropping off the back of the race – because the speed is so high and there's not much shelter; the main part of the bunch is still 250 metres up the road.

It takes us until four and a half kilometres to go to reach the main body of the peloton. Shelter at last, but I'm running out of time. Got to get my head together and get really focused.

I have to win, forget about the rest.

My teammates are shot, so it's up to me to get to the front. There's a corner coming up, and I fly up the right-hand side in the gutter. No brakes – no time to slow down – nobody had better get in my way. I pass 70 guys in one go. Back into the middle of the bunch, past another 20 blokes. All I am seeing now are gaps – opening for a fraction of a second as riders shift their positions momentarily, but enough time for me to squeeze into them and get my shoulders in front of the hole before it closes up. I'm not even seeing riders any more, just gaps. Always moving forwards.

Through a couple of roundabouts, diving through the corners

and swooping past half a dozen riders at a time, I've killed myself to get back towards the front of the bunch, but I still need to sprint. A kilometre to go, and I'm still in 25th wheel. There's a roundabout ahead, and riders are going left and right, while I seem to float straight over it, past another dozen, and at last I'm in position, about 12th back with 600 metres to go.

I'm pleased to be back where I should be. What a comeback.

Snap out of it. Focus. You can win this.

What was the finish? Uphill, kink round to the left, don't wait until you can see the finish line before sprinting or it will be too late. Hit the front at 200 to go. Ignore the rest.

But it's hard to ignore the rest when they are riding like jumpy racehorses. Robbie Hunter, a South African guy who won't pull off the win with a surprise long-range effort, hits out from about 500 metres to go on the uphill. Way too early, but it is a real leg-burner following him. Of course, everybody panics and a heap of guys jump after him.

As Hunter figures out he is about to blow, things kind of tail off again – nobody wants to take the lead, and the peloton concertinas. There are still 275 metres to go, and the only certain thing is that if anybody goes now, they won't be the winner.

But somebody will crack – they always do – and it's the Austrian Bernie Eisel who goes, right past me on the right-hand side. I think, *That's my free ride.* It's a bit of a manoeuvre to get his wheel, and I have to give the Spaniard Francisco Ventoso a little bump. I barely feel it. He's not a real contender for the stage; he's just in my way.

I have Eisel's wheel, on him for 50, 60 metres, and then I hit off him with absolutely everything that I have got just as we're coming up to that final bend.

Races are won and lost by the way riders take corners. As the others take the inside line and swing wide, I go the opposite way, starting wider and cutting back in ahead of them so I take the bend more tightly.

They all miss my wheel, plus I am going faster than them because I've jumped 30 metres before them, exactly where I'd planned.

And there it is – the gap. Clean air, no slipstream between my back wheel and those of my rivals. Hit them again – just 100 metres to go, and the rest can't live with me.

Holy shit, I'm about to win the stage.

I have a quick look back. I am winning. Have won. Sit up. Arms up. Disbelief.

What I did in Canterbury, what my team did, was impossible, a miracle. I felt like the fastest man in the world.

2

The Eight-Year-Old Pro

ACCORDING TO RECEIVED WISDOM, I have never been the fastest sprinter in the world. But, funnily enough, I have often been the guy who is able to beat the fastest sprinter in the world.

My career has spanned a golden age of sprinters. I became a professional racing cyclist in 1996, and in my first month I came up against the Uzbekistani sprinter Djamolidine Abdoujaparov – and beat him. In subsequent seasons, I raced against Mario Cipollini from Italy – beat him; Tom Steels from Belgium – beat him; Erik Zabel from Germany – beat him; and the Italian Alessandro Petacchi – beat him. Tom Boonen, Óscar Freire from Spain and Thor Hushovd from Norway – beat them. Manx Mark Cavendish? Let's just say I would have liked to have had the chance to race against him more before busting my knee up in a crash in the Tour of Belgium in 2009, but when I won the stage in Putte at the Eneco Tour in 2007, he was back in fourth, so I've beaten him as well. That said, I've lost count of how many times I've been beaten into second place by all these guys during my career.

I love winning. I'm a competitive little bugger and have been so ever since I can remember. On school sports day in grade one, Robert McEwen, aged five, turned up with that tight feeling in his stomach, sweaty hands and slightly queasy from the adrenalin, taking it *extremely* seriously. Thirty-four years later, I've learned to manage it better and use it positively, but I still get a little twitchy when I'm in a race, or playing pool, or cards, or anything I want to win. I can't remember exactly where I came in the Tour of Taiwan, which I rode as an amateur, but I do remember winning a peanut-eating competition using chopsticks after one of the stages.

There's not much point in being super-competitive and sucking at sport, however, and as a child I quickly worked out what my strengths and weaknesses were. I was sporty at school, but not in the traditional crickety way. Anything involving hand–eye coordination wasn't my thing – I wore glasses from first grade, and I could hardly see the blackboard, let alone fast-moving balls. I once faced a cricket ball from my brother and it cracked me right in the ear – I hadn't even seen it coming. You only have to be hit in the face once or twice by cricket balls before deciding that you don't really want your features to be unnecessarily and painfully rearranged any more.

But I was energetic, fast and strong, and running and swimming suited me well. I was always small for my age, and this prevented me from being the fastest runner in my grade, but I was good; I was a trier, and I never gave up. In fact, I've always believed that being forced to try to keep up with stronger, more mature individuals, all the way up to my early 20s, has made me a lot better at cycling.

I grew up in the suburbs on the south side of Brisbane. The

area wasn't so developed back then, and it was rural enough that I can remember looking out from my first house in Kingston in the morning and seeing kangaroos licking the dew off the grass. We moved a couple of times, but most of my childhood was spent in Daisy Hill, in the house my parents still live in now. I'll tell you some important things about my family later on, but all you need to know now is that I had a very happy, energetic and outdoor-focused childhood.

My dad was an army brat – his dad was in the RAF and was stationed in Malaysia and Aden before they moved to Watford in England. My mum grew up in Bushey, just nearby, and my parents met at high school in Watford, getting married and moving to Australia in 1968, wanting a new life. It's a good job my mum has a strong character, because within eight years she was outnumbered four to one by the McEwen males. My older brother, Ross, was born in 1970, I was born two years later and my younger brother, Cameron, arrived in 1976.

Maybe that's what makes me so competitive: middle-sibling syndrome. I spent my entire childhood trying to keep up with and preferably beat Ross at whatever we were doing. Plus, I had to keep an eye on what Cameron was doing – I was defending and attacking at the same time, on two fronts. And when we weren't fighting each other, we were ganging up on Mum. One of our favourite playing spots was a natural pond near the house, perfect for swimming and splashing around. We'd get home in the evening muddy and stinking like wet dogs, ready for dinner. Sorry, Mum.

My brothers and I fought, argued and did all the things that brothers do, but we were tight. Cameron's speciality was splitting his head open. Riding his first bike, with training wheels, he tripped over the lip of the garage floor, head falling straight onto the reflector of his bike, opening it right up. He bled like a stuck pig.

Another time, probably when I was about 12 years old and he eight, we were home alone and he tried to nick the batteries out of my remote-controlled car. He ran, naturally I chased, and instead of looking where he was going he was looking back at me to assess the situation. Boom! Right into a wall, head bleeding everywhere. It looked like I'd murdered him.

Ross and I were closer in age and initially closer in our interests. And, since I was eight onwards, that meant BMX.

Virtually everything I have achieved as a cyclist is built on the foundations of BMX. It's not as simple as saying that BMX and road cycling are the same thing. I might be good at turning pedals around faster than the next man, but that's not the important thing. Essentially, from the age of eight, I have been training, thinking and acting like a professional athlete.

It helped that we lived about a minute's walk from our school. Back home in the evening and we were straight off on our BMXs. Half the time, we went back onto the school grounds, where we built jumps. We had a 250-metre run-up, built up as much speed as possible, up the rocket jump, and back to do it again. We'd probably do that 60 times a day. That kind of training regime would kill a grown man, but we were just kids; we were young and carefree.

We built tracks everywhere in the bushland around our house, doing these crazy intervals without even realising it. We sprinted everywhere and started getting strong. Strong enough to enter races.

My first big race was the state championships in Bundaberg,

a 450-kilometre drive from home. I was eight and a half, and I'd only just started, but somehow I managed to persuade my parents to let us go. We went as a family for a week, making a trip of it.

I took it very seriously. There were five or six heats, and it was all calculated on points, with the best 16 going through to the semi-finals and the top eight riding in the final. It wasn't the first across the line in the final who would win, either; it was still judged on points, accumulated through the whole day.

I can't remember where I ran in the final, but at the end I was equal on points with a kid called Shane West, who was far and away the best rider in the state. I was just some kid, while Shane had factory sponsorship and a bike that was probably half the weight of mine. Since we were equal on points, there would be a sudden death run-off, mano-a-mano, to find the best eight-year-old BMX racer in Queensland.

I was inexperienced, but right from the start I was a competition beast. Put me in a race and I'll ride right through you to win it. And I'd learned very early about handling the nerves and pressure. Somehow, I've always been good at channelling my nerves and converting them into forward motion.

So we sat on the start line, me and Shane, and I readied myself for the biggest race of my life so far. I tensed, waiting for the starter's signal, holding all my energy in, ready to explode into the race. The start gate dropped, and even before my conscious brain had absorbed the information my legs were punching the pedals, arms wrenching the BMX from side to side to generate more power. First into the first corner, still focused, fast in, good line through, and accelerating out.

But my inexperience showed through one of the corners. The

margins are tight in BMX races, which are over in less than a minute, closer to 30 seconds. All it took was a little slide and Shane was past me. Beaten.

But second in the Queensland state championships at my first go? I was pretty good at this. I'd stumbled into a sport I was naturally suited to. I remember thinking, *This is what I'm meant to do. I want to do this for the rest of my life.*

I was hungry to race again and move up to the national titles. I got some sponsorship, read magazines about the American pros and rode my BMX every day – sprint to the jump, do the jump, sprint back, sprint to the jump, jump, and repeat 50 or 100 times. No wonder I was fast improving.

Then I went to the next year's state titles, was leading through the last race and crashed out, just as I was about to win.

I didn't particularly enjoy losing those state titles – I'd stuffed up my first two – but I was like an empty hard drive; I was downloading information by the megabyte: tactics, training, skills, even psychology. I'd blown that second state title by enjoying the win before it had happened. All I had to do was stay on my bike and I'd win, but instead I went for the glory. I wouldn't make that mistake again.

I wasn't a particularly fantastic starter, but I was very fast down the straight to the first turn. I also had good endurance, so I'd still push out a full sprint on the last straight. I almost never blew up in a race – I had trained myself to be able to sprint full bore for 30 to 35 seconds. Try it some time – it's not an easy thing to do.

But, just as importantly, I had good technique. I was good over the jumps, good at throwing my bike around and maintaining total control. I had good coordination on the bike and I was smart tactically – I intuitively knew which lines to take, which side of a jump to take so that I'd land in the best place to go hard into the next bend, how everything fitted together, how to pick my moment to pass somebody. I think I had to develop all these skills fast because I was small compared to some of the other kids.

There were some real gorillas winning BMX races during my early teens. When I was 15, a guy called Adam was winning races. He had muscles on his muscles. No shit, he looked like the German pro cyclist André Greipel. He was way stronger than me, but unchannelled, too. He'd go a million miles an hour to the first jump, then hit it wrong and be sideways in the air. I'd be ahead of him even before he hit the ground.

A lot of guys who mature really early are killing everybody for years, so riders like me have to work out how to beat them using smart tactics. By developing my tactics and skills, I became their equal, then when I matured and caught up physically I went ahead of them. They'd been relying on brute strength for so long that they didn't have anything to fall back on.

My brothers and I raced BMX all the way through school, and I was still thinking I could be a professional BMX rider. I used to come back after Easter holidays all through primary school with trophies from the national championships, which were a pretty quality show and tell.

I wouldn't have got very far in BMX without the support of my parents, however. The first national championships I did were on the Gold Coast, 45 minutes' drive from our house, but the next year they were in Perth, 4000 kilometres away. A week of hotels plus flights is a big investment for a working family, so my dad did a deal – he'd take us, but we'd do it properly. We were going to prepare for them.

It wasn't an East Germany-style sports school or anything, but we started training. We were up at six to go for a four-kilometre run – this was when I was 11 or 12 – then sprints on the road on the BMXs. Dad would stand by the house with a stopwatch; we'd start 200 metres away and do half a dozen full-on sprints. We did push-ups, upper-body work and step-ups onto a stack of bricks while holding a pair of two-litre cordial bottles full of water – three sets of two minutes at a time. I never realised how much serious training we were actually doing – I loved it.

I also started working when I was 12, doing the worst job I've ever had, folding and delivering pamphlets around the neighbourhood for 30 bucks a week. That enabled me to save up for some dumb-bells and weights, which I used to train even harder.

And I noticed two things happening. First, I was starting to get much more pronounced muscle development in my upper body. Second, we were running out of shelf space for the trophies I was winning.

Ross didn't persevere at BMX but Cameron had managed to stop splitting his head open for long enough to start racing himself. The two of us more or less took it in turns to do well at the national championships. Cameron actually started even younger than I did – I remember watching his first race when I was about nine years old and he was only five. I made the final in 1984 and 1986, and Cameron made the final in 1985 and 1987. Then, in 1988, I won my first national championships, and the following year the world championships were held in Brisbane at Chandler Velodrome – my first and only worlds as a BMX rider, aged 16. I made the final, but I didn't get a good run and ended up sixth. I was still suffering from my size – the guy who won was a huge Dutch bloke with a moustache.

Sixth in the world championships was the pinnacle of my BMX career. After that competition, I felt like I'd done what I'd come to do. I could have persevered and done better, maybe even won the worlds, but I was about to finish school and felt that I needed a break. I'd been training and racing since the age of eight, and I decided to have an ordinary life for a bit, before it was too late. I'd also worked the whole way through – delivering pamphlets, then cooking burgers and fries at Hungry Jack's restaurant, and finally pumping gas at a service station.

I got a driving licence, bought my first car with some of my savings, and discovered alcohol, girls and parties. I started hitting the beach and going surfing, and, in order to look more impressive on the beach, I started working out quite seriously with the weights at a local gym. I wasn't training with the same focus I had applied to BMXing, but I really started putting on muscle. At 17, my system was a raging torrent of testosterone, and I was developing quickly.

I got so lean and was getting such good muscle definition that my gym buddies somehow managed to persuade me to take part in a bodybuilding contest, which was short of junior entries. I wasn't big, but I had muscly legs and good abs, and at least you could see which muscle was which.

If I'm going to do something, I'll do it properly, so I did the whole fake tan and oil thing. I kind of regret the skimpy purple swimmers I wore, and my old school mates rightly rip the piss out of me about the whole thing to this day. Some guy who looked like the Incredible Hulk won, but I was second. Second!

However, it was my first and last foray into the world of competitive bodybuilding, and I stopped going to the gym soon after, because it was cutting into my beach time in summer. I was looking for something else.

In December 1989, my mate Darren Smith, a former BMXer, invited me over to Chandler Velodrome to see the track racing. Darren had started track cycling when he was 15, and he reckoned I should give it a go.

3

Darren

DARREN SMITH WAS ONE of the most outrageously talented bike riders I've ever met. If you had to categorise Darren as a rider, you'd have to damn him with faint praise and describe him as an all-rounder, but only insofar as he was bloody good at absolutely everything. He was just like the Italian Classics specialist Paolo Bettini – he had big, muscular legs but he was very compact in the upper body. Darren was strong, snappy and very nippy in the sprint, but he could also time-trial and climb. I'm a rider of specific skills and talents, to whom hard work and well-directed focus has brought a bit of success. Darren, on the other hand, was pure gold.

The two of us were good, well-brought-up, friendly young blokes, but what we also had in common was that we both had sufficient inner bastard in us to win races. He was a few years ahead of me, but I recognised in him the rider I wanted to become: successful and talented. Everybody liked Darren – they saw him as their talented little brother – and he didn't have a single enemy.

But never mind how good he was. The first thing you have to know about Darren Smith was that he was my best mate.

Darren raced with the Surfers Paradise Cycling Club. I hadn't ridden a bike in six months when I went to see him at a Wednesday-night session at Chandler Velodrome. He suggested I give it a go, and I went and did a few laps on a borrowed bike that was several sizes too big.

That was fun, I thought. *See ya next week.*

I turned up the following Wednesday, borrowing a bike that fitted me a bit better, wearing running shoes and shorts, and with my feet strapped into the pedals. I came out and blasted everybody in the first sprint after five laps of a 150-lap/30-sprint points race. *That went well*, I thought, before they ripped my legs off, chewed them up and spat me and my legs out the back – race over.

I decided I liked the feeling of blasting people in sprints more than I disliked the feeling of having my legs ripped off. Just as I'd caught up with and overtaken kids who were twice my size and strength in BMX, I suspected that once I'd got a bit fitter and used to cycling for longer periods I'd be able to outsprint people right through a race, rather than just in the first couple of laps. In a BMX race, I'd make one all-out effort for 30 seconds or so, and the race would be over. In a track race, with multiple sprints, I'd be racing hard for 15 minutes or longer, and it took me a little while to get used to that. Road races last even longer – from one hour all the way up to five or six.

I had a friend at high school, David Thomson, who had got into cycling about the same time as me, and he'd already got all the kit. He persuaded me to join him in an event that was going to take place up and down the brand-new Logan Motorway before it was opened to cars. I borrowed Dave's old bike, a ten-speed Repco Traveller with old-fashioned clips and straps on the pedals, and showed up in my shorts and T-shirt.

It was just a fun ride, but, as with any fun ride, many people, including me, were taking it quite seriously. It started off leisurely enough, but not many serious riders can resist the opportunity to start showing off in front of their mates, and they started swapping off on the front and increasing the pace. No worries; it was nothing I couldn't handle. Faster and faster, until Dave got popped out the back. I was still chugging along with the front guys of this little peloton that had formed, up to the first turnaround, and they started looking at me a bit funny. Put yourself in their shoes – they're busy trying to impress all their non-cycling friends with how fast they can ride, while some idiot with hairy legs and board shorts is sitting on their wheels and making them look slow.

So they did what any right-thinking cyclist would have done: attacked the shit out of me and disappeared up the road. But it had taken them most of the race to do so. I was pretty pleased the real cyclists had to try hard before they could drop me.

Next stop: the bike shop, so I could buy myself a bike and start training. I invested eight or nine hundred dollars in a second-hand bike and went out to do a 40-kilometre road ride. These days, a 40-kilometre ride is what I do on a rest day, but back then it was like asking a 100-metre sprinter to run a marathon. I didn't think to take any food, ran out of energy halfway round, crawled home completely wasted, dragged myself into the kitchen and ate a whole box of cereal. And all I could think of was when I could do it again.

I had become a cyclist.

I still lived in Brisbane, but I decided to join Darren's club in Surfers Paradise, 45 minutes away. I'd drive over to the coast in my old Datsun station wagon and train with him and a few other blokes who lived locally. They were my mates – Darren, Wayne, Sebastian, Stuart and Brett – but they were also my teachers, especially Darren. I learned how to ride from them – how to pedal, how to sit on the bike, how to sit close behind the rider in front to save energy and when to expend that energy, and a thousand basic things that are now so ingrained that I don't even have to think about them.

I was also instantly addicted to the lifestyle – meeting with a bunch of friends, going for a spin, stopping for coffee and a cake, hitting the beach for the afternoon, then going to a couple of bars in the evening. Cycling, you see, is more a lifestyle than any other sport I know. People play cricket or soccer and usually describe it as a hobby – only the pros describe themselves as 'cricketers' or 'footballers'. A cyclist, no matter if he or she is at the top of the sport or an occasional weekend rider, is a 'cyclist'. It's part of the identity of virtually everybody who does it.

I settled into the routine. I was still at school during the week, but on Friday afternoons I'd chuck my bike in the back of the car along with enough clothes for the weekend and stay at Darren's house. I'd go for a quick spin with whoever was free on Friday, then we'd all head out to drink two-dollar jugs of beer at one of the bars before hitting a nightclub, trying to meet girls and coming back at two in the morning.

We'd get up at six, feeling a little dusty, and head over to the sewerage works where the club ran training handicap races on the private road that led to the main plant. Instead of all starting in a bunch, small groups, in ascending order of fitness and ability, set off at intervals. The Saturday-morning shitfarm races were legendary. There was a long false flat (a road that looks flat but actually slopes slightly) down to the works, then we went around the witch's hat and a couple of kilometres back up the other side. It was at these races that I learned the first and most important lesson of cycling – that everyone suffers. The handicaps were unglamorous, and they were bloody hard. They'd set off the veterans first and give them a 15- or 18-minute head start. They'd ride at around 32 kilometres per hour, which meant that we were killing ourselves to catch them – 44 kilometres per hour up the false flat, then 54 down the other side, just to catch them in time for a sprint.

Then we'd hit the beach, and maybe some more bars that evening. When things got more serious, we'd do the Saturday-morning handicap at the shitfarm, grab something to eat, then ride 50 kilometres to Murwillumbah, do another 60-kilometre race, then ride 50 more kilometres back home. On some days, we were riding over 200 kilometres.

I was seeing constant improvement, and I found that the routine suited my character just fine. I love box-checking: setting a goal, working out what to do to reach it, doing it, achieving the goal, then using that as the starting point for my next goal. My first aim was just to finish a race. Then to win a race. Then to finish a longer race. And to win a longer race. The progression pleased me – I'd gone from not being able to ride even 40 kilometres to being able to win 70-kilometre races.

Our coach was Bob Panter, and he and Darren taught me everything. Bob was eccentric, tireless and far too generous with his time – as all true coaches are – and he has been one of the biggest influences on my entire career.

Bob had been to Belgium as a young man and done the racing, and now he wore the XXL T-shirt to prove it. He'd been a pretty tidy rider, and he loved Belgium and Flemish racing – it's a gritty, tough man's scene where elbows are sharp and knowledge is passed down through generations of racers.

Bob was the source of knowledge, delivered in concentrated, pithy instructions. Don't stand if you can sit. Don't sit if you can lie. Eat before you're hungry. Drink before you're thirsty. It's not the energy you use but the energy you save that wins you races. That kind of thing. Bob was great at simplifying things, which is often the best thing to do in cycling.

Bob was generous with his knowledge. He was a go-any-where, do-anything-for-anybody kind of person, and it really helped me when I was finding my feet as a cyclist.

He saw me at my best and my worst, and supported me unconditionally through both. He once drove me and Darren to a national series race at Glenn Innes in New South Wales, 600 kilometres from the Gold Coast, on a freezing cold, soaking winter's day. In the race, Darren had a mechanical, I got dropped, and Bob drove around the circuit behind me, helping me, encouraging me and giving me advice. And not once did he tell me to get in the car, because he knew that just getting to the finish of a hard race was a learning experience for a young rider. He was a great coach, not in the sense of setting me training targets – hit this number, ride for that length of time at such-and-such a heart rate – but for general advice and mentoring. I've encountered a lot of coaches who are real experts on sports science but who are not real experts in everyday life or common sense like Bob is.

I didn't win a lot at the beginning, although I was always good at criteriums – short races around tight circuits that involved lots of fast cornering, fast accelerations, fighting for position and sprint finishes. They were basically longer versions of BMX races. When I started racing, it was to try to win the club handicap, then the local crits, then the regionals. I never hung around long enough to dominate any one category – my improvement was constant and pretty fast. I went from D-grade to C-grade to B-grade, and at the same time increasing my distance limits by ten kilometres a time, still being there at the end after 70, then 80, then 90 kilometres. That's what cycling is all about. At first, the extra distance kills you, but then it makes you stronger. I made steps up from one level to the next all the way from when I started cycling right through to the mid-2000s, when I was at my peak. Even now, as I approach the end of my career, I'm still learning.

My first big success was when I got the chance to ride the eight-day Golden West Tour in Queensland in 1991, where Darren helped me win a stage. I'd been given special dispensation to ride with the A-grade riders, even though I wasn't technically at that level yet.

The bunch hared around the final corner with me very near the front, and with 400 metres to go – a long way for a sprint – all the blood rushed to my head and I jumped off the front. Darren saw me go, and, instead of getting involved in the sprint himself, he sat in the wheel of another fast sprinter, riding shotgun on him. It's a very common tactic in cycling. Two against one should always win, given riders of similar strength. One rider from the pair attacks, and then the individual rider has a choice – either chase the attacker down and take the attacker's teammate to the finish with him, or don't chase the attacker, in which case the attacker wins. That's the situation Darren and I were in.

In a way, he sacrificed his own chance of winning so that I could do so, even though at that point he was considerably better than me, but that's why we were strong as a team. Although it's normal in cycling to give teammates wins where possible, it was still the equivalent of passing the rugby ball to a teammate right near the try line, and I appreciated it.

That was my first road stage win in a high-standard Tour, and the only person more pleased about it than me was Darren. He'd already won plenty of races, and he was as happy to see his mate win as he would have been if he'd won himself.

Not long afterwards, Darren joined the national cycling program at the Australian Institute of Sport (AIS). In 1992, he went to Europe to race, coming second to the Netherlands' Erik Dekker in the Bicicleta Vizcaya Bira in Spain and gaining selection for the Australian team at the Barcelona Olympics. He was already one of the best young amateurs in the world.

I'd got a scholarship to the Queensland Academy of Sport (QAS) in 1991, where Peter Day was my coach. Peter's knowledge complemented what I'd learned from Bob Panter – while Bob had taught me about life and cycling, Peter taught me about myself and my body. I learned to train and peak, and started working more scientifically. I was winning sprints left, right and centre, and in 1992 an opportunity came up to do a camp in Adelaide with the national track program. Peter told them I was very fast but pretty raw – remember, I'd been cycling for fewer than three years, while my peers had twice as much experience in the sport. But why not? Where Darren had led, I was going to follow.

And, three days after I arrived in Adelaide, the comfortable, straightforward, successful, happy life that I'd been leading was violently upended.

Darren was dead.

Seeing those three words on the page, almost 20 years after it happened, still makes me feel rage in a way I've rarely experienced. It's a horrible, vertiginous anger that is all the more wretched for the fact that nothing I can do or say will ever make it better. I don't do 'can't' – I'm a person who, in adversity, rolls up his sleeves and organises his way out. But, as I stood in an office at the AIS and the news was broken to me, my companions were an empty, lonely sadness and frustrated confusion. I wanted to understand, to know why, but I never would.

Darren had been cycling back to the Gold Coast from his girlfriend's place in Brisbane, along the main highway – a road I'd often cycled myself. It was a fast road that people might wrongly describe as dangerous, because to describe it that way is to mitigate responsibility. As with every 'dangerous' road I've ever encountered, it's the way people drive along it that makes it dangerous.

He was hit by a small truck and killed instantly. There was an inquiry; the guy lost his licence for a period of time and paid a fine.

I rode along that highway three times a week, while Darren did so only very rarely. I'll never stop feeling guilty about that.

When Darren was killed, a whole future was stolen. He was going to be a Classics winner; I am absolutely certain about that. He should have been sitting here, writing a book about his own career, about the stage wins at the Tour de France, about the world-championship gold medal sitting in his drawer. He'd have stopped Paolo Bettini winning Classics, he was that good.

But that doesn't matter. I'd lost my mate, and Darren's parents had lost a son.

4

Charlie

IT'S SAFE TO SAY THAT CHARLIE WALSH and I weren't exactly on the same wavelength.

Charlie ran the track program at the AIS when I first joined, and he pissed me off almost from the beginning. In fact, no, he didn't piss me off; he was bloody lucky I didn't hit him. At the news of Darren's death, I immediately started sorting out my trip home from Adelaide. I wanted to go to the funeral, to see Darren's family.

Charlie took me aside and advised me not to go. He was of the opinion that it would destabilise my training. I told him to forget it. I meant it; if I wasn't coming back as a result, then so be it.

He wasn't a bad guy, but he wasn't big on the human side of things. With help from the German coach Heiko Salzwedel, as head coach Charlie had developed the Australian track team into a world-beating force. But he was the real tough-nut killer coach, like you see in the movies. His method was like the old East German way – throw a load of eggs against the wall and keep the ones that don't break. With the team pursuiters, he'd push and push and push, until there were six left – four riders and two reserves. Then he'd push some more, see who were the four strongest, and that was his team.

Charlie's thing was 'character'. You either had it or you didn't. And if you didn't, you wouldn't last long with him. Great. I'm all about showing character, but if it means not recognising when riders are tired, or on an off-day, or over-trained, then it stops being effective coaching and just starts being a bad way to deal with people, in my opinion.

He was big on numbers and measuring physical output – something I recognise to be an important aspect of cycling but see as only one piece of a very complicated jigsaw puzzle. Numbers and measurements, such as VO_2 max (aerobic capacity), were everything to Charlie. If you were a very good bike rider but only had a VO_2 max of 65, you'd be packing your bags.

He was also very big on diet, or, more specifically, on his riders losing as much weight as possible. I remember him coming up to me one day and saying, 'I saw you this morning at the buffet, like a little piggy.' I'd had some avocado, the morning of a 200-kilometre training ride.

At the AIS, we lived in a fantastic beachfront place just out of Adelaide, in Henley Beach. The cricketers lived there as well. Charlie had us up doing roller sessions – putting our bikes on stationary indoor trainers, like a runner's treadmill – at 6 am. Ten minutes at 100 revs per minute, ten minutes at 120 and ten minutes at 140. A quick shower, breakfast, then we were ready to go out training on the road. We'd do strength intervals up the 10-kilometre-long Norton Summit, get back after midday and the bloody cricketers would just be getting up, with bed hair, for a leisurely breakfast. They didn't have to watch what they ate, but Charlie was constantly prodding at us with the skinfold callipers to check we weren't getting fat.

There was a simmering psychological war between the riders and coaching staff. While they demanded discipline and mental fortitude, we were busy hatching plans to go out partying without them finding out about it. One Friday night, we hit Adelaide, and it was raining cats and dogs – we were convinced there would be no training the next day. Midnight, and it was still pissing down, so we decided to stay for another one. One o'clock. Yep, bring us another jug of beer, barman. Three o'clock, still bucketing down – bring it on! Best night in the world! We crashed into the house some time after four, laughing our skinny backsides off that there'd be no training that morning.

Six-thirty, and the day dawned with a beautiful blue sky. And we guessed that the coaches suspected something when they announced a 180-kilometre ride. That'll cure a hangover.

I was getting strong, though. At a race at the Adelaide track one evening, I beat Stuart O'Grady and Brett Aitken in a scratch race – a track event in which the first rider across the line at the end wins – and that was just not done. Stuey and Brett were the two kings of the track squad – Charlie's angels, local Adelaide boys as well as Olympic and world-championship medallists. Nobody turned up on their turf and beat them, but I did. It caused the tiniest bit of friction. They were both incredibly strong, but I just had the edge on them in terms of pure speed. I started coming out and beating them in the sprints on our road rides, too. That said, at everything else – the long rides and strength efforts up hills – they killed me. And a week or two after I'd beaten Stuey and Brett, Stuey reminded all of us of the pecking order by pulverising us in the 80-kilometre points race at the track. The points race suited Stuey right down to the ground – there's a sprint every five laps, and the winner is the rider with the most accumulated points. Stuey's fitness and experience were too much for me at that point.

But while I was getting strong, I was also getting tired. Charlie was driving us hard, and I just hadn't built up the years of kilometres and training to make my body resilient enough to stand up to the tough schedule. Another coach would have allowed me to back off, recuperate, then hit the training hard again once my body had adapted. Not Charlie – he could sense that I wasn't showing the necessary character, and if he just cranked it up a little more he'd know whether or not I was going to become one more broken egg, sitting at the bottom of the wall.

We went to Mexico for an altitude-training camp in January 1992, and that is where it started to go a bit pear-shaped for me. I didn't deal too well with the altitude to start with, and the training went a bit too hard a bit too soon for me. I just about came through it and started going really well. The coaches were starting to talk about taking me to Europe as part of the squad, to do all the road racing before going for medals on the track.

But the very next thing on the schedule was a ridiculous 280-kilometre ride.

Who on earth does a 280-kilometre road ride in January? That's more than I ever do now, as a fully fledged road professional. But for a track racer, with only a few years of cycling under his belt, it was way over the top. If you're going to take 20, 21, 22-year-old cyclists out for several hard days in a row, culminating in a 280-kilometre ride, you're going to blow their doors off.

My doors were duly blown off coming to the last part of the ride, and after the others dropped me I just slowly forced myself to ride back to the hotel, on my own.

The road curved around to the left ahead of me, with a little offshoot road straight ahead. As I took the bend, I went past the turning, and suddenly I was lying in the grass by the side of the road – I'd been hit by a bloody bus, probably going around 90 kilometres per hour. He had just missed hitting me with the front of the bus, which would have killed me, no doubt, and had smashed into me with the side of it instead. I'd flown up into the air and landed on my left side.

My left leg has actually never been the same since – I've done my whole pro career with a left leg that's not quite as strong, or as big, or as coordinated as the right. I did some kind of damage to the nerves, muscles and fascia, which I was never able to sort out.

Charlie didn't seem to give a shit, however. Next day, I had to be out on the bike. We had no medical check-ups, although Charlie did make the concession that I could take it a bit easier and only ride 60 kilometres. I was off colour for the rest of the camp, unsurprisingly. It broke me, and at the end Charlie summoned me for an assessment of my situation. I still felt positive about doing the road season in Europe – it would have been tough, but I thought I'd be able to deal with the challenge. Charlie didn't feel the same way.

'Spend a season concentrating on racing at home. Just enjoy yourself,' he said. 'I don't think you're cut out for being a top-level cyclist.'

And that was that. My time was done in the AIS track program. I looked Charlie in the eye and said that I'd prove him wrong.

I never felt the need to go and find Charlie afterwards to rub it in – my results and achievements speak for themselves. I didn't see him again until the 1996 Olympics, where I was representing Australia in the road race. I ran into him at the athletes' village. To be fair, he congratulated me: 'Well done. It takes a lot of character to do what you've done. It's a credit to yourself that you've made it to where you have.'

Yeah, thanks for nothing.

5

You're Wrong, I'm Right

I TAKE A GREAT DEAL of satisfaction from proving doubters wrong. You'd think people would have learned by now not to tell me I can't do something, because it winds me up. And then it winds them up when I go and do it, proving them wrong.

But my absolute favourite thing in the world, apart from my family, is winning. Winning is what hooked me on BMX at the age of eight, and it has kept me coming back for more and more through 30 years of competitive cycling. Winning is something I will never be bored of, and it's my primary motivation. Yes, I like cycling, being fit and many other aspects of the sport, but I think about winning the same way I think about my morning coffee – life without it is dull, colourless. I guess that I'm addicted to winning in the same way – and I realise that saying this may be a little politically incorrect in cycling's current climate – that some people are addicted to recreational drugs.

Take these two things – the love of proving people wrong and of winning – and add them to what I've already told you about being unusually competitive, and you'll get an equation something like this:

(Liking winning + Enjoy proving people wrong) × Competitive bastard = Race wins for Robbie McEwen

I won 25 races in 1993, after Charlie deemed that I was not capable of being a top-level cyclist. I went straight back to live at home after Mexico and back to the QAS program with Peter Day. I was basically back at school, and, because I still had so much improving to do, my progress was exponential.

In a way, Charlie did me a favour. Although he was wrong about my ability and, more importantly, my potential, his throwing me off the AIS squad meant that I just had that little bit of extra motivation to do well. The success of the Aussie track team was looming over me constantly – I didn't begrudge them their success at all, but I was determined to prove that I too would be on that level. I remember the morning of the Queensland state championships in 1993. We'd just heard that the Aussie team pursuiters had won the world title in Norway, in a world-record time. Good on them – there was a real buzz around the start of the race that morning. Good times for Aussie cycling.

But, again, I thought, *I'll show you*. The race took place on a really hard circuit, with a really steep hill. I got in the breaks, split it again and won a three-up sprint by about 50 metres. It wasn't a world title, but I'd dominated a hard national-level race. And I'd not only won, I'd also just proved a little point to anybody who'd been paying attention. I went to bed that night feeling a little smug.

In 1993, I also won the national criterium championship. And the National Series. And, against a major international field, I won the sprint classification at the Commonwealth Bank Classic. I didn't win a stage, but there were points during the race where I beat everybody for an intermediate sprint, or won a bunch sprint when the breakaway had just managed to stay away. I was definitely one of the fastest there. Germany's Jan Ullrich, who would later go on to win the Tour de France, won overall.

My results weren't shabby at all, and this, along with all my other wins and big results, got me a place back at the AIS, only this time in the road program, which I felt would suit me like a tailored shirt. I'd actually won a scholarship – there was guaranteed entry to the program for the winner of the National Series, which I was particularly proud of, because it was a scholarship in the name of Darren Smith. But my other results would have got me in anyway.

The road program was based in Canberra, and it was run by Heiko Salzwedel, who I felt would be a better coach for me than Charlie. Heiko's a talker, but he's also a listener. He'd come from the strict, hard East German program, and when the Berlin Wall came down he took his expertise to Australia.

He quickly understood that the East German method couldn't be directly applied to Aussies. In a regimented, closed society, it might have been okay to drive riders to breaking point and beyond, but Aussies aren't the same. He realised that Aussies are weaned on the three Bs – barbecues, beaches and beer – and you can't deny these three basic rights to Aussie athletes. He also understood that the boys in the Aussie programs would work harder than anybody, as long as they were allowed space to play hard as well.

I was ready for Canberra – I'd soaked up Peter Day's training advice and scientific coaching methods, and I had an extra year of experience and kilometres in my legs. I was starting to add a deep layer of aerobic strength to the anaerobic ability I'd nurtured from the age of eight, and I was ready.

We might just as well have been a professional team, although we had the square root of stuff-all money. We lived together, raced together and trained together, with a sponsor – Giant – team clothing and proper support from the management. There was no such thing as under-23 level back then – just professionals and amateurs, and the line dividing the two wasn't as clearly defined as you might think. We wouldn't be participating in the Tour de France or anything of that level, but we would take part in many pro-am races, against some of the biggest teams in the world.

The other important thing was that we were a great bunch of mates. David McKenzie, who'd go on to win a stage in the Giro d'Italia, was on the team. Jay Sweet, Henk Vogels, Pete Rogers, Nick Gates, who became my best mate in cycling, Damien McDonald, Jonathan Hall, Kelvin Martin and a few others all rode on the squad. We were out to have a laugh; we were also out to win races, and we'd fight to the last for each other. Jay, especially, made me laugh. He had a good career, riding the Tour de France for a French team, Big Mat, and he was a bloody good rider. Cycling couldn't tie him down, and he had various careers. He was a car salesman, and he had a go at boxing and deep-sea fishing. He laid into each new job with the scrappy intensity with which he rode his bike.

For pre-season training, we were in Canberra along with athletes from many other sports, and we got on well with them – especially the netball players. At the start of 1994, we began a trip to Europe, going via the Tour of Taiwan, which was a real eye-opener for me.

I was in great form in Taiwan – I won three stages – although my main memory is of a killer stage from sea level that climbed for 60 kilometres right up to the top of a mountain at 3000 metres. The Kazakh team, including Alexandre Vinokourov, absolutely pulverised everybody – they came first, second, third and fifth.

But Taiwan also symbolised the fact that I was on a new adventure – it was exotic and different. I'm an Australian – I'm used to spacious suburbs and wide open spaces between the cities. Taiwan was polluted and crowded, and everybody lived on top of each other. Where I come from, cities are where people go to work, then you can go home to a nice place, where you live. In Taiwan, I found it claustrophobic, just the sheer number of people crammed into such a small area around the coast. Twenty million people, and it's half the size of Tasmania. I just wondered how they all fitted in.

Everything there was overwhelming – people were constantly bumping into each other, and nobody even seemed to notice. In Australia, if you bump into somebody, you're in a fight. And then Taiwan surprised me again, with the real open space of its interior. The middle of the island is a proper rugged mountain range, with forest and peaks.

The Tour of Taiwan field was a very good one, and after winning my three stages I remember thinking, *How good is racing?* My wins all came in sprints, but the one I was most proud of came on a day when we'd crossed two category-one climbs and only 60 riders made it to the finish.

I was obviously good, but even at this point I wasn't giving much thought to becoming a professional. I'd started watching the Tour de France in 1991, but it was as a cycling fan, not thinking that I'd one day ride it or win stages. I'd particularly noticed Djamolidine Abdoujaparov, who'd won a lot of stages in the early 1990s – I enjoyed watching him sprint; he was really exciting and interesting to watch. But I didn't have heroes. I was so concentrated on being good and getting better, and winning today, that tomorrow was hardly on the radar. Most European riders wanted to be professionals all through their teen years, but I hadn't come from a cycling background, so I didn't have an idealised vision of where I was going to finish up. I just wanted to sprint lots, win lots, get better and, most importantly, see the world and have a heap of fun with my mates.

Next stop: Europe. If we were expecting a cosmopolitan and sunny life on the Riviera, or glamorous Italy, we were soon brought down to earth. Heiko proudly announced that our European base would be an old sports school – a *Sportschüle* – in the greyish and uncosmopolitan city of Cottbus, about 100 miles from Berlin, occupying an uncelebrated sliver of land between old East Germany and Poland.

Not much had changed since the Wall had come down, and initially we considered that a bunch of young Aussies showing up was probably the most exciting thing to have happened there after reunification.

But that was before Pete Rogers discovered the nude sunbathing lake out in the forest. He'd had an extremely convenient injury, and we'd noticed his cyclist's tan had become a suspiciously uniform all-over brown. The lake became our regular afternoon recuperation spot, although, being mainly shy boys, we tended to stay in the non-nude part of the beach, just over the border from where naked Germans played volleyball, swam and generally accidentally wandered into our field of vision.

We also didn't take long to find the local nightclub, maintaining the Aussie tradition of occasionally sneaking out for motivational beers. The trouble was, Heiko had taken on more Australian habits than we'd realised. One evening, he decided we'd worked and trained hard, and deserved a break from the routine. He took us to a restaurant, which made a nice change from cooking our own food in the sports-school canteen. Then he rubbed his hands together and promised us a special treat.

'What do you think, guys?' he asked as we walked into the same bar we'd spent the whole of the previous night at. Great, we agreed, as we frantically tried to stop the barman from greeting us like old friends.

At the end of April, we went to our first European race – the Peace Race, held in the Czech Republic. The Peace Race was about as bloody hard as amateur racing got – we'd be up against the cream of Eastern European riders, from all the old Communist Bloc countries. They were as hungry as us and twice as mean.

It was like being in an old movie, where all the colour and brightness had been washed out of the landscape. We rode through bleak rural backwaters, staying in empty boarding schools and living off rice and hunks of tough grey meat that we couldn't quite identify. There were no vegetables to speak of, and the culinary high point of the entire nine days was the soigneur (team helper) going out and managing to find a bunch of bananas, which we fell upon like starving monkeys.

But I was on fire. I won three stages. On the first day, I got in a break with Germany's Michael Rich and Jens Voigt, and

Poland's Tomasz Brozyna and Dariusz Baranowski. They were absolute monsters. Bloody hell, Rich had leg muscles on his leg muscles, and a facial expression that didn't ever, ever change, even if he was tanking along at 50 kilometres per hour. He did that a lot. Jens Voigt was a lanky, big, incredibly strong guy. Heiko had warned us about him, saying he was about the strongest cyclist he'd ever encountered. He ended up winning the whole race, which wasn't surprising given that he could essentially use his teammate Rich to ride on the front of the bunch all day every day. They also had another German, Uwe Peschel, on the team, who was a carbon copy of Rich. That first day, we rode harder than I'd ever ridden before, and they popped me right out the back, just by brute force.

But two days later, I got my chance. The Germans were hammering away on the front, as usual, with a Russian guy about a minute off the front and a Bulgarian halfway between. I attacked over a climb, passed the Germans, picked up the Bulgarian on my way past and joined the Russian, to make three at the front. We increased the lead to two minutes, dropped the Bulgarian, and then, with ten kilometres to go, the Russian stopped riding. He just sat in my wheel, and because we had no way of communicating with each other I had no way of finding out if he was stuffed or waiting to outsprint me. I just kept on riding – the Germans were really closing us down in the last few kilometres.

With a kilometre to go, I was all over the road, shouting back at the Russian guy to fucking come through, but he didn't even change his facial expression. We got to 200 metres to go, and I just wound up the biggest sprint I could, riding him right out of my wheel. I'd won my first race in Europe.

Three days later, in the pissing rain, I got in a five-man break and won the mini-sprint again. Two-man break; five-man break: I was a breakaway artist! And on the last day, on an uphill finish over some rough setts, I was right in position as the bunch sprint opened up. Boom! Three stage wins, and I couldn't put a foot wrong.

The others on the team said they'd never seen anything like it. Australian teams had been to Europe in previous years and won a few races, but never three in eight days like that. My total for the year was already six.

And then, in the next race in Holland, the Olympia's Tour, through crosswinds, rain, chaos and madness, there was a huge crash and I got right in the middle of it, sliding along the asphalt and cracking my back on a concrete kerb. Here is where the stretched logistics of our small team made life difficult, because I was in no shape to continue the race but had to get home. The plan was for me and Dave McKenzie, who was also out of the race, to go and stay with some people who knew somebody who knew one of the team staff. No going to hospital to check out my back or anything. Oh, and by the way, it's 100 kilometres across Holland. And, sorry, you've got to ride there.

So there were Dave and I, traversing Holland, looking at a crappy map and trying to work out where the hell we were, on the way to some guy's house. One week, I'd been winning multiple stages in the great Peace Race. The next, I was travelling around Holland like a backpacker. That's cycling. You can go from the penthouse to the shithouse in a matter of seconds.

6

Pros and Cons

I'M A PRETTY DECISIVE PERSON. I don't sit around agonising about decisions I have made, and I'm bloody stubborn as well. I listen to the opinions of others, but I'm happiest when I'm the one making the decisions, and if I think I've got the right way of doing something I'm going to do it that way. Once my mind is made up, that is that.

Which is why it was pretty easy for me to turn down an offer to turn professional with the Big Mat team in France at the end of 1994, soon after winning a stage at the Tour de l'Avenir, which was probably the biggest pro-am race in the world at the time. The offer coincided exactly with the flowering of my ambition to be a professional and my realising that I was able to compete on that level. I'd been riding free of charge, and suddenly someone was offering to pay me!

My list of pros and cons was as follows:

PROS
50,000 dollars

A car
An apartment
Taking part in bigger races
Being a professional cyclist is the pinnacle

CONS
Am I experienced enough to take this step?
I don't get to hang around with my mates any more

Sorry, I told the Big Mat management. I was going to do another year with the Australian team.

I wasn't ready to strike out on my own yet, which was a little uncharacteristic – I'm a bit of an individualist, and I don't suffer from a lack of confidence in my abilities. Plus, they were offering me fifty grand, a car and an apartment, and the chance to ride lots of races. I'd been racing for nothing, living off my savings and a small amount of prize money that we were sharing from our results, but that still didn't tempt me enough.

Mateship is an important thing for me. I've never seen it among other nationalities in cycling, only with Australian riders, and I was having such a good time with the AIS boys that it would have to have been something amazing to tear me away. What Big Mat were offering was good, but not amazing.

Most young cyclists are ambitious. I was ambitious, even though I hadn't grown up dreaming of turning professional. But I was also smart enough to realise that my longer-term ambitions would be better served if I was patient and realistic about my development. Nobody is born the fastest sprinter in the world – they develop organically over time. You don't harvest fruit before the tree is grown.

I'd also seen that there were bigger and better teams out there. If I screwed up with Big Mat, which was a small team, there was no safety net – with one injury, or a spell of bad form, my career could have been over. If I waited a year, improved, and got a place in a bigger team, at least if I stuffed it up there'd be the safety net of teams like Big Mat.

I'd got it all in order in my head. I felt I could probably have done it physically, even if it would have been tough, but I needed to know for certain that I was ready, just in case. Waiting a little longer wouldn't do any harm, because if you are good the talent doesn't disappear.

Apart from just enjoying it and being good at it, the two things I was getting out of cycling around the end of 1994 and into 1995 were a rewarding process of improvement and the camaraderie. The boys in the AIS team were happy to ride for each other, and having a sprinter like me on the team who was winning a lot was good for morale. We'd come home from races with trophies and flowers, crack open a bottle of beer back in Cottbus, train hard, go to the next race and win again.

We didn't win everywhere, obviously. At the Commonwealth Bank Classic in 1994, I held the leader's jersey going into the hardest stage. It was Jens Voigt who ambushed me. Going up a tough climb, the Germans shredded us in textbook style. They sent a couple of guys up the road before the climb, then Jens attacked and dropped me, along with Michael Andersson, a Swedish rider with a glass eye, who was very susceptible to attacks on his right-hand side and would go on to win a silver medal in the world time-trial championships. We didn't see them again until after the finish.

But we were winning enough for it to be a confidence-booster.

Like any group of competitive individuals, our team wasn't without friction, and we used to wind each other up on an almost daily basis. A prime example was when Nick Gates caught Jon Hall doing secret interval training on a set of rollers hidden behind some bushes in the garden and raucously called the rest of us to have a look. Jon's form had been poor, he'd been acting kind of weird about it, and the last thing he probably wanted was Gat mocking him for trying to do something about it. But the team spirit and mateship easily smoothed things like this over. I was with good mates, and I wanted to do it again next season. I thought if my rate of improvement stayed consistent, teams would come back with a much bigger offer the next season.

And, sure enough, 1995 was like 1994, only better. We had the same group of good mates, riding and playing hard, piling into the races like steam trains, hitting our rivals hard and collecting wins like stamps on our passports. However, we weren't so cocky when it was confirmed we'd got a start in America's biggest race, the Tour DuPont.

We had raced against some talented opposition around Europe, but the Tour DuPont was a fully fledged international professional stage race. Let me list some of the riders who would be kicking our skinny butts over the course of the race: America's Lance Armstrong and the Motorola team; Switzerland's Tony Rominger – he'd won the Vuelta a España three times and was building up to winning the Giro d'Italia; and Djamolidine bloody Abdoujaparov – one of the best, and certainly the most aggressively focused sprinter I've ever seen.

God knows what we were doing there – Heiko had riffled through his extensive contacts book and blagged the team an entry in 1994 from Mike Plant, the organiser, and after a good showing by Henk and the boys we got invited back for 1995. There were all these proper pro riders there, plus a bunch of amateur Aussie chancers.

We weren't going to waste our opportunity, however, especially as there were some outrageous prizes on offer – five grand for a stage win, two grand for an intermediate sprint. The stage into Charlotte was worth ten grand, and I came very close to winning it. I won the bunch sprint, just behind Franck Jarno, a French rider who'd jumped away before the sprint started. He won 10,000 dollars, while I took home 800. If I'd just got him, we could have lived off that for years back in Cottbus.

For one intermediate sprint, the bunch was together, and I thought, *Right, I'm going to have a go here*. I saw Abdu and thought, *Well, I've seen you on television*. I glued myself to his back wheel as he flew up through the bunch, and I received the biggest sprinting education I've ever had. He went through the middle, out to the left, back through the middle, up the inside, then opened up the sprint. I followed him through, saw the line, came off his wheel, drew level, then beat him in the throw. Holy shit, I'd just beaten Abdu. My teammates almost fell over backwards – as I went back through the bunch, they were saying to me, 'You beat Abdu.'

One of the great things about racing in America is that everybody loves an event. You could hold a potato-throwing event and you'd get a whooping crowd there. The crowds at the Tour DuPont were huge. And the other great thing about racing in America is that they like to go over the top with the prize presentations. I didn't manage to win a stage, but I did get a third place, behind Abdu and Italy's Massimo Strazzer, and because it was America the top three got to go on the podium at the end of the race, instead of just the winner. I was wearing the sprints jersey, which had a great big picture of a cheetah on it, and as well as my prize money I won a suit, which I decided would never be coming back into fashion and donated to charity via a clothing bin.

But on the whole we were out of our depth. We were nowhere near as strong or as organised as the big teams, unsurprisingly, and our top fives were achieved by sheer determination. When the bunch wound it up into the finish, we were like tiny boats getting tossed about in a rough sea, with big boats going right over us. We got pummelled, really, and the tiredness made me get so sick with bronchitis that I had to pull out of the race. We had no team doctor, and by my final day I couldn't even get out of bed.

My results were starting to get me noticed among team managers at the bigger teams. You don't stay unknown for very long when you've beaten Djamolidine Abdoujaparov, even if it was only an intermediate sprint.

And at the next race, the Postgirot Open (Tour of Sweden), which was also a pro-am race, I met Jan Raas, the manager of the hugely successful Novell team. Actually, I hardly noticed Raas, but he couldn't help noticing me one day when we were about 40 kilometres out from the finish. I was feeling really crook, my stomach was killing me, and I really needed to stop, preferably for at least five minutes, in a comfortable, clean executive washroom with soft music playing and a good book. Since that option wasn't open to me, nor was stopping at the side of the road (I would never have caught back on), I had to be resourceful. I managed to manoeuvre my bib and braces off underneath my cycling jersey, and while the bunch cruised along at a speedy 45 kilometres per hour I took the initiative, went to the back of the bunch, pulled down my shorts, hung off my bike, relaxed and left the contents of my bowels on the road. It was the hugest relief I've ever felt in my life.

First car in the convoy, right behind me, was Novell, driven by Raas.

Done. I had no toilet paper, so I used my cap and threw it away. Then I got my shorts back up, moved back up the bunch, sprinted and finished third or fourth.

That evening, one of the Novell mechanics, Chris Van Roosbroeck, approached me and said, 'Hey, Jan has been watching your results and was really impressed with how gutsy your day was. He said he's never seen anything like it. When his new sponsor signs, he says there's a place for you in the team next year.'

Unreal. I had the Collstrop team asking after me as well.

I won more races. I won against amateurs, and I won against pros. Eight months before, as 1995 started, I wasn't ready to turn professional; now I was.

But I wasn't finished winning yet. In September 1995, at the Tour de l'Avenir, I took one stage win, in Rennes. It was raining, and the bunch was extremely disorganised, which suited me just fine – I've always thrived when sprints are chaotic. As we came into the velodrome for the stage finish, there was a group just off the front, and at the bell they still had quite a lead. I thought, *If we're going to catch them, I've got to go.*

I wound it up and just went, around the top of the group I was in and down the banking into the back straight to give me an extra acceleration. I passed the group into the final bend and then held off the bunch. It's funny, whenever Aussies win chaotic sprints, or do well on the rare occasions when road races finish in velodromes, armchair experts will always say, 'Well, it's the Aussie track experience that makes the difference. The Aussies all grew up racing track, so they always do well in velodromes and sprints.' And it's true I had a fair bit of track experience.

But it had nothing at all to do with my win in Rennes – it was pure speed, pure grunt, and the fact that if I didn't go when I did I wouldn't have won. It would have played the same way out on the road. Track experience didn't help me in the amateur Championship of Zurich that year, which finished in a velodrome, when Switzerland's Niki Aebersold jumped at the finale of the race and I got shut in by another rider. That wasn't very clever track riding at all, and my track coaches would have shaken their heads if they'd seen that.

The evening of my win in Rennes, I got a call from a representative of Jan Raas. They'd called my mum in Australia, and she'd given them the number of the hotel. Raas's representative told me that the sponsor was in place and there was a spot on the Rabobank team for me in 1996 if I wanted it – a two-year contract along with a starting salary of 65,000 guilders, or about 45,000 Australian dollars.

I should have played it cooler – maybe I could have chiselled more money out of them – but I basically bit their hand off. 'It sounds good,' I said. 'Where and when do I sign?'

We met at a hotel near the airport in Paris. Jan arrived, showed me where to sign and shook my hand.

I was a professional cyclist.

7

Sprinting (I)

I AM A SPRINTER.

Every sprinter is different, so I'm not about to explain why other sprinters are good at sprinting or how they sprint. What's true of me isn't true of my rivals, and vice versa. But to understand why I'm so good at it, you need to know that, mostly, people have got me wrong.

People have made assumptions about my character for a long time, based on the way I sprint. They see me ripping into the final hundred metres of a stage, rubbing elbows with my rivals, subtly leaning on them if that is the way the sprint is going, grimacing so horribly it looks as if the veins are going to pop out of my head, and fighting the bike and myself for every last bit of momentum. They extrapolate from that and assume that I'm the same person outside of that situation. They see the way I sprint and assume that I must be doing laps of the room after a race and smashing stuff. Especially when I've lost.

But I'm like that in a sprint because I need to be like that to win. I'm like that for 15 or 20 seconds a day, 40 or 50 times a year. For the other 99.99 per cent of my life, I'm a very normal bloke, probably more patient than the average, with fairly uncomplicated needs. Give me a beer, sit me down with my family and friends for a barbecue, and I'm happy.

Even during a bike race, before a sprint, I'm as cool as a cucumber. Staying cool saves energy, and I'm incredibly anal about saving energy during bike races. Every last drop of energy saved, even if it's not even noticeable at the time, is a bit of extra energy I can use in the sprint, and it will make the difference between winning and losing. I focus on staying out of the wind, holding my position and not wasting energy – for hours at a time. It might look like I'm just cruising along, but really I'm cruising along and concentrating very hard on expending the minimum energy possible overall. That's the complete opposite of what I do in the sprint, and it means I have to subconsciously flick a switch – it's like I become a different person for that handful of seconds.

Me turning from Dr Jekyll into Mr Hyde doesn't just happen. I have to psyche myself into it. Other sprinters operate on anger – I've seen certain sprinters picking fights, and I think it's to gee themselves up and get angry, because it helps them go a tiny, tiny bit faster. They can't get the best out of themselves unless they're a little bit pissed off. Some riders need to hate their rivals, but there's never been anybody in a race who I've hated.

I'm not like that. All I want is to beat people. I build the focus, then flick the switch. My inner bastard comes out. And from that moment on, I will smash straight through you to get to that line first. I will hammer myself, force my body to hurt itself so badly that the next day I won't be able to walk properly, and standing up will make me feel dizzy. In the sprint, my legs and arms will burn acutely from the effort, my throat feeling like I'm forcing sand into my lungs. And still I'll try to squeeze more out of myself.

It's not anger, aggression or rage. It's a very extreme and highly channelled focus, which builds up over the course of a race. The focus starts wide, and by the time I'm in a sprint it becomes tunnel vision, and you can't allow anybody or anything else in. If somebody is drifting into my line, I'll gather myself, bang them right out of the way and go back into my tunnel. My inner bastard knows what he has to do, and nothing else matters.

As a sprinter, I have more chances to win than other riders do, but even the best sprinters lose far more races than they win. I ride up to 100 races a year, including all stages and one-day races. Some are too hilly for me to win. Others are time trials. I'll be involved in 30 or 40 sprints a year, and the best I've ever done is won 20. Even ten is bloody good going. In a good year, I'll win ten per cent of the races I start – if a football team won only ten per cent of its games, they'd sack the manager, and the players.

And I'm one of the lucky ones – other riders get far fewer chances to win. But the flip side of me having more opportunities is that there's more pressure. People brush over it fairly lightly – they'll see it's a flat stage in a race and say 'You can win today'. But it's not that simple – there could be crosswinds, or no will from other teams to chase. People don't always realise what goes into a sprint and how difficult they are to win. It's not a case of simply getting to the end and then going as fast as you can for a couple of hundred metres.

Most races that I'm interested in winning can be divided into three phases: the first few hours, which are relatively straightforward, although that's not to say that I'm ever just relaxing during this part; the lead-up to the sprint, which is probably the most interesting and crucial section of the race; and finally the sprint itself. If I do the first two parts right, I've got no excuse for not winning, other than somebody was faster than me – and I will be the first to acknowledge that to be the case, if it happens.

During the first part of the race, which goes from the start up to about 30 kilometres to the finish, I'm obsessive about energy saving. If the bunch crosses a hill, I'll make sure to be right at the front when it starts, then tap up as slowly as I possibly can, at a steady pace, so that ideally I'm the last man over the top. If I go down the other side without touching my brakes, I can catch back up to the front, and I've actually used half the energy I would have done if I'd tried to stay at the front while climbing. In some cases, I'll have climbed the hill a whole minute slower than the leaders, but by the bottom of the other side I'll be back up with them, having saved that energy. Multiply that energy saving by five hills and I'll be much fresher than the idiots who dance up at the front trying to look good for the television cameras. I learned that technique from the Danish racer Rolf Sørensen at Rabobank.

I've become famous in the peloton for the 'drift' on hills. I remember starting a hill at the Tour de France and Lance Armstrong shouting at me, 'I know what you're doing – you're sandbagging,' as I carved my way backwards through the bunch. Fabian Cancellara, the Swiss rider and multiple world-time-trial champion, sometimes does it and says he's 'doing a McEwen'.

The way I corner saves energy. There are many guys in the peloton who just don't take flowing lines through the corners

– they're kind of zigzagging through and losing speed. And every time you lose speed, you have to accelerate, which uses a lot more energy than if you hadn't lost speed in the first place. In the course of a race, you might go around 100 corners, and if I can use 0.1 per cent less energy on each one, it's 10 per cent more that I'll have to sprint with.

At every single moment, I'm focused on saving energy, so much so that I don't even think about it any more – I know myself so well that my body automatically does it for me, just in case the energy I spend consciously thinking about it detracts from my sprint. I detest braking unnecessarily, because slowing then surging back up to speed again saps energy.

Meanwhile, there will be politicking going on within the peloton over who is going to manage the gap to the break and then chase it down. In a stage race, the convention is that the team of the race leader will control the first half of the stage. It's a fair deal – they do half a day's work to defend their rider's lead. Then it's up to the sprinters' teams. That said, if the overall race leader's team has let the lead go out too far, the sprinters' teams will tell the leader's team to get back on the front and do another 100 kilometres. In general, you're looking for a collaboration, where everybody's got something to gain, but it's not easy to organise or execute.

At any one race, there'll be ten or 12 guys who could be described as sprinters, but you can narrow it down to three or four who have a real chance of winning. Those four sprinters will donate a couple of riders each to pull the break back.

Phase two is more complicated. There's a little bit of aggression involved, because I'll be defending my position near the front of the bunch. Everybody wants to be at the front, and because the other sprinters know that I'm one of the best at positioning myself for a sprint, everybody wants to be exactly where I am.

Imagine you are walking through a crowded shopping mall in a straight line. There are people bumping you, and you have to be able to move, so you use your balance and momentum to brush past them without losing any of your speed. That's what it's like coming towards a sprint – there's contact, bumping and outright aggression, and I will do everything I can to minimise the effect of all this on my own speed and position. That includes barging people right back if they try to lean on me.

I'll be riding along, really focused, and sitting on the perfect wheel. Bang! Somebody will shoulder me out of it, to take my place. When that happens, I use their momentum to help me swing out, then I swing right back in and bang them back, just as hard. I'm not scared. I won't fall. You will not take my place. It goes as fast as you are reading these words. Bang. Swing out. Swing in. Bang. Focus. And I'm back where I was.

If I have to be, I'll be more insidious about it. Somebody's where I want to be in a line, so I'll move up slightly ahead of them and gently move my hip into their brake lever, just the slightest touch. Most riders aren't keen on that kind of contact; they'll move out, and that's it. Where they once were, I am.

It's actually a very aggressive move, but it's done ever so gently, and remember we are cycling at 55 kilometres per hour. You can't go banging into people's brake levers hard, but the slightest touch is usually subtle enough to steal a rider's position in the line. On the other hand, you have to know who you can and can't do this to – Jaan Kirsipuu from Estonia, one of my rivals in the late 1990s and early 2000s, was a brick wall on a bike. No matter how strong or good you were, he was absolutely immovable in a line of riders. Alessandro Petacchi tried to shunt him out of the way once and ended up on the ground with a broken collarbone.

It's sometimes a fine line between what's dangerous and what's acceptable, but most riders, including me, know exactly where that line is and will not cross it. You don't want to injure somebody, or yourself, but you do want to have your bloody way.

The final 15 kilometres are full of constant, nervy nudging. Guys nudge me; I nudge them back. Sometimes, I need to go through a gap. My handlebars are 44 centimetres wide, so I really need half a metre between riders to safely get through. But my confidence in my bike-handling abilities is high enough that if I see a 46-centimetre gap, I'm going to go through it anyway. As long as I get my handlebars through, I'm past the gap.

I can sometimes see the gap before it opens. A fast-moving peloton is like a case study in cause and effect, and I think I understand the dynamics of the ebb and flow of riders in a group as well as anybody – I'm very observant, I have a very good memory and I'm very experienced. I can see the slightest movement several riders in front, and I can predict the ripple down the lines of riders resulting in a gap. And by the time the gap opens, I have accelerated and am through, with my hip lightly resting against somebody's handlebars while they let me in. I know what's going to happen, because I've stored a bank of memories and experience from my years as a cyclist, and apart from freak events and a few wayward riders, very little happens in a peloton that isn't predictable.

The sprint itself can be very complicated or very simple, depending on the road, weather and the other teams. If a team is trying to organise a train, it's a straightforward concept, but, at the same time, it's actually one of the hardest things to do. You have to organise a group of different riders into a drill, all doing the right thing at the right time, at the same time as other teams are trying to do the same. Getting into a line when there are half a dozen riders between you and your next teammate needs to be planned – you can't just do it.

Into the finish, when I think the time is right – generally the furthest point from the line that I know I can hold my top speed, although this all depends on what my rivals are doing as well – my focus narrows and I turn it in on myself to force the hardest jump possible. My primary weapon is my jump. When I was at my peak, I think it was the best in the world.

I hit the pedals as hard as I can, bunching and tensing my body to anchor my legs, and for a few pedal strokes – maybe four or six – I'm putting absolutely everything I've got into squeezing all the forward motion I possibly can out of my bike. It's like a deadly combination of punches in a prize fight – left, right, left, right, left, right, bang, bang, bang, each fiercer than the last. There is nothing else in my world – it is at this point that the focus has narrowed almost to a singularity.

And I am flying.

I've accelerated from 55 to 70 kilometres per hour in a matter of metres, and if I have timed it right, which I usually do, the sprint has been decided. I hold my top speed and I know that my jump has already put me past the rider in front, and that nobody will be able to pass me from behind. I'll be going that hard sometimes that I start to see stars – everything goes a little dark, and the focus can almost go to a blackout.

And then the outside world starts to leak in, because I have done everything I can and nothing will change the result now. I sense the line approaching, the focus starts to widen, I see that nobody is with me, and the realisation that I am going to win allows me to sit up, take my hands off the bars, raise them aloft and experience whichever emotion has pushed its way out. It could be joy, relief, satisfaction, a little bit of told-you-so or a mixture. I never know until it happens.

I am a sprinter.

8

A First for Everything

THE FIRST THING I DID upon signing my Rabobank contract towards the end of 1995 was go straight out with a few of the Aussie boys in Paris, to spend some of my 60,000 guilders. I was flying to Flagstaff, Arizona, for an altitude-training camp ahead of the world championships in Colombia, and I saw no problem whatsoever in my first act as a professional cyclist being to get absolutely hammered with my mates, pull an all-nighter and go straight to the airport the next morning.

But my euphoria lasted as long as it took for me to crash out on the plane and wake up in Dallas. I had gone to sleep fine and woken up with a knee that was totally blown up, stiff and swollen. I could barely walk. I arrived in Flagstaff hoping it would come good, but I was getting sharp pains from nowhere.

The problem didn't go away, even with only light training, so I pulled out of the worlds and went back to Australia. Still no improvement. I tried racing in a couple of crits, but it was excruciating. I went for an MRI, and the doctors informed me I had a cartilage tear, which is the kind of injury footballers get from twisting. I still, to this day, have no idea what caused the injury – maybe a flight attendant jammed a trolley into my knee while I was sleeping on the plane, or maybe an old injury just flared up. I booked an arthroscopy, and they cut the tear away, which wouldn't have any long-term impact, but I had to take it easy when I should have been building a big base for 1996.

So much for hitting the ground running with Rabobank – with my dicky knee, I wasn't even hitting the ground walking. In fact, I was just hitting the ground and lying there, because I had to fly back over to Europe to do the team photographs, just when I could really have done without a 24-hour flight and nine-hour jetlag, then back again. Rabobank being a predominantly Dutch team, and the Dutch riders being renowned for taking bonding extremely seriously, we went out for some team-building drinks the night before the photoshoot. This would have been fine, except that at one point or another I rolled my ankle, spraining it, and it blew up so big I could hardly get my shoe on for the shoot the next day.

Back in Australia, I tried to prepare for the season as best I could, but to recover from my knee operation I had to take it easy all the way through December.

Without the base of long training rides over winter, form tends to be unpredictable. By January, I was training again, and even going quite well, but it wasn't the ideal start to the year.

In February 1996, I lined up for my first ever race as a professional cyclist, the GP Etruschi in Italy. Etruschi is a sprinters' race. I'd be up against Mario Cipollini, probably the fastest sprinter in the world. Time to see how I measured up.

Cipollini rode for the Saeco team. Or, rather, the Saeco team rode for him. Saeco's main tactic – in fact, their only tactic when

Cipollini was in the team – was to string out the bunch towards the end of the race by riding extremely hard on the front. All the team members save Cipollini were used up in this way, with the last one, if all went to plan, swinging off the front with about 200 or 250 metres to go, at 60 kilometres per hour. Cipollini would jump, and he was so strong and fast that coming around him was extremely difficult – it would actually take me the best part of seven years to really crack him, and even then he was bloody difficult to beat.

What really struck me at Etruschi was that while I was keen to take it as seriously as possible, the more experienced riders were definitely there for training only. Riders such as Italy's Franco Ballerini and Andrea Tafi were in their full winter gear.

Sure enough, at Etruschi, Saeco put themselves at the front of the bunch with ten kilometres to go and basically had the whole bunch on the rivet for the rest of the race. But I was close to Saeco coming into the sprint. With about 350 metres to go, I thought, *Bloody hell, I'm still in it.* I got a rush of blood to the head and hit right out over the Saeco train. I could sense them looking over at me, thinking, *What does he think he's doing?* Possibly followed by, *Who the hell is he?*

I hit the front, and there I was, in my first professional race, leading into the final metres. I hit the pedals hard, put my head down and sprinted as hard as I could. I was going to win. I was really going to win.

Then they all blew past me. At much the same time as the second or third rider came past, I started tying up quite badly. Italy's Fabrizio Guidi won. I ran eighth, some distance behind.

I may have ridden like a bit of an idiot, but not many riders get eighth place in their first race, and even being there and figuring at the end of a race was important. Then I went to the Tour of the Mediterranean and got blown away. In a couple more one-day races in Italy, I didn't even get near the finish, getting one kicking after another, probably thanks to the lack of training in November and December.

But then came the Tour of Murcia in March, and by then I'd started to feel good. I'd be up against Abdoujaparov again and some other extremely strong sprinters: Czechoslovakia's Ján Svorada, Jeroen Blijlevens from the Netherlands and Stuey O'Grady, who'd turned pro the year before. I ran third in the first stage, my best placing yet. And three days later, out of the clear blue sky, came my first professional win.

Stage four, which finished in a town called Yecla, was so suited to me that I might just as well have gone out and designed it myself. There was a kilometre of false flat up to the finish, with a tailwind – fast but hard. At 250 metres to go, I was in around eighth wheel, possibly three or four back from where I'd have liked to be, but good enough. I could see the line, and I felt it was time to go. I came out of the wheels and went straight up through the guts, passed everybody and kept going.

I noticed the blokes I was passing and thought, *Well, this is pretty good*. There was Abdu – he'd already won Tour de France green jerseys and had given me a lesson the previous year, which I was putting to good use. Svorada and Blijlevens were giving it everything. But so was I, and I was in front of them. For the final 200 metres, I was perfect – I was aware only of the straight line between my front wheel and the finishing line, and my form, hitting the pedals each in turn, well on top of the speed. As I approached the line, I knew.

You beauty, I thought. *I'm away*. I had won stage four. But then

I went absolutely shithouse in my next race.

Not many riders win a race as a 'neo', a new professional. If you win one, it's fantastic. I won ten in my first year, starting with a crit on New Year's Day in Fremantle, Western Australia. In 2007, Mark Cavendish was really obsessing about beating my number, because during that year he kept on riding up to me and asking me how many I'd won in my first year. Every time he asked, the number had gone up – eight, nine, ten. He ended up winning 11 – good on him. But nobody else in the last 20 years has come anywhere close to us.

If it was 2010, and some new professional outsprinted, say, me, Cav and Alessandro Petacchi in his first season, it would be headline news. When Cav beat me at Scheldeprijs for his first big win back in '07, the cycling world went ballistic. But when I'd just beaten Abdu, Svorada and Blijlevens five weeks into 1996, nobody gave it much attention, least of all my own team. They should have realised what they had and put some resources into me winning races.

Instead, the next real contact I had with the management was when they gave me a bollocking over my performance in the Setmana Catalana, the following race. I'd stayed down in Spain to do a week of training in the good weather along with Stuey and Canadian Gord Fraser, but I think I overdid it and made myself tired for the race, where I struggled. The management took a bit more notice of me now I was going badly, and they hinted that they thought we'd been down there partying. They didn't trust me at all.

I'd had my first win and my first bollocking from the management, and I made it a hat-trick of new experiences when I got my first disqualification at the Teleflex Tour. There was a sprint finish, and I hit the front maybe 30 metres before I should have. I'd left a nice little gap on one side, perfect for somebody – it turned out to be Germany's Sven Teutenberg – to come up and try to pass me.

I kind of sensed somebody was approaching, so I did what any sprinter in my position would probably have done and drifted right across the road, all the way to the barriers on the right-hand side. It was instinctive, more to prevent the possibility of being passed than to cut off someone who was actually passing. Sprinters are in the business of maximising their chances of winning. As a first-year pro, I wasn't dominating people and riding them out of my wheel, so I saw the fine line that separated legitimate advantage from actively preventing one of my rivals from winning, balanced right on it and might have put one cycling shoe down on the other side of it. I didn't absolutely need to do it – I probably would have won anyway – but the adrenalin got the better of me.

The good news was that Teutenberg didn't crash. The bad news was that the race jury didn't enjoy my little display of lateral thinking (and riding) and relegated me. I held my hands up in faux outrage and told them it was bullshit, but I knew what I'd done. It's been done to me, and I've done it to others – you don't actively slam the door in somebody's face in a sprint, but you can gently and inexorably ease it shut. Sometimes, there's a disqualification, and sometimes there is not. I liked Raas's reaction, though. He was one of the world's best and wiliest riders in the hard old-school of the 1970s, and he'd seen it all. 'Ach, nothing wrong with that, boy,' he said. I liked Raas – he was gruff and straightforward.

I'm not a dangerous sprinter. I know exactly what the limit of my ability is, I know what is possible and I will never go beyond it. Nor will I ever deliberately endanger any of my competitors, and every sprinter subscribes to the same code – they won't last long otherwise.

But I do everything I can to win, and sometimes it impedes my rivals. If it's dangerous or unfair, I'll get disqualified, because in going up to the limit of what's legal, sometimes the only difference between right and wrong is down to one commissaire's opinion. I've been rightly disqualified and wrongly disqualified. The Teleflex disqualification was one of the more subjective ones.

I got another disqualification in the Tour of Denmark later in the year, when one of my rivals did crash. I went a little far out, and there was a strong crosswind, which meant riders were getting a free ride on the leeward side. So I swung all the way back over to the right-hand side of the road, to stop anybody coming on the sheltered side – if they wanted to come past me, they'd have to go into the wind. Trouble was, I hadn't seen Fabrizio Guidi trying to come past me. By the time I got to the barrier, he had his wheel up to my bottom bracket. His handlebar and brake hit my thigh, and from that situation there isn't really much recovery. He went down like a sack of spuds and unfortunately broke his collarbone. I won. I was disqualified. The danger wasn't deliberate, but it was my fault, unintentionally.

However, it's the wins that were the big story of my debut season. There was never any notion of the management sending me to the Tour de France in 1996, although it would have been an interesting experiment looking back, because I was absolutely flying during July. I went to the Rheinland Pfalz Tour in Germany and won a stage there. In the finale of stage two, down in the hills near Luxembourg, I rode Germany's Olaf Ludwig out of my wheel, and joined his countryman Andreas Kappes and America's Darren Baker. Dropping Ludwig was pleasing – he's a former green-jersey winner at the Tour de France, and he had leg muscles that were about the same size as me. There was a descent into Trier, a three-up sprint, and I won by about 15 metres from Kappes, who was a bloody nippy sprinter himself. Baker got dropped as soon as we changed gears for the sprint, but I absolutely pulverised Kappes.

I could tell I was starting to get a reputation in the bunch, however. A couple of days later, I got in a break with five riders, including Olaf Ludwig, and he taught me a real lesson – never take your eye off an experienced pro. There were four Germans and me coming to the finish, and I had just ended my turn on the front, with about a kilometre and a half to go. Just as I came off the front, he hit us like a ton of Olaf Ludwig. I looked at the others; they looked back at me. Second place.

I've always been a sprinter, but the funny thing about 1996 is that I was winning in sprints, small groups, breaks, wherever. I was no climber, but I was doing well in harder races. I went to the Lük Cup in Bühl, which used to be a one-day race before it became more famous as a two-up time trial. The circuit it was held on was absolutely filthy – a 20-kilometre lap with two climbs. I got into a 20-man group, which whittled down to 18, 16, 14 . . . Every climb, a few more riders got popped, and it was me on the front doing the pacesetting. Our manager for that race was the Dutchman Joop Zoetemelk. I didn't know much about cycling history back then, but I kind of knew that he'd won the Tour de France and that not many people have done that.

Joop's about the quietest guy I've ever met – a man of extremely few words. He'd called up Raas from the car, gushing effusively about how he could not believe what he was seeing – McEwen: sprinter, climber. In the end, I got it down to a three-man sprint: me, Dimitri Konyshev from Russia and an Italian rider. Konyshev tried to offload me on the last climb, but I was going too well – I rode next to him all the way to the top. Chalk one more up for McEwen – by 20 metres – although Joop had gone back to his usual taciturn self by the finish. 'Good job. Very strong,' was his assessment.

It was a bloody good year, 1996. I didn't find it easy, but I started winning immediately and seemed to be able to convert good situations into winning situations. I knew I still had a lot to learn, but, the way I see it, you start at the shallow end of the pool and make your way to the deep end. I was some distance off winning stages in the Tour de France, but I was on the right freeway. It's just a shame that what Joop was saying to the other managers in Germany – you've got something special here – was being ignored.

9

Angélique

I'VE LIVED IN BELGIUM for 15 years. It's just about clear on the other side of the globe from Brisbane geographically. And culturally. And climatically. I like sunshine, barbecues, beaches and beer – luckily, Belgium makes up for its lack of the first three with very high quality control on the latter.

Raas told me that I'd need somewhere to stay when I joined Rabobank, and he suggested that, as my mate Henk Vogels had already been racing with the team for a year, I might as well go and live with him in Belgium. I just nodded and said, 'Yeah, I s'pose.' I'd never raced in Belgium, so I didn't know much about the place. If they'd told me to go and live in Italy, or somewhere else, I'd have gone there instead. I was just following orders.

I got to Belgium in January, and one of the Rabobank managers, the Dutch former racer Theo De Rooy, drove me from the team presentation to my new home. We drove down these tiny potholed roads built out of concrete slabs, and I really did wonder if he was just taking me somewhere to have me killed.

It was grey and freezing cold, and I remember my initial reaction: fuck.

I've developed a love–hate relationship with Belgium. I'll never get used to the weather. I'm solar-powered, so the deal is this: I live in Belgium while I'm a professional cyclist, and then I'm moving back to the Gold Coast. There were times early in my career when I came home from a race and was going badly, or was sick, or injured, and I just sat alone in my apartment watching the rain hit the window for a few hours or days. That said, I'm in Australia from November until the end of January every year, so I miss the worst of the Belgian winter. During the season, I'm away in warmer places for weeks at a time, and if the drizzle does set in while I'm at home, I can get on a plane and go somewhere nice to train for a few days.

I like the way cycling and cyclists are treated here, however. There's no better country on earth to be a professional cyclist, just for the respect and depth of knowledge of the fans. Cycling's the biggest sport in Belgium, especially in the Flemish part, where I live. To give you an idea of just how popular it is, look at the Tour of Flanders, which is the biggest race in Belgium – 260 kilometres long, and through the towns the fans are 20 or 30 deep. The MCG holds 100,000 spectators. The Tour of Flanders will pass by a million people.

I've embraced the culture to a certain extent – I've learned to speak Flemish, and that goes down exceptionally well with the media, who treat me as an honorary Flandrian but without heaping on the pressure that they load onto the Belgian riders. The locals also pretty much treat me as one of their own. Just down the road from my home in Brakel, there's a bar that is home to the Belgian Robbie McEwen fan club.

I also like Belgian cyclists. They've got a keen sense of the sport, see hard work as something to be embraced, and you don't get the poseurs that you find in some French or Italian teams.

But lastly, I've stayed in Belgium because, soon after moving here, I met the woman who would become my wife.

I was all over the place through early 1996. I was racing or training in Spain, Italy, France and Spain again, and I only really got back to Belgium in April. I'd run out of contact-lens solution, so I found a shop in Brakel that sold it, but between my non-existent Flemish and the non-existent English of the shop owner, I managed to leave the shop without the solution. Luckily, there was another optometrist in town, and I somehow guessed enough international sign language to ask the man who worked there if anybody spoke English. 'My daughter,' I think he must have said, because he called a tall, beautiful blonde woman from a back room to do our translating.

She was stunning, and I was determined to ask her out. Unfortunately, I was hopeless at asking girls out, and my chat-up line consisted of mumbling, 'Can I have some contact-lens fluid, please? Thank you.'

I paid up, left and walked around the corner, kicking myself.

Fate gave me a second chance, however, and a few weeks later I saw her walking through Brakel with her niece. I said hello, found out her name was Angélique and told her I needed some new contact lenses. 'Do you need an eye test?' she asked. I stammered that I did not – which, looking back, was the wrong answer, given that it would have involved her looking very closely into my eyes. I told her I'd be along to pick them up in six weeks. It was probably the least impressive chatting-up of a Belgian by an Australian in the history of romance. I could tell that she was expecting never to see me again.

I had to race in Germany, then go to the Olympic Games. I was planning to come back after Atlanta, but I got sent directly to the Tour of Denmark, then they put me straight in a car to the Regio Tour. It was about two months later that I finally got back to Brakel. I went to pick up the lenses, and Angélique seemed surprised but pleased that I was back. She gave me the lenses. I paid the bill. Said thank you. Walked out. And almost punched myself in the face. I actually said out loud, 'Just go in and ask her.'

I took a deep breath, turned around, went back into the shop and committed myself: 'Would you maybe like to go out for a drink some time?'

Angélique's response will stay with me forever: 'How old are you?'

I'd timed it perfectly. She'd just come out of a long relationship and didn't want to commit to another immediately, so I gave her a week (I was actually at the Tour of Holland, anyway), then we were on the phone virtually every day. I made a shocker of a first impression. I'd had such a heavy race schedule, doing all those stage races through the summer – the Olympics, the Tour of Denmark and the Regio Tour – that I was absolutely on my knees. We went dancing, and, as I sat there not actually doing much dancing because my legs hurt so badly, she must have thought I wasn't very keen. But I had a different feeling from the start with her. I said to myself, *Robbie, don't screw this one up.* We got engaged 18 months later, then married in 1999.

Being married to a professional cyclist is like a full-time job. We've got three kids – Ewan, Elena and Claudia – but really there are four kids in the house, because I need to be looked after as well. Angélique is unconditionally there for me, for the good, the bad and the in-between. It's easy to be Mrs Robbie McEwen during the good moments – when I've been winning races and becoming a famous cyclist. But she's there when I've been hurt, injured, in hospital and operated on, or had tough times with lack of form, management troubles, team problems and contract difficulties.

Professional cyclists aren't easy to live with. We train hard, and we rest hard, and that basically means I do bugger all around the house. I'm not particularly proud of it, but resting, i.e. sitting on my arse, makes me a better cyclist, and me being a better cyclist is what earns us money and a good living.

She's done my motorpacing – sitting shivering on a motorbike in front of me while I ride. She does all my shopping. She cooks for me and tidies the house and garden. She has to be a wife, mother, cook, psychologist, soigneur, cleaner, physio and confidante, and my career wouldn't have been what it has been without her.

It's not very easy to be the son or daughter of a professional cyclist, either. While it looks great when I'm on the podium of the Tour de France and Ewan is there in his little green jersey milking the applause, you have to realise that being Ewan's father is not like that for the rest of the year.

I love being a father, and I wish I had more time and energy to put into it. But the kids realise that I'm away a lot. I can come home after a race and spend time with them, but being away so much affects your relationship with your children. It creates distance, and when I walk back into the house after a week or more away, I can't just pick up where I left off. After every Grand Tour I've done, I've had to rebuild my relationship with my children.

They don't quite understand why you've disappeared, especially when they are younger – it breaks trust and damages the relationship. When Ewan was three or four, it really affected him. They can be cold when you get back, and it's heartbreaking, because, deep down, you know they are right.

Kids are very perceptive. When my big suitcase comes out, they know I'm going to be at a Grand Tour and be away for three and a half weeks. Ewan used to cry when the big suitcase came out. If it was just the holdall, he knew I'd be back in a few days and didn't get so upset.

I feel bad for the kids, and I feel bad for myself, that we miss out on a lot of family stuff together. But there are benefits. When times are good, Ewan is my number-one fan, and he thinks it's pretty cool being the son of Robbie McEwen. Until he was five, he never called me daddy. He always called me Robbie, because he always heard people shouting my name for autographs or photos.

Every year, he comes to watch me finish the Tour de France in Paris. When I've won the green jersey, he's been up there on the podium with me. When I've done my parade with the other riders up and down the Champs-Élysées, he's been on my handlebars, really milking the applause.

I've done my best. I've been at the births of all three of my children. And later on, I'm going to retire and be around all the time. Then they'll be sick of the sight of me.

10

Bank Withdrawal

MAYBE IT WAS THE FACT I was an Australian on a Dutch team that made me suspect that Aussie wins weren't quite as important as Dutch wins to the Rabobank management. I dropped enough hints with my results that maybe, if they got behind me and supported me in the sprints, rather than leaving me to my own devices, they had something special in me. I won plenty of races in 1997 and 1998, and did everything except win a Tour de France stage in my first two appearances in the race.

In my first Tour, I was doing the sprints totally on my own, and I got a fourth and a fifth. Ditto the next year, except I got a second and a third, and several top-six places, which resulted in fourth place in the green-jersey competition. The green jersey is the points classification at the Tour, the second-most prestigious competition in the race, behind the yellow jersey. While the yellow jersey – the general classification – is calculated on time, the green jersey is calculated on points allocated at stage finishes and in bonus sprints held through the stage. Since so many stages finish in sprints, the green-jersey competition favours sprinters.

Rabobank's self-image was of a Classics team, an attack-ing team. Their reputation was for tactical smartness, because they would always get a man in the break, but sometimes the smart tactical thing to do is sit back, look after your sprinter and help him win. The philosophy at the Tour de France was 'Let's get into the break so we don't have to work'. My idea, mostly ignored, was 'Let's do it this other way and maybe win'. Sprinters win more races than attackers. The management kept telling me that I had to prove myself for the team to work for me, but, to my mind, proving myself would have been a lot more straightforward if I'd had a decent leadout, rather than having to come up alone against guys like Erik Zabel, Cipollini, Svorada and Blijlevens, who had all their teammates helping them.

I ended up becoming one of the best and most consistent sprinters in the world from 2002 onwards, after six years as a pro. Maybe if the Rabobank managers had believed more in me, I could have reached that level much sooner, wearing their team jersey instead of somebody else's. I got on fine with Raas, who'd signed me for the team, but his work was more focused on sponsors, and we didn't have much to do with each other. At the races, I was working with Theo De Rooy and Adri Van Houwelingen, who was also from the Netherlands, and I found it frustrating.

The problem was that while Rabobank did have some extremely strong and experienced leaders, there was a real hierarchy, at the bottom of which were all the new riders, like me, jostling for position. Riders such as the Dutchmen Aart Vierhouten and Léon Van Bon occasionally did some good work for me in the sprints, but they were also ambitious and were trying to prove themselves by having a go.

Things got ridiculous in the 1998 Tour de France stage to Neuchâtel, where I was fourth, and we had two other riders in the top ten. I told the team, 'Fellas, we cannot work like this. It's better to have the winner, and everybody else in the last eight places in the bunch, than to finish second, third and fourth.' In cycling, winning is everything. If the energy that Van Bon and Vierhouten expended in coming sixth and ninth in Neuchâtel had been put towards my sprint, I could have won.

And there's something else that stopped me from winning so much in 1997 and 1998. I wasn't stupid, and I knew something was up, but look at what it turned out was going on back then doping-wise. I'll accuse nobody directly, but with the subsequent admissions by certain riders it's clear I was pissing in the wind thinking I was going to go out au naturel and beat everybody. I ignored it, but it's no coincidence that after a load of riders and teams got busted in 1998, I started going better again. Or maybe it was the others just going worse.

Reading back over this, it sounds like I was having a really bad time at Rabobank, which isn't true. The team were right behind me at the Tour of Holland, where I won two stages apiece in 1997 and 1998. For once, the management didn't care who won for them, Dutch or not, just so long as they were wearing orange. When Rabobank went right, it was a great team.

At the Tour of Holland in 1997, the team got it together to organise a sprint train, and I was on fire after finishing the Tour de France. In fact, the team was pretty active on all fronts at the Tour of Holland. Léon Van Bon, who was a good sprinter himself, was doing these incredible leadouts where he'd end up running second or third – I loved being able to finish off the boys' good work and ride the last 25 metres with my hands in the air. And at moments like these, I thought, *Now the team will believe in me.* I was beating riders such as Blijlevens, a Tour de France stage winner, at the Tour of Holland. The team should have seen that they had a sprinter who would win Tour stages for them.

I did learn a huge amount from experienced leaders and proven winners such as Rolf Sørensen, Russia's Viatcheslav Ekimov and Erik Breukink from the Netherlands. In fact, Sørensen, though he was a completely different rider to me – he was an attacking Classics specialist while I was a sprinter – had a similarly anal approach to planning, and I took a lot from him. He was always motivated, and he always had a plan, just like me. But with Sørensen, it wasn't just a case of *having* a plan; everybody had to *believe* in the plan. He'd get the team right behind him.

If a team leader has a plan and says 'This is what we need to do to help us execute the plan', it empowers the whole team. That way, we make the race unfold the way the leader wants it to. It's what Cipollini did, what Zabel did, what Armstrong did, what I went on to do and what Cavendish is now doing, and it's incredibly effective. I've lost count of the number of riders I've encountered who would have achieved great things if only they'd realised that a united, motivated, organised team were a foundation for their own ambitions, not a backup in case things went wrong.

Maybe I should just have recognised that Rabo weren't a sprint team – they just didn't have the mentality to put all their eggs in that one basket, even if I was pretty confident I'd have got them a dozen wins a year. They were Dutch, and they were into Classics. I even talked with De Rooy about it, and he suggested that I focus on the semi-Classics, because, in his words, there was 'always someone faster' at the Grand Tours.

But I knew I was fast enough to beat just about anybody. I just needed what my rivals had: someone to hit the wind for me at certain places, so I could save my energy and put it all into one sprint, instead of me being isolated, having to make four mini-sprints to move up to the front and wasting my legs.

But Raas still wanted me in the team, maybe because they'd seen I'd still get wins with very little support. A week before the 1997 Tour, I was invited to sign a new two-year contract, and it was very strongly implied that I wouldn't be riding the Tour unless I signed it. Back then, it was unheard of to break contracts, so I signed, rode the Tour and committed myself to two more years of the same.

I was my own manager at the time, and I probably sold myself short and signed for way less than I should have, but Raas was a bloody intransigent negotiator. The discussion was relatively short and sweet. We met in the Holiday Inn out near the airport in Antwerp, and the contract was basically identical to my first one, only with a bigger number on it.

I went in and said, 'I'd like this many guilders. I've done well, and I want 220,000.' I wrote it down on a piece of paper for him.

He said, 'I won't pay you this.' And he drew a big line right through my figure, almost going through the paper. 'I'll pay you this.' And he wrote down 200,000.

Okay. With Jan, that's what it was like. I wasn't frightened of him, but I did know not to bother negotiating. The good thing about Jan was that you always got a definite answer. There was no beating around the bush, just yes or no. You could always ask straight questions to Jan and he'd give you a straight answer, even if it wasn't the one you wanted to hear. Yes or no. Done. Next.

I reckoned I was worth more, but 200,000 guilders was still a lot of money. I now had enough to buy a house in Australia, paying cash.

My performance in 1997 had been much the same as in 1996 – I got fewer wins, but I did ride and finish my first Tour de France. And 1998 in turn was much the same as 1997 – a few wins, some results at the Tour, but I wasn't seeing the fast improvement I'd had every year before I turned professional. The next year, 1999, was going to have to be better.

However, it started even worse, and things began to come to a head with the team and my frustration with their tactics.

I went to Paris–Nice in March and proceeded to injure myself by banging my knee right against a metal table leg in the team bus. Afterwards, when I put my full weight down on it, it was excruciating – the last thing you need when you're doing a hard, hilly race in bad weather.

The other riders on the team went well in the race, however, although to my mind they made a pig's ear of the first road stage. They dominated, getting seven riders in a ten-man break that finished almost two minutes ahead of the rest of us, but they still didn't get the stage win. Nevertheless, we were very well set up for the overall win.

Rabobank were happy, because my teammate Michael Boogerd, another Dutchman, went into the lead on stage five. We had to ride and ride on the front of the bunch, and it was windy, cold, hilly and snowy. I told them I was having real issues with my knee, but Van Houwelingen insisted I was to ride on the front.

I ended up pulling out before we got to Nice, because my knee was in agony. Van Houwelingen was really pissed off at me, even though Boogerd went on to win the race. He thought I couldn't be bothered.

I'd done my knee in so badly that I needed another operation, and I only just got myself going again in time to scrape into the Tour de France team by winning a stage in the Tour of Luxembourg and the Route du Sud. They were hardly major victories, but they served their purpose: getting me into the Tour, where I'd hopefully be able to advertise myself to a new employer. I wasn't staying at Rabobank – that was almost certain. I was getting stale.

Unfortunately, the 1999 Tour was business as usual for Rabobank, who refused to commit resources to their best chance of winning a stage: me. But the boys were going really badly themselves – they couldn't buy their way into a break, and they got smashed in the mountains. To top things off, I was feeling flat. Mario Cipollini was murdering everybody in the sprints – he won four stages on the trot in the first half of the race.

But here's the difference between me and almost everybody else who was on the Rabobank team bus: they gave up; I didn't, even though I felt like I was sprinting through treacle.

We were only 12 days in, halfway through, and the others, with the exception of my Aussie teammate Pat Jonker, were treating the Tour as a good training camp for the Summer Classics after the race.

Even the managers had the same attitude – they'd written off the race. De Rooy and Van Houwelingen were down because the team were doing badly, and morale got so bad they weren't even doing a pep talk in the team bus before the stage. Just, 'We'll go out and ride and see if we can get in a break.' Which nobody ever did because they had bad morale. I could see the team falling to pieces in front of me. I'd only run fourth or fifth a couple of times in the first fortnight, but there was still a week left.

And then, during that last week, I started to feel good again. I was feeling the same heavy Tour fatigue as the others, but I came through it and started improving. Sometimes, form is like that. It can come and go at very unpredictable times, and I was about to inexplicably hit some good form. The others were still down in the dumps, which was starting to give me the shits. I told them, 'Bloody hell, this is the Tour de France. The Tour de France! All we have to do is win one stage, out of six or seven, and the Tour will have been a good one.' But I was pissing into the wind, because the others were already psychologically on the plane home from Paris.

On the fourth-last day – a flat finish into Bordeaux that favoured the sprinters – I ran second to Tom Steels. I'd come so close. I was riding well, I felt good, and I really believed I could win. I'd finished really strongly. I'd come from a way back and just ran out of road to overtake Steels. I was still pissed off, though, because I'd asked the team to ride at the front to chase the break, and the only two guys who had the motivation to help me were Pat Jonker and Switzerland's Beat Zberg. I don't know whether it's coincidence that the three of us were the only non-Dutch riders left on the team. I'd asked the others to ride, and their answer was just 'Nah – can't be arsed'.

The next day, a 13-rider break stayed away, but I won the bunch sprint, ahead of Zabel and Stuey. With a time trial the next day, there was one more chance – Paris. And I was going to smash my way through a brick wall to win that stage if I had to. I was so pissed off.

After my second place in Bordeaux, I'd done an interview with a couple of Dutch journalists, during which I said that yes, I was pleased with my second place, but I felt I could win. I went on to say I was disappointed that the team seemed to have a defeatist attitude, and had carried it for over a week, just because things hadn't been going well. The Tour wasn't over yet, I pointed out. I knew I could win a stage, even though there was only one real chance left.

One of the journalists pretty much wrote what I'd said, and I was fine with that. I stood by every word. But the other, from *De Telegraaf*, had a bit of an agenda with the team; he was looking for anything with which to criticise the team managers and Dutch riders because the team had underperformed in the Tour. He took what I'd said, added some other stuff and generally ran with it as far as he could go. I'd given him the lead, and he filled in the rest, making the story what he wanted it to be.

Into the papers it went, and the article as it appeared heavily criticised the team managers, saying that they were unprofessional and weren't motivating the riders. My quotes were what I had said – that it was a pity I was feeling good and the rest of the guys were feeling down, because it's not over until the Champs-Élysées. But Van Houwelingen read the rest, assumed that it was all from me and went ballistic. He was absolutely ropeable.

For the first time that Tour, I actually saw some passion from Van Houwelingen, but unfortunately it consisted of ripping right into me on the bus in front of everybody. Van Houwelingen was doing all the talking, or shouting, and De Rooy was standing there tutting and nodding. He threw the newspaper down in front of me. I had a look and said, 'Well, I said this and it's true, and I said that and it's true.' The rest was the journalist's words, so Van Houwelingen could take it up with him if he felt strongly about it. I basically told him to get over it. If he wanted to take the word of a journalist over one of his own riders, that was his problem.

Then he brought out his trump card, which was pretty redundant, given that I was looking for a new team anyway. 'Maybe there's no place on this team for you next year.'

I told him to stick it. He thought he'd scare me by saying I wouldn't have a job next year, but I didn't want it anyway. I felt so strong and confident in my ability at that point that I didn't need Rabobank, even though I hadn't got a contract sorted for 2000 yet. It was suddenly very quiet on the bus. Van Houwelingen just walked out. That was that.

And then I proved my point by winning the final stage of the 1999 Tour de France.

The boys couldn't wait to get to the end of the Tour, grab their suitcases and go home, but I was a bundle of nervous energy. I couldn't wait to sprint – I thought that if I was anywhere near the front of the bunch at the end of the stage in Paris, I was going to win. I had that familiar feeling in my stomach of anticipation mixed with excitement, and I concentrated hard on balling it up inside me, ready for it to explode into forward motion in the sprint.

The early part of the final stage in the Tour de France is about as close to relaxed as bike racing gets. I was cruising along, chatting to Udo Bölts, a German rider, when he hit a cat's eye. In a freak occurrence, his hands slipped off his handlebars, his bike went 90 degrees sideways and he took us both down. I went right over the handlebars, landed on my back and burst a packet of Extran energy gel, which squirted all up my back, into my hair and helmet. But I was more worried that I'd fallen quite heavily.

I scraped myself up, got on the bike and carried on. The sticky gel would run down my face and back for the rest of the day. I was demoralised and pissed off – it had been a bad Tour, and my crash had been the final indignity. I was even talking to myself: 'Why this? Why now? Why me?'

But then I started thinking about the confrontation with the management, and how I'd felt when I told Van Houwelingen to stick his contract. I got angry at how badly the Tour had been going. I got angry that I'd crashed, almost blown everything and got covered in energy gel. At the same time, we started speeding up and arrived on the Champs-Élysées.

Arriving on the Champs every year is one of the best moments I experience as a professional rider. The crowds, speed and atmosphere make the hairs on my arms stand up. As we came through the finish line for the first lap, a rush of adrenalin hit me. It mixed with the anger I was feeling, forming a potent combination. I had it all ready, focused into a bundle of energy and force. And the best thing of all? There were five Rabobank guys riding on the front of the peloton on the Champs-Élysées. They'd taken what I'd said the right way. I felt a wave of optimism and power. I was like a coiled spring.

The setts on the Champs-Élysées are often quite heavy to ride on, but I felt like I was gliding on a cushion of air a centimetre above them. I could go where I pleased and choose the wheel I wanted to be on. It was like following an invisible line through the bunch and around the course, and I came haring across the Place de la Concorde for the last time, right where I wanted to be, in Erik Zabel's wheel. Around the corner and

Sporting a cheeky grin and a pretty good blonde-hair helmet back in the '70s.

Riders ready, pedals set! The gate call in 1985 at Redlands BMX, Queensland.

Winner of the 9/10-year-olds' Trophy Dash at Ashmore
BMX on the Gold Coast, circa 1983.

At 15, I won my first National BMX title in 1988 in Alice Springs. A
year later, I dominated again, winning the 16-year-olds' title.

17 November 1992: a tragic day when I lost a great mate and the world lost an exceptionally talented cyclist. RIP Darren Smith.

1994 and 1995 were two fun, successful and educational years as a member of the Australian Institute of Sport Road Squad based out of Canberra. I won about 40 races while travelling the world with a bunch of mates.

Any opening for a prank wasn't wasted in the AIS team. Nick Gates looks after the baggage while sleeping off a night out on an end-of-season bender in Hawaii.

Baden Cooke nicking the green jersey in the final sprint of the 2003 Tour. The picture looks like we're all over each other, but this was well after the finish line.

(Graham Watson)

I met my wife, Angélique, in Belgium in 1996. I don't know whether she fell for my charm or my persistence. We got married in November 1999.

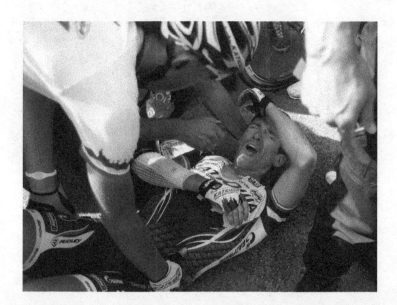

The last thing I needed in the 2010 Tour, having crashed once and lost a lot of blood, was to be knocked off my bike again, this time by a television technician.

(Graham Watson)

My trademark wheelies are normally reserved for the hardest
mountain-top finish in the Tour de France. This one is celebrating
victory in the final stage of the 2000 Tour Down Under in Adelaide.

(Graham Watson)

There are plenty of incentives to perform. Race leader
of the 2011 Tour Down Under after stage two.

(Graham Watson)

My son, Ewan, is still my number-one fan.

(Graham Watson)

A game of backyard soccer at home in Belgium with the boy.

I really miss my family when I'm away racing. Claudia, Angélique, Ewan, Elena and I, August 2011.

1999 Tour de France, stage 20

My first Tour de France stage win. I was about
100 times more excited than I looked.

2002 Tour de France, stage three

Long overdue confirmation that I was one of the fastest in
the world, in the champagne capital of Reims.

2002 Tour de France, stage 20
Winning on the Champs-Élysées and clinching the green jersey after a race-long battle with Erik Zabel. You can see how exhausted I was.

(Graham Watson)

2004 Tour de France, stage two
A victory on home soil, or Belgian at least.

2004 Tour de France, stage nine

Sprinting, and winning, with a broken back. One
of my most painful ever victories.

2005 Tour de France, stage seven

The second of three stage wins in the 2005 Tour. A chaotic sprint, which you
can see from the number of riders spread across the road just behind me.

2005 Tour de France, stage five

I'd already been written off after four road stages in 2005, which
made winning stage five in Montargis an absolute pleasure.
The gesture meant, 'Don't forget I'm in this race too.'

2005 Tour de France, stage 13

The Davitamon–Lotto team at its best. My boys had chased for 100 kilometres, and Fred Rodriguez (just behind me) gave me a superb leadout into Montpellier.

2006 Tour de France, stage two

Thor Hushovd pulled his foot out of his pedal in the final few metres in Luxembourg, but I'd already done enough to hold him and Boonen off.

2006 Tour de France, stage four
Winning easily after a super leadout from Gert Steegmans.

2006 Tour de France, stage six
My best victory celebration – the *Dumb and Dumber* 'running man'
– which I did as the result of a bet with Levi Leipheimer.

2007 Tour de France, stage one

The miracle in Canterbury – possibly my best ever win. I was flat
on the floor 21 kilometres from the end, but my team somehow
got me back into contention, and instinct did the rest.

2004 Tour de France green-jersey winner

On the Paris podium with overall winner Lance Armstrong, best climber
Richard Virenque and white-jersey-winner Vladimir Karpets.

2002 Tour de France green-jersey winner

My first green jersey. Also on the Paris podium: Armstrong, the winner,
Laurent Jalabert, the king of the mountains, and Ivan Basso, white jersey.

into the final straight, and I knew my moment had come.

I came out of Erik's wheel and was almost seeing the finish in slow motion. I could hardly feel the pedals, but I was punching them bloody hard. High speed, high cadence – I was totally on top of it.

As I rode past Zabel, I got an extra rush of adrenalin. I could see the line coming up, and I tried to stay focused, even though my mind was starting to tell me, *I'm finally going to fucking win my Tour stage, and, when I do, I'm going to go bloody mad.*

And then – the single most exciting moment of my whole career. Everything that went before had been building to that single second. Everything that came after was built on it. On that last pedal stroke onto, and across, the line, it was as if the whole world went totally quiet for that single second, followed by an explosion of white noise.

The next thing I remember is being off my bike, punching the air and screaming 'Yes!' again and again. Dignity had been left behind, along with the other sprinters. I sat down on one of the plastic barriers in the middle of the road past the finish while the press came running up, and the whole thing collapsed underneath me. The press got to me a bit too early, and I don't think I was making much sense. I see the interviews now on video and I think, *What a goof.* I was absolutely incoherent. But I'd won my Tour stage, and I felt that I'd proved a point to a lot of people.

The podium was different. I'd had a moment or two of reflection, and from the presentation area I could see Angélique. I was very emotional, but this time without the adrenalin and excitement. I was almost in tears. From here on in, I felt, things were going to get a bit easier.

In cycling, the winner is always right. Rabobank had had some negative publicity, catalysed by my quotes after Bordeaux, but the management reacted by being critical of me, rather than assess my words and take a hard look at the situation. I'd rescued the Tour for Rabobank, not that anybody said thanks. The team basically packed up and disappeared, although Theo De Rooy managed a grudging congratulations when he bumped into me at the doping control.

My win also inadvertently gave the same journalists fuel for their fire when they took the angle that I'd rescued the Tour for Rabobank in spite of, not thanks to, the team management.

It wasn't personal, but I had issues with all the team managers at Rabobank, for different reasons. The main problem was that they were so conservative, which didn't suit my style. Van Houwelingen was a domestique as a rider, and I maintain that, in many cases, domestiques make the best team managers, because they have much better empathy with the riders. Team leaders make bad managers – they've been so self-centred their whole career that they don't understand others' weaknesses.

Zoetemelk told me he'd only ever pulled out of one race, when he'd fallen right onto his head. He never got sick, but his problem as a manager was that he didn't understand that other people sometimes do get sick. He used to drive up in the team car to ask us why we were getting dropped on climbs. The answer: because we're going uphill. It really is the last conversation you want to have when you're being dropped.

De Rooy was very highly strung, twitchy, talking a lot and always going at 100 miles per hour. He was a protégé of Peter Post's – the manager of the Panasonic team in the 1980s – but while Post was a natural authoritarian De Rooy was a bag of nerves. He tried to act like Post, but I never really found it very convincing.

Van Houwelingen, it seemed to me, was permanently stressed, and it didn't create a good atmosphere. He was a large, soft-natured guy who got anxious that things might screw up while he was in charge, and it blocked him up. He was actually a good manager in terms of his tactics when things were calm, but they weren't often calm.

We had one more terrible argument at the Vuelta in 1999, and I didn't speak to him again for five years. The funny thing was that normally he'd hardly raise a shout. He's not a naturally aggressive guy, but I think I brought it out. He's a nice guy, and I speak to him now, but the stresses of the Tour can change a man, and if somebody cares to point it out, it can bring out the worst.

All the managers were tactically sound, because they'd been racers and they knew what to do in a race. The team also had a lot of experienced riders, so in general the Rabobank tactics were pretty good. They definitely took far too much notice of the press, though, especially when it involved criticism.

I represented the team well after that. I won a stage at the Tour of Holland, but I was coming to the end of my time at Rabobank. The Vuelta a España didn't go well for me and the team – my form was dipping and I was unable to win a stage, pulling out after nine days. I was too tired, and the next few days were in the mountains. I told Van Houwelingen that I was finished and that there was no point in continuing. He said, 'Very well. It's going to be your last race for Rabobank.' My attitude was, *That suits me just fine.*

I was in talks with a rival Dutch team, TVM, whose sponsor was changing to Farm Frites, about a contract for 2000. They were losing their own sprinter, Jeroen Blijlevens, and I was a perfect fit. I sneaked out of the bus one morning at the Vuelta to go for a meeting with Cees Priem, the team's manager, who'd got his driver to go and park their bus well down the road from ours. It was a pretty straightforward negotiation. He told me his team were looking for a sprinter. I told him I was a sprinter looking for a team. It took about three minutes.

We agreed that I'd be paid 250,000 euros and shook on it.

11

Feeling Average

I'M NOT SURE EXACTLY when I realised I hadn't landed on my feet at Farm Frites. Rather than a sudden epiphany that things were going pear-shaped, it was more of a slow-burn realisation. There was just a general feeling of non-specific dread that started pretty early on.

I'd liked Cees Priem when I met him, and I'd seen that the team were pretty good at setting up Blijlevens – he'd won 11 Grand Tour stages with TVM by the end of 1999. We were similar riders, and if they could carry right on doing for me what they'd been doing for him, I felt I was going to win more Tour stages. Paris was only going to be the start.

But at the beginning of the season, Priem was pushed out in one of those mystery off-season manoeuvres that sometimes happen in cycling teams, and Jacques Hanegraaf was put in as general manager. Hanegraaf was a former rider who'd won Amstel Gold and had a fairly decent career. Farm Frites was his first cycling-management job, and his intention was to make a big impression. His attitude was, *There's a new boss in town, and it's me.*

That was when the problems started. A lot of things had been arranged, the season had been sorted out and everybody was happy. Then Hanegraaf waded in and scrapped everything that had been decided – not because things needed changing but because he had the idea that he needed to assert himself as the big boss.

I've got no problem with people being assertive. I'm pretty assertive myself. But Hanegraaf went way over the top, in my opinion. There's assertive, and there's being a dictator.

We had the Belgian rider Peter Van Petegem in our team. Peter was one of the strongest, most intelligent and well-organised riders I had ever encountered, and his speciality was the Classics. When I joined the team, he was the defending champion of the Tour of Flanders, he'd won Het Volk twice and he was coming into his peak years. Peter knew exactly what he was doing, but Hanegraaf treated him like a junior: he couldn't trust Peter to train and prepare; he started laying down the law about how he should be doing it. Hanegraaf also wanted Peter to ride the Tour. There was one rule with Peter Van Petegem, and that was that Peter Van Petegem didn't ride the Tour de France. He was a Classics specialist, and the Tour, which mostly consists of mountain stages or flat-out sprints, didn't suit his abilities.

Peter was an excellent example for me – hugely experienced and confident in his methods, incredibly focused on his targets, and able to stop living like a monk and enjoy himself properly once his targets had been achieved.

Peter couldn't stand people hovering over him and checking on what he had been up to, which is precisely what Hanegraaf was doing. Peter trained bloody hard, but after a race or training camp he'd enjoy a glass of Leffe, Belgian beer. Hanegraaf decided to make an example of him, by dictating that not one glass of beer was to be drunk by any of the riders under any circumstances. The thing is, Peter's also extremely headstrong – push him and he'll push right back. I think Hanegraaf saw it as a challenge, but my opinion was that he lost the dressing room at an extremely early stage.

The team got a couple of good results. Geert Van Bondt, from Belgium, won Ghent–Wevelgem, largely thanks to the fact that Van Petegem was clearly strong. While Van Petegem's rivals sat on him, Van Bondt was able to nip away and win. Two weeks before, exactly the same thing had happened in the Harelbeke race, except our Russian teammate Serguei Ivanov had won. It wasn't good management; it was a very good set of riders doing well in spite of bad management.

But apart from these, the results were very average, and I was making a big contribution to that. I'd won races early in the year – a stage at the Tour Down Under and a stage at the Tour of Mallorca – but at the next race, the Ruta del Sol in Spain in February, I felt myself starting to come down with something. I felt absolutely horrible.

There was very little medical support within the team, and I was told to push through and get well soon. But every time I went out riding, I was nailed to the road. I felt like I couldn't even get out of my own way.

Farm Frites had organised a training ride in March after the Ruta del Sol, on the course of Het Volk in Belgium, the first major one-day race of the year and a hugely important one for the team, given that Van Petegem was one of the favourites. I rode ten kilometres from my house to the start of the ride to meet my teammates, and it almost wiped me out. I had to apologise to them, turn around and struggle home. I felt like I was going to fall over. I rested for days after that and still felt like death warmed up.

Apart from a few isolated patches of good form, I've always been bad in March. I think it's the way that I've always structured my year. I train well in Australia in extremely good weather through November, December and January, usually winning stages at the Tour Down Under at the end of that period. Then I really hit the ground running in Europe in February, win more races, have a bit of a dip in March, build up again in April, and I'm ready to sprint at the Giro in May. It's a very comfortable and healthy routine for me to be in, but it does always seem to result in poor form in March. In 15 seasons as a prolific winner, I've won a total of six races in March.

But this was different. It wasn't a dip in form; there was something seriously wrong, and it went on for months. I was just bad at cycling, for no discernible reason. The team kept on giving me mini-breaks – but not for long enough to shake whatever was wrong with me – and then putting me back in races. I had a week or two off, my body would start to recover, then I'd get put back in a race, with no training, and knock myself right back into a rut. I got through Tirreno–Adriatico in March, but I was pack fodder. I never got anywhere near the front. A lot of the riders I'd beaten back in Paris were now sprinting well, but I was getting dropped on the run-in to the finish. I felt like I had the flu without any of the symptoms, just the tiredness.

I should have had the initiative to go and have some blood tests, because I'm convinced I had glandular fever, but nothing ever got diagnosed. My morale was on the floor, and then I got sent to the Giro d'Italia to make my debut in the event. I had to ride a three-week stage race, but I'd hardly strung together three days of training since February.

Predictably, I couldn't even get close to the front of the race. I don't think I got into the top ten once, and I took an absolute walloping in the mountains. In one mountain stage, I was dangling off the back of the gruppetto at the very back of the race, with a couple of Dutch teammates: Miquel Van Kessel and Martin Van Steen. And what really pissed us off, apart from being absolutely stuffed, tired and generally being halfway through a Grand Tour, was that many of the Italians in the gruppetto were just hanging on to cars and disappearing up the road. Me and the others looked at each other, and we couldn't believe it. We were killing ourselves to try to stay in the race, but by the time we got over the first climb we were a long way behind.

Miquel said to me, 'We're going to be out of the race here.' Every single other rider was well up the road. There was a long flat section, and we heard the gruppetto was four minutes ahead. We looked at each other, and we knew what we had to do. When in Rome, do as the cheating bastards do.

We held onto the team car for the flat section. A hundred kilometres an hour for a few minutes, and we were back in the race. I hated doing it, but if the Italians hadn't all been doing it we wouldn't have had to.

I'd been planning to drop out on the 14th stage anyway, which was in the Dolomites, but the decision was made for me when I got dropped by the entire field early on. I was rooted, off the back again, and this time I think my legs meant it – they weren't going to get me to the finish. There was just me and a team car, struggling along at something less than 20 kilometres per hour, up an early climb.

I had planned to pull out at the feed zone, which was another 20 kilometres up the road. I told Omer, the team helper who was driving the car, that I was going to pack at the feed, and he suggested it might be an easier ride for me if I were in the group just a little way up the road. I didn't care whether I packed alone or in a group, but it was going to make his day easier because he wouldn't have to be waiting around for me, so I grabbed onto the car and Omer drove me 50 metres up to the back of the group. It was the first time I'd touched a car since I'd been spat out the back with Van Kessel. We came around the corner and virtually drove straight into a commissaire, who was on a motorbike.

He went ballistic. He jumped out ahead of me, waving his arms and shouting, 'You! Yes, you!' in Italian.

I felt like I was back at school. He carried on yelling. 'You're disqualified. You're out! Get out! Give me your number!' He was livid.

I was over it. I was dead. I snapped the number off my bike, asked him if that was the number he wanted, then frisbeed it right over the edge of the cliff.

He went bananas, yelling and shouting that he needed my number.

I said, 'Fucking well go and get it,' got in the car and was out of the race.

I'd been brought into the team as a leader for the sprints, and, six months into the season, I'd hardly sprinted. It was Rabobank all over again, as I felt there was zero support for me from the team management. In fact, it was worse – at least I could sprint when I was riding for Rabobank.

Hanegraaf should have treated me more like the team leader I'd been hired to be and helped me get back to the level I'd proved I could ride at, but it never happened. It was a lack of good management. Anybody can be a good manager when riders are winning races, but to be a good manager you need to be able to deal with riders who are sick or injured. Management is about getting the best out of people, but Hanegraaf only seemed interested in ordering riders around and putting them down when things went wrong. He was too busy projecting an image of being a tough businessman and autocrat to actually take a step back and understand what his job was.

Somehow, I managed to get a ride in the Tour de France, but I was a shadow of the sprinter who'd been so confident riding into Paris the year before. I was getting dropped on the run-ins to the finish – and that *never* happens. I was getting beaten up in the mountains, just surviving.

I'd been feeling crappy for five months by then. But, just like the previous year, I started coming round a little in the final week. I started getting points on stages, doing intermediate sprints, and I even got up to second place in the green-jersey competition. I wasn't good, but I was consistent.

I ran second to Erik Zabel in Troyes, on the penultimate day. He got me by half a wheel, because I'd just made a little mistake in my positioning. I went up one side of him but the door closed, so I had to go back, around and up the other side – I could really have won. That could have made the whole year good, by winning there. Nobody ever remembers a second, third or fourth if you've won a stage at the Tour de France.

It was really eating at me – a different feeling from the previous year, when I'd been annoyed but also very confident. I didn't have the same self-assurance on the Champs-Élysées, and then the Mapei team really caught us out, with three of them going for it from the Place de la Concorde. They split the field and hit out over the top of everybody while the rest of us just looked at each other. The Italian rider Stefano Zanini won by half the length of the Champs-Élysées, and they still got three in the first seven. I was eighth. And that was my Tour, in a nutshell. Mediocre.

But I finally felt like a bike rider again, and I went to the Tour of Holland determined to pick up my season, with my sights fixed on the Olympic Games in Sydney. The Olympics were about the only thing on my mind from the end of the Tour de France onwards. Few riders have the opportunity to compete in a home Olympics, and I desperately wanted something to go right with my season. Why not there?

Instead, I crashed in Holland and snapped the ligaments between my left collarbone and shoulder blade. I now had a matching pair of bad shoulders, having done the right one in 1998 in a kermesse race. But with the Olympics coming up five weeks later, I was going to have my work cut out to get into shape.

My legs still worked, so I was on the stationary bike straight away. In early September, I rode virtually the entire Tour of Poland one-handed. Poland has got terrible roads and heaps of cobbled sections, and I took a battering. I spent most of the week riding along with the hand of my bad arm just above the handlebars, in case I really needed it, but the road shock was putting me in considerable pain. I couldn't hold the bars with both hands, I certainly couldn't sprint and I couldn't stand on the pedals, but I desperately needed the kilometres in my legs.

I pulled out on the final day, in agony so intense I could taste it at the back of my mouth. A day later, I spoke to the Australian Olympic team selectors, to whom I hadn't explained the extent of my injuries. I would be fine, I assured them.

I returned to Australia, bashed myself in training for another week, just to try to get some form, and just about felt normal by the day of the road race. I rode okay but had three bike changes and a puncture, finishing 19th. Top 20 wasn't a bad result at all, considering what I'd been through to get there, but I was beginning to feel severely victimised by bad luck. It was special to represent Australia in the Sydney Olympics, but I wish I'd had a better lead-up to the race, and no mechanicals.

I was exhausted by it all, so I pulled up stumps and finished the season. I didn't go back to Europe; I just stayed in Australia. I'd had a terrible year, and I'd hated every second of it. I'd felt ill, had underperformed, suffered bad luck with crashes and injuries, and had lost all respect for my team manager. I wanted 2000 to be over as soon as possible, so I could move on.

Only one good thing happened. Hanegraaf left, after a group of influential riders apparently voiced their displeasure directly to the sponsors. I was glad to see the back of him. In my view, his arrogance screwed the team and turned what was a bad season for me into a total disaster.

The circumstances of the team changed, too. Farm Frites underwent a sort of merger with the Domo team. A lot of riders were leaving, and Domo needed a second sponsor for their team – it suited Farm Frites to go with that.

Domo was run by the famous Patrick Lefevre, one of the most highly regarded managers in cycling. I had the option to leave, but with the results I'd had in 2000 even I wouldn't have signed me for the same money. My contract would be honoured, and, what's more, I'd be riding for Lefevre. I had seen what he had achieved at the Mapei team, which was basically win a huge number of races. They'd dominated, and my expectations were extremely high.

Then he called me to his office for a meeting and said, 'McEwen, you are overpaid.'

12

All Trained Up and Nowhere to Go

MONEY'S A BIG MOTIVATION for me and always has been. It's probably because I saw how hard my parents worked to do everything they could for us. Our BMX careers were expensive, on top of the normal household bills, and I was always very conscious of what it cost. There was a large net deficit. What do you get from a childhood winning BMX races? A few trophies and the memories.

My parents worked their backsides off to pay for us to fly around the country racing, and that made a big impression on me. It must have done, because I've worked since the age of 12, and not only worked but worked hard. There was the pamphlet-folding and delivering job – slave labour. For a single pamphlet delivered to 300 or 400 houses, I'd clear $5.20. On some days, I'd have to deliver more than one pamphlet, so I'd double or treble my money, but I'd have the extra folding work too. I was taking home 25 bucks a week. Peanuts.

But, after two years of this, I had two grand in the bank.

I've got a funny relationship with money. I like earning it, but I'm not flash. People who know me would probably try to describe me as a notorious tightarse. But I'm not tight; I think I'm just too lazy to have all the latest stuff and cars. We've been living in our house in Belgium since we had it built in 2000. At that point in my career, I'd had two years at 65,000 guilders and two years of 200,000 guilders. We built the house when I got my first good contract at Farm Frites, which was 575,000 guilders, or 250,000 euros.

We could have bought somewhere bigger, but in cycling you know how much you're earning for precisely the next two years and no further. You could get a great contract, buy a whacking great house, get a massive mortgage and end up injured, and suddenly you've got to sell up and get a job paying a quarter of what you were earning before. Our house is nice, but it's nothing special, and I'm happy with that.

I'm not into flash cars, either. I don't really enjoy driving, because I hate sitting in the car in a queue behind a tractor, getting slowly from A to B, which often happens in Belgium. To me, a car is functional, and spending a load of money on the latest one, just because it's newer than the one in the garage that works just fine, doesn't make sense.

I've consciously built a house to a budget in Belgium and not overcapitalised, so we can offload it when we move to our dream house on the Gold Coast. I plan to get a bit flash and put a nice sports car in the garage, too, but in general I prefer subtle style over bling.

But I do like earning lots of money, and I think that over the course of my career I've demonstrated my worth to my sponsors, which is why when Patrick Lefevre told me I was overpaid, I was taken aback.

Lefevre was – is – a very respected and experienced team manager, but he also used to be an accountant. In Belgium, they call it a *beroepsmisvorming* – it translates as a 'professional deformity', but there's no real equivalent in English – when somebody has been doing something in their profession for so long that it becomes a personal trait. I think that's what Lefevre was like – he never lost the habit of adding up numbers and penny-pinching.

That wasn't all. 'You're not going to ride the Australian national championships. We need you at the team training camp instead,' he added.

I'd wanted two things from Lefevre in 2001: confidence and support. I could see that I wasn't necessarily going to be able to rely on him for either.

The good thing about Lefevre was that he was organised. The team staff gave me a new training program, which had been developed for the team by Dr Peter Hespel at the University of Leuven. It was incredibly scientific, with coded spreadsheets covered in numbers. A certain day would have a set of numbers, and each referred to the intensity, cadence used or length of the session. I modified it a little. It was set up for a European winter, but I'd rather ride out in the Australian sunshine, so when an indoor ride was prescribed I'd just do it outside. But apart from small details, I was pretty faithful to it. And it resulted in absolutely the best form I'd ever had up to then, right from the start of January.

I rode the Bay Series criteriums in Australia in January, and I won the first three – bang, bang, bang. They might sound like training races, but I was beating top-level Aussie professionals such as Stuey, Graeme Brown and Mark Renshaw – it was a proper sprinters' field. I had to let other riders win the last two because I felt bad about winning so easily. I reckon I'd have been a shoe-in for the national championships and probably two, three or four stages at the Tour Down Under. But I had to go to training camp during the former, and Domo weren't sending a team to the latter.

Instead, I had to waste my fantastic form at the Domo camp at Calpe, in Spain. We did some simulated races up a climb on which I was riding the entire team out of my wheel. The Belgian cyclist Johan Museeuw, Lefevre's number-one star, couldn't keep up with me. I was in the best form I'd ever had. I wanted to show Lefevre that every euro would be accounted for with my wins that year.

I went straight to the Tour of Mallorca, where Erik Zabel customarily ruled the race with an iron fist. You never, ever beat Zabel in Mallorca – except that, one day, I did. I got over five or six climbs, there were only 40 guys left, and I won. Straight after Mallorca, I won another stage in the Tour of the Mediterranean. Two wins – great.

And that's when it started to go wrong. Cycling has a funny habit of kicking you right in the face just when you think things are going well. The very next day, I got into a crash and fell very awkwardly, bashing up my left knee and hip. I struggled a little after that.

A couple of weeks later at Paris–Nice, there was a bunch sprint in the rain on the second day. A big pile-up happened right in front of me, and down I went, onto my back. It bloody hurt. At the next race, up near Antwerp, in the pissing rain, somebody went down. I rode into him and ended up with a load of riders on top of me. I was going from crash to crash to crash.

You can get away with falling off once. You'll be stiff and sore for a few days back on the bike, and it will hurt, but your form will still be there or thereabouts. But fall off three times and it's going to seriously compromise your fitness.

Two days before Ghent–Wevelgem – a realistic target for me – Lefevre phoned up and told me I wasn't riding. The Latvian rider Romans Vainsteins was to be the leader instead.

That really pissed me off. Vainsteins was one of Lefevre's golden boys – the reigning world champion – but he wasn't a fast bunch sprinter like me. He had an interesting career. He came from nowhere to win the worlds, had about two good seasons then pretty much disappeared. But, in early 2001, he was the world champion, and he wanted to lead the team in Ghent–Wevelgem, so that was that. Lefevre told me to focus on building up for the Tour de France.

I've done 15 seasons as a professional cyclist, and I've only missed the Tour de France three times. I was a late starter, so my old boss Joop Zoetemelk's record at the Tour – 16 starts, 16 finishes – isn't under threat from me, but a dozen Tours and counting isn't bad.

Then again, it should have been more. In 1996, I was a first-year pro, and Rabobank didn't even consider taking me. Maybe I could have done something, but not many first-year pros start the Tour, and even fewer finish it. I don't really have any complaints about that, although there's a fashion these days for taking young riders to the Tour for ten days or so – that would have suited me down to the ground in 1996.

Another time I missed it was in 2009. It started six weeks after one of the worst crashes of my career, and my knee was in pieces. I wasn't even capable of walking to the bike, let alone riding it. And then I missed selection for RadioShack for 2011.

But when Patrick Lefevre left me off the Domo Tour team in 2001, for no reason, I thought he needed his head examined.

Hendrik Redant was the one who broke the news to me. Hendrik was a team manager with Domo, who would also go on to be my manager at Lotto. He's one of the best I've ever worked with – he knows exactly what he is doing. We were at the Tour of Switzerland, and I'd got a third place in one stage, after just getting rolled in the final 25 metres. I was coming into some really good form, and I was ready for the Tour.

But Lefevre had suddenly changed his mind. Or maybe he never even intended to bring me. He certainly didn't have the courage to come and give me the news himself that I wasn't riding. He sent Hendrik to do his dirty work.

'Listen, Robbie, Patrick's told me to tell you that you won't be going,' Hendrik told me, and he was as surprised as I was.

They were going to take Vainsteins as the sprinter – and he'd started riding really averagely by this point. There would be nobody for the general classification (GC), just a bunch of guys who might have been able to slide into a break.

Let me tell you about the Tour de France. It's a predictable race. Before the 1990s, it was a bit more of a free-for-all, and you never knew what was going to happen. But it's a major international sporting event now. The level is higher, as are the stakes and the pressure. This means the flat stages are controlled by the sprinters' teams, because they want to be in a position to win a stage. You'll get a good eight stages – that's almost half the whole race – settled in a bunch sprint. The mountain stages – another five or six – and two time trials belong to the riders going for the yellow jersey. That leaves four or five stages for breakaway-style riders, but you have to remember that breaks tend to number between four and ten riders out of 180. Put it this way – if you go to the Tour without a sprinter or GC rider, it's going to be a long three weeks.

I was extremely pissed off. I spoke to Lefevre and said, 'I should be in the Tour team. You told me to get ready for it. You told me I was going to be in it.'

The problem was that Vainsteins wanted to be the sprinter at the Tour. He didn't want any competition within the team. But, in a Tour sprint, Vainsteins wouldn't stand a chance; he just didn't have the speed.

I wasn't finished.

'The team you've picked, you're not going to have a good Tour,' I told him.

Lefevre took criticism badly, but not as badly as I took being left out of the Tour team.

I went straight home, ordered 12 tonnes of gravel to be delivered to my house and spread the lot on my drive in a single day. I was that annoyed.

I was also flying. I went to the Uniqa Classic in Austria, up against a whole load of other pissed-off riders who hadn't been selected for their Tour teams, and won two stages there, plus another race at the end of August at the Tour of Wallonia. I was winning with one leg, it was so easy. Meanwhile, the Domo team were busy not winning anything at the Tour. They squeezed out a couple of top tens, and the best overall rider was Axel Merckx, from Belgium: 22nd place and almost an hour behind the winner. It could all have been so different.

And then I had an interview with a Belgian journalist from *Het Laatste Nieuws*, who must have had something against Lefevre and caught me at a good moment. I believe my words were,

'With the form I've had this month, I was definitely worthy of a place in the Tour.'

I think that's a fairly uncontroversial thing to say – just a little statement of opinion, backed up by pretty hard facts. Unfortunately, like the Dutch journalists with Rabobank in the 1999 Tour, this guy took a bit of a liberty with it and gave Lefevre the full works, along the lines of 'the team were shit and I knew they'd be shit'. He fluffed it up to the point where he was virtually saying Lefevre was an idiot. The Belgian press had a pretty bad relationship with him anyway and took any opportunity to pull his feathers. I just happened to be the fall guy this time.

Lefevre was, predictably, furious. The situation was probably exacerbated because he knew I was right and that he had been wrong. He pointed out that I wasn't winning races, while I pointed out that I had won six races so far (and I would win another three before the end of the year). His retort was that I didn't win big races – like the Classics and Tour stages, presumably. But if he was going to pull me out of Ghent–Wevelgem and the Tour at the last moment, then winning them was going to be tricky. I think Lefevre was frustrated at Vainsteins not providing the wins he'd been hired for, and he was taking it all out on me.

I rode the Vuelta a España that year with two small worries at the back of my mind: my form was dipping, and I didn't have a contract for 2002 yet. Without a ride in the Tour de France, I couldn't easily put myself in the shop window. I didn't win a stage in the Vuelta, although I do enjoy telling people that I was, in fact, first in the race. First to finish in Madrid, that is – the race finished with a time trial, and as I was last overall and time trials are held in reverse order, I was first. But by this point, I was just disillusioned. I'd won several races and wasted some extremely good form on doing a few small races through July and August.

Back in Australia, nobody was returning my calls about a new contract. This was very worrying. I got myself a new manager, who talked to absolutely everybody, basically offering them a sprinter who could give them consistent wins through the year, could finish Grand Tours and win Tour de France stages. He should have had his hand bitten off, but there was zero interest, and we couldn't understand why. My manager made some discreet inquiries and heard that I'd been described as a troublemaker. I don't know by whom.

It got so late in the day that I had to get on the phone myself to the teams, while I was riding the SunTour. The really stupid thing is that I was winning stages out there and still getting no interest. But then I spoke to Christophe Sercu, the manager of the Lotto team, and he said straight out that he'd be interested, but there was no money left. 'I want to give you a spot, but I can't promise anything. It's a long shot,' was how he left it. That was better than no shot at all.

November is not the time to be looking for a job in professional cycling. I was facing the end of my career. I could have gone back into the amateurs, but I had a house, a wife and a child on the way. It was either Lotto or go and get a proper job.

13

The Best Job in the World

FROM THE OUTSIDE, it probably looks like being a professional cyclist is the best job in the world. The racing hurts, obviously, and you can see from our faces, from the scars and the fresh wounds, that it's a tough, tough sport. But the lifestyle must look pretty sweet to most people who press their noses up against the window, looking into the world of professional cycling.

When we're not racing, we're relaxing. In the days before a race, we'll be in a hotel and maybe go out for a nice one- or two-hour spin with the rest of the team. We'll stop at a cafe and drink a coffee in the sunshine – cyclists are good at drinking coffee. Or we'll hang out at the hotel, occupying the lobby in groups of skinny, sunburned men, laptops out. Life is pretty good.

However, that's just the bit that you see. You don't see the training, or feel the fatigue, or realise just how intense the life is.

The difference between being a professional athlete and being even an amateur weekend warrior is the difference between going out and playing nine holes of golf on the local goat-track golf course and playing at the US Masters, or kicking the soccer ball around with your mates on the beach and playing against Manchester United at Wembley Stadium.

In the peloton, you've got the absolute best of the best. Everybody wants to win, and just about every rider has the capacity to win. Everybody is strong. And at any one race, somebody is flying. Or, more likely, quite a few people are flying, making life extremely difficult for everybody else. From January until October, you'll come up against riders at their absolute peaks, and they want to hurt you so badly that you can't stay with them. That's the point of cycling.

The suffering is such a daily occurrence that no one day really stands out from another. As a sprinter, I'm having to hang on well beyond what I think I can tolerate, because most riders don't want to sprint against me; they want to break me before the finish. While it looks like I'm just sitting comfortably in the bunch, cruising on my teammates' wheels, it often feels like I'm one or two minutes from popping. To be involved in a sprint, first I have to go through the pain barrier to get there, and that's before I have to make my body push the bike past 65, even 70 kilometres per hour.

Fans often see us out for a group ride the day before a race. The sun is shining, we're chatting away and it looks great. But you can guarantee that at least one person in that group is absolutely stuffed, from racing the whole week before or from a heavy training week. They'll be wishing they were doing anything except going out for another ride.

And when we get back to the hotel, our job is to rest. It's easy to vegetate, just watching TV or staring at a computer screen. Resting is work. We can't go for a walk because it prevents us from resting. We can't go and kick a football about. It can get pretty dull.

But we can't switch off, because racing is 100 per cent concentration every day – not just on the race itself but also on the other riders, on oneself and on the road. We can't stop concentrating during the five or six hours of a race, especially in Belgium, where the roads have a big slit down the middle between one side and the other. There's always somebody whose concentration lapses and who disappears down a pothole. If you're not sharp, he'll bring you down too. Or the riders in front will block your view of a big crater in the road, and your first sight of it will be when you are flying towards it over your handlebars. Avoiding getting into that kind of situation is tiring. Concentrating hard for six hours, while exercising equally hard, is incredibly fatiguing. It's constant low-level psychological stress, added to extreme physical stress.

Now I've made it sound like the worst job in the world. But when I was faced with losing it in November 2001, I was desperate.

By the time Christophe Sercu called me back, ten days had passed since I'd first contacted him. I wasn't just in the last-chance saloon; I'd been drinking there for several hours and they were looking at throwing me out.

'We can give you 65,000 euros, plus win bonuses,' he said, and he was almost apologetic. On the one hand, it was the best possible news – I was still in the game. But in the wider picture, the whole situation had been a kick in the guts, because I'd been on four times as much, and I'd ridden a pretty good season, with lots of wins. But I still thanked him very much, and I meant it – he'd saved my career. I was now a Lotto rider.

I think if Lotto hadn't worked out, I might have jacked it in. I'd had a lack of support at Rabobank, shocking management at Farm Frites and then arrogance from Lefevre at Domo. If all teams were like this, it would have been unsupportable. But I was determined to make a fresh start at Lotto. I followed the same training program as I had the year before. Domo might have been a bad experience for me, but their winter-training program had been an exception to the general rule.

If anything, I was in even better form in 2002 than I had been in 2001. I won two of the Bay Series crits without too much trouble. One of them doubled as the national criterium championships.

At the national road championships, on a very hilly, tough course in Ballarat, I ended the race a little bit poorer but with the national champion's jersey on. My fellow Queenslander Nathan O'Neill was ripping the race to shreds. He'd been out in front alone, while the best 20 or so guys in the country, including all the Europe-based professionals, coalesced into a group behind him. I attacked them and went straight across to Nathan.

He told me he was battered, but as we were from the same state he'd give me whatever he had left. He rode that hard that by the end he really had me on the ropes, but I stayed with him, won and he was second. My prize money, plus a little bit from me, went straight to him.

I'd been on my new team for two weeks, and bang! I'd won two national championships. You beauty. Next!

Lotto were already in a good mood with me, and they turned up to the Tour Down Under ready to support me. I was almost too good. I got four stage wins, although I missed out on winning the overall classification. My break was caught one day, and the next one to go was the one that decided the race – I finished well down in 26th thanks to that. I've finished second, third and fourth in the Tour Down Under over the course of my career, and something's always stopped me from winning.

But I had six wins in the first month of the season, and I'm not sure that cycling has ever been that easy for me before or since. I was imperious – my form was a boulder picking up speed as it rolled down a mountain.

What's more, for the first time in my career I was having a great time with my manager. Lotto had sent the Belgian former pro cyclist Walter Planckaert over to the Tour Down Under, and we hit it off immediately. He could see that if the team worked for me, I was as close to a sure thing as you can get in cycling, and he put his trust in me. It had taken until my seventh season as a professional cyclist for somebody to do that.

Walter was relaxed, but he made everybody aware of what was expected of them, and he always came to a race with a strong plan. Instead of ordering riders around, he'd motivate us by saying, 'We can win this if we ride for Robbie.' He'd been a smart tactician when he was a rider – very sly. That's the same as me, and that's why I worked well with him. We think the same way. It wasn't about flicking people but about taking advantage of situations. Brute strength isn't enough to guarantee race wins, but a clear head often is. And if it went wrong, he'd never get angry, but we'd discuss it afterwards to see how we could prevent it happening next time.

In fact, I got on well with the entire management team at Lotto. Christophe Sercu was the big boss, the general manager. He didn't get involved in tactics, selection and the everyday details; he allowed the team managers to do their jobs and kept everything running like clockwork behind the scenes, just like a general manager should. He made sure we had equipment, that we were paid and that we were able to do our jobs, which isn't difficult, but you'd be amazed at how bad some people can be at doing these simple things.

I also worked well with Claude Criquielion. He was always a bit quiet, but he knew what he was doing, and he knew that the riders knew what they were doing. And Jef Braeckevelt had a soft spot for me because Lotto were always big rivals with Patrick Lefevre, and Jef could have a good laugh that I was doing so well now I wasn't riding with him. The management team at Lotto knew what they had and made sure I was happy.

None of my cycling seasons have been identical – sport by its very nature is too unpredictable for that to be possible – but since my first year at Lotto there has been a pattern. Lotto allowed me to build my season on the foundation of me going back to Australia for three months to train. I would hit the ground running in the Australian races in January and race through to the end of March or early April, picking up as many wins as possible. Then I'd take a short break and build up to the Giro, hopefully winning some stages there. I'd pull out after two weeks, rest, build up again and go to the Tour de France for stage wins. After the Tour, I'd take a short break, ride some exhibition races through August, then peak for one last push through September. In this last part of the season, I'd try to win as many races as I could before my form went on holiday for the winter.

I'm the kind of person who likes routine, whether it's the micro routine of my daily life or the macro routine of my cycling season. Most days are similar for me: up, breakfast, get the kids to school, surf the net, go for a ride, coffee and lunch, back for a rest, kids, dinner. I'm comfortable in the routines I've carved out for myself, and they work well for me.

Perhaps it was because 2002 worked so well for me that I settled into that routine. I left Australia after the Tour Down Under, and Jef booked us into a hotel he knew down in the south of France for a series of races there. They were happy times. Angélique was pregnant, so Jef arranged for her to stay at the hotel as well, and she was with us for a few days.

I felt like I'd been cut loose at Lotto, and I went into the French races like a steam train. At the Étoile de Bessèges – a tricky five-day race held on compact loops around the arid southern end of the Ardèche, covering horrible, gravelly roads – I was first, third, then second three times. I won the race overall, so I now had eight wins for the season – that's a total that only a handful of riders can match over any whole season, and it wasn't even mid-February.

I wasn't only sprinting well; I was climbing fast too. I'm not physically predisposed to climbing, and it's not something I've ever particularly worked at, beyond making sure I'm good enough to survive mountain stages in the Tour so that I might be able to win a sprint the next day. But I think my form was so good in early 2002 that I was able to climb at the front of races anyway.

Following Bessèges, we went to the Tour of the Mediterranean, where I got eighth – a very good finish for a non-climber like me – on the stage that finished up Mont Faron. Faron's a steep, winding piece of singletrack asphalt, climbing up above the harbour in Toulon. It's renowned as a real early-season battleground for riders who aspire to winning the Tour de France later in the year.

I had no right to be anywhere near the front of the race as it climbed Faron, but I could hardly feel the pedals going round.

I even attacked. Going into the climb, I was so surprised that I was anywhere near the front that I thought, *What the hell?* There's a nice little technical section into it, and I felt just like a BMX racer again as I hit over everybody, went through the corners five kilometres per hour faster than the others and got a head start on the climb. I held a good lead until the final two-kilometre section, where the Italian rider Michele Bartoli just legged it past me with a small group of others.

Jef could see that there was no point in just holding me back for the bunch sprints – I was capable of winning almost any-where, and his faith in me was a new experience. I'd been put in the squad for the Tour du Haut Var, another exceptionally hilly one-day race held on a double circuit in Draguignan, in the south of France. The year before, I'd started it with Domo, and I lasted about 15 kilometres before the peloton hawked me up and spat me out.

Jef said to me the evening before the race, 'You can win this.'

I was so surprised that I didn't even believe him. *Steady on, let's not go overboard*, was my reaction.

But it turned out that Jef knew a lot more than I did. I got over the climbs and was feeling better and better as the race went on, which is a rare thing. When many of the favourites went into a break on the final short lap, I was right in the middle of it. I eyeballed everybody in the group. Laurent Jalabert was there – one of the best riders in the world, he'd been fourth on home soil at the Tour de France. Alexandre Vinokourov – also one of the best riders in the world – was there too. Davide Rebellin from Italy – ditto. I watched them, they watched me, and they rode hard, but they couldn't drop me up the last climb.

But then, just over the top, Jalabert attacked with Vinokourov, and a Russian rider, Alexandre Botcharov, got in between me and them but couldn't follow. I couldn't pass Botcharov on the twisty descent – in that moment, the race was lost. It was only a five-metre gap, but the race was that hard that nobody could close it. I easily won the sprint for third, but I think if I'd been on their wheels when they attacked, Jalabert and Vinokourov wouldn't have dropped me. And I'd have outsprinted them. But even so, me finishing on the podium in Haut Var would be like a Tour de France contender, some climber, coming third in a bunch sprint finish. Or, to give a non-cyclist an idea about how unusual a result it was, it would be like a 1500-metre runner coming third in a marathon.

And so it continued. I was fourth in Het Volk, behind Peter Van Petegem, who'd also signed for Lotto that year. I took two stage wins in Paris–Nice. I won Scheldeprijs.

Even better, my win bonuses were starting to mount. Bessèges only got me a couple of thousand euros or so, but my two Paris–Nice stage wins got me 12,000 euros each. I was getting towards a hundred grand for the year, which was more like it.

Here's the thing, though: my form was a little better in 2002 than in 2001. But my results were significantly better. The two differences were luck – I crashed three times in 2001 and didn't hit the ground once in early 2002 – and management. I was treated well at Lotto and had landed in a team that reflected my values. It was a family at Lotto.

The managers loved it when I was at a race. We'd have a plan – me to win the sprint – and the whole team would do their best to ensure that happened.

I wasn't the only guy winning everything in 2002, however. Mario Cipollini was winning a lot too. We came up against each other at the Giro d'Italia.

Cipollini was the best sprinter I have ever raced against. Full stop. Nobody was as difficult to beat. He was just so bloody difficult to come around. He was very strong and fast but also rock solid, and very big – he took up a lot of room on the road and sprinted with his elbows out, which meant going an extra distance when coming around him. And his team took him to 200 or 150 metres to go, so that when he jumped you had just eight to ten seconds to pass him. It was almost impossible. Almost.

And at the 2002 Giro d'Italia, Cipo was at his best. But he was obviously worried about me. Towards the end of stage one, he was in second position behind his countryman and teammate Giovanni Lombardi, while I was right in his wheel – perfect position. I hit him hard, before he had a chance to launch his own sprint, and I was going past him like a rocket. Lombardi clocked what was happening, swung off and proceeded to ride me all the way across the road into the barriers, squeezing me into them so I had to slow. I was ropeable – Lombardi knew I was likely to win, so he made me lose. In the next sprint, somebody put his foot into my wheel and took ten spokes out of it. I was lucky to stay upright.

It sounds like I was having a bad time, but it was actually good as well. I got pissed off, and when I get pissed off I tend to win. Just like I had in Paris in 1999. People looked at the results, saw Cipollini's name at the top and assumed he was the fastest. That's when I'm most dangerous. I had a point to prove. Not him. Me.

In Strasbourg, for stage four, Cipollini's team rode perfectly again. It was textbook, and they were absolutely flying into the finish. I couldn't believe how fast we were riding, even before the sprint. Lombardi took Cipollini to 150 metres, and Cipo opened up.

But this time was different. Cipollini did nothing wrong – he rode his usual sprint and was going bloody fast. But I was so pissed off at having not won yet that I just wasn't going to accept it again. I refused to be beaten – and that can be worth a yard or two in a sprint. I made sure I had his wheel coming in, came off him and wrenched every last bit of energy from myself, swooping around him on the line. The moment I'd taken off, I knew I'd timed it as well as I could, that this was my moment and that if I was fast enough I'd beat him. You can see his expression in the photographs of that finish – he's kind of looking over at me as if to ask, 'How? How can this be possible?' He rarely got beaten in that position, and I'd just nipped him on the line.

I'd just beaten the best sprinter in the world, and I even won another stage at that Giro – an uphill sprint that Cipollini didn't make it to the finish for. I didn't have to look back on that day to know that I'd won by a clear four or five bike lengths. I don't know if two sprinters who were both so close to their peak have come together like Cipollini and I did in that Giro for the last 20 years or so. The floodgates had opened, and my next big race would be the Tour de France. I'd waited four years to win my first stage at the Tour, and it had now been three years since that had happened. I was going to make amends.

14

It's Not that Easy Being Green

MY CAREER HAS SPANNED a golden age for road sprinters. When I started, Djamolidine Abdoujaparov, Erik Zabel, Tom Steels and Mario Cipollini were dominant – all of them incredible talents. Then Alessandro Petacchi and Óscar Freire came along in the early 2000s, followed by Thor Hushovd and Daniele Bennati, and in the later part of my career there's been Mark Cavendish and Tyler Farrar. But one period in particular stood out. There's probably never been such depth in sprinting talent as there was in 2002 and 2003, when Cipollini, Petacchi, Zabel, Freire and I were all competing for limited resources.

I've already said that Mario Cipollini was the hardest sprinter to beat, one-on-one. But Erik Zabel gave me as many problems, because he was so consistent. He was possibly the only rider I've sprinted against who hated losing as much as I do. If you beat him one day, he'd come right back at you the next. And the next. And the next. He was like a piece of iron. He never gave up. He was never ill. He rarely crashed. He never smiled. And he was fast.

Zabel won six Tour de France green-jersey competitions in a row, between 1996 and 2001. I'd actually come second in 2000, somehow, but it was an extremely distant second, given how mediocre my form had been. He was considered unbeatable in the competition. The green jersey is given to the most consistent finisher – usually but not always the best sprinter in the Tour. Points are awarded at the end of stages: 35 for the winner, 30 for second, 26 for third, etc. There are also two bonus sprints a day, giving six, four and two points for the first three over the line. The bonus sprints come during the stage, usually in a town or village en route. (The points scale has been changed for the 2011 Tour de France.)

It wasn't just outsprinting Zabel that was the problem, although I felt I was faster than him in a flat sprint. It was his ability to sprint hard for two bonus sprints every day, then again at the finish. Plus he could climb. He'd gain points on mountain stages, while that was impossible for me.

The green jersey is a strange beast. It's only a points competition, so it rewards consistency over occasional brilliance. But, at the same time, for a sprinter it is the holy grail.

I never went into the Tour with the aim of winning the green jersey – my first priority is always winning a stage. But if you win enough stages, you should generally also win the green jersey, unless something untoward, like a disqualification or a crash, prevents you from scoring points. That's why consistency is also important. One first place and one last place gives a rider 35 points. Two second places will give a rider 60 points. But I'd still take the win over two second places, even though it's less useful for the green jersey.

Sometimes the best sprinter in the Tour wins the green jersey, and sometimes he doesn't. Sometimes it's the luckiest guy. Sometimes it's the strongest and most consistent man. What I will say is that the three times I've won the green jersey, I have been the best sprinter in the Tour. And I've been the best sprinter in the Tour and not won it, as well. Each time I've won it, I've won at least two stages. Some green jerseys are greener than others, though. If you're really deserving of it, you've got to have won a stage.

My first priority in 2002 was to take a stage victory. It had been three years since my single Tour stage win, and I knew I was worth more than that. Even though 2000 had been bad, I still almost won one. I was flying when I was forced to sit out 2001. Three years pass pretty quickly in cycling.

Lotto were right behind me. The plan for the Tour was for me to win sprints, while Belgium's Rik Verbrugghe and Mario Aerts would have leeway to get into breaks. The expectation was that I would win a stage, and my own opinion was that there was no way I was coming away without a victory.

I've only once ever won the first stage of the Tour de France – in 2007. Every year, even through my peak, I've found the first stage a difficult nut to crack. It's a very nervous stage. Everybody's jumpy because it's the first sprint of the race and they don't know how they are going compared with everybody else, so it's often a bit anarchic. There was an uphill sprint into Luxembourg for the first stage in 2002, and some young guy none of us had ever heard of – Rubens Bertogliati, from Switzerland – outwitted us and escaped with a kilometre to go. I was third, with Zabel having got his wheel in front of mine. I cocked it up the next day, too, coming second behind Freire. I was bouncing off the walls with frustration.

Third, second, do the math, I thought to myself as I started the next day into Reims. Reims is the home of champagne production in France, and I was bloody well going to have something to celebrate at the finish. It was a tricky run-in to Reims, but the boys must have been looking forward to the bubbly after the stage, because Rik, Mario, Hans De Clercq and Serge Baguet (all from Belgium) were on the front of the entire peloton from five kilometres to go. I told them to just go as far as they could, because it would keep me out of trouble.

My last man was Aart Vierhouten – a good sprinter but an even better pilot fish. He'd guide me through the final kilometre and a half, taking me through gaps, holding his place in the line and shielding me from the wind. Into the final kilometre, I felt invincible. Aart dropped me off near the front at the last corner. I sat in the wheels, hit out over the top of everybody and absolutely pummelled the pedals through the final 100 metres. I tried to keep my focus right on the finish line, but I was getting distracted on two fronts. I was right up against the barriers, and as I sprinted along I was getting hit in the head by the big cardboard hands the PMU company gives out as publicity material to the fans by the road. I moved away from the barriers, then a small part of me could sense a rider right on me, not giving a single inch. I didn't turn, didn't look. I knew that if I maintained my speed to the line, I'd win. But who was it?

I moved just the smallest amount, not to discourage him from passing but more to let him know that I knew exactly where he was, then I hit the line. In three days, I'd been third, second, and now . . . first. I raised my arms. Just behind me, I could sense a flash of green out of the corner of my eye – Zabel. He had crossed the line right on my shoulder. There were 19 days left in the Tour, and 2718.5 kilometres left to ride. Little did I know that Zabel would spend a good proportion of them right there on my shoulder, where he'd finished in Reims.

I hadn't looked at the green-jersey competition yet. Zabel was in both yellow and green that evening, which meant that I'd ride the team time trial the next day in the green jersey. (The yellow takes priority, so if one rider holds both, the rider in second place wears the green jersey.) I hadn't earned it, but it was the first time I'd ever worn it, and I remember thinking, *I like how this looks and feels. I want this for myself.*

I'd had a win, a second and a third: 91 points. Zabel had had two seconds and a third: 86 points. But there was one difference: he'd also been picking up points at bonus sprints – ten in total. He was going for it, and if I wanted to win the green jersey, I'd have to all but physically rip it off his back.

Against Zabel, I knew there'd be little leeway for making mistakes, which made it especially annoying that the team made a bad decision a few days later. In stage six, to Alençon, I'd killed Zabel in a bonus sprint – I'd won, and he was third. I was now leading the competition.

But my legs had burned for far too long after that sprint. Normally, the sensation disappears after a few kilometres, but this time they felt heavy for a worryingly long time. I told the boys not to chase the break – it had one of Zabel's teammates in it, so he wouldn't chase either. Tactically, it suited me to be sprinting for seventh instead of first, because my legs felt so bad. If Zabel beat me, as I suspected he would, he'd only gain one or two points on me, instead of five or nine if we were sprinting for first.

Claudy Criquielion was the manager in the car, and he told

the boys to chase over the race radio. I wasn't wearing a radio – I rarely wear one, preferring to make my own decisions rather than be controlled by somebody who can't even see what is happening.

It came to a bunch sprint. Zabel won, and I was third. I was livid, because I'd just lost nine points to my biggest rival. You can't give nine points to Erik Zabel – it will take you a week to chisel them back out of him. I told the whole team that if I'd said not to ride, it was for a good reason.

'Don't change my tactic, and don't doubt me,' I told them.

I'm not one of those guys who says he's going terrible then wins a race. If I say I'm feeling bad, then I'm not going to be up for sprinting.

That was the last time Erik Zabel beat me in a sprint in that whole Tour, although I was about to find out just how difficult he was going to make life for me.

The next few stages were very tight. Me fourth, Zabel fifth. Me eighth, Zabel ninth. Me 13th, Zabel 14th. Two bonus sprints: me first, Zabel second. Every time I turned around, he was there, on my shoulder. It got so that I expected him to pop up over my shoulder in the mirror when I was brushing my teeth in the evening. He made me fight for every point. And I finally took the jersey off him, by one point, in Pau, the day before the Pyrenees started.

But Zabel had a plan. The next day, he caught back onto the lead group after the huge, 1709-metre-high Col d'Aubisque climb – something I didn't have a cat's chance in hell of doing – and nabbed four points in the bonus sprint. But it hadn't just been brute force that got him to that sprint – he showed how well he knew cycling's black art of team cooperation.

Cycling isn't like other sports. Alliances between different teams are so common that nobody who knows the sport bats an eyelid at them. Some alliances can last over several races – sometimes teams of the same nationality club together to help each others' riders win. Sometimes, it's entirely temporary – my team and another sprinter's team will work together to bring a break back so that we can sprint for the win. Or a team may do another team a favour one day, to call it back in when they need it a few days or weeks later. You'll sometimes see a team working for absolutely no apparent reason – chances are they're paying back a favour owed from some other race.

It happens all the time; it's part of the sport. And Zabel played me like a violin when he seemed to get a huge favour from Lance Armstrong's US Postal team on that mountain stage over the Aubisque.

I'd had a run-in with Armstrong a few days earlier, on some shitty little road in Brittany. The bunch had been quite jumpy, and on those tiny, gravelly roads, I thought, *I need to be at the front – there are going to be crashes and I need to be in front of them.*

The road was wall-to-wall with riders, so what else was a former BMX champion to do? I saw a grass verge alongside the road. *Right, this is me,* I thought, and I bunny-hopped onto it, passing Armstrong and his teammate and countryman Floyd Landis, and coming back onto the road in front of them.

Rather than compliment me on my excellent skills, Armstrong got really sarcastic, calling out, 'Everybody, look. Here comes the fucking champ,' in that Texan drawl, while Landis laughed.

I told him to get fucked.

The trouble is, a few kilometres later he got caught up in some crash, which he probably associated with me going past him, having got one up on him. He was pissed off, and it carried on for a few days. I wasn't scared of Armstrong. To me, he was just another rider. He didn't like that, because he was the big boss of the peloton. We get on fine now that we're riding for the same team.

Back to the Col d'Aubisque, and Zabel had been dropped on the climb but wasn't that far behind the leaders over the top. The lead group, led by Armstrong's US Postal team, eased up, and here's why: Zabel's Telekom team arranged a working partnership with US Postal to wait for Zabel. Once he was on, Telekom would do the work on the long valley road to the sprint and to the bottom of the final climb. Zabel would get the points, US Postal would get a break from doing all the work, plus Armstrong could get one over on me. The only losers were Laurent Jalabert, who might have gone on to win the stage if Telekom hadn't chased, and me. It was a typical cycling tactic. All the points I'd gained in sprints for eighth or 13th place, plus the bonus sprints, over the past few days were wiped out in one go. I was monumentally annoyed about it.

But, after another bonus sprint and another sprint for 13th place, Zabel and I finished the 13th stage tied on 229 points. The funny thing was that, for the next five days, neither of us would score a single point. The race went into the Alps, and neither of us was likely to get close to many bonus sprints. Sometimes, Zabel and I would have ten kilometres left before a sprint, we'd be eyeing each other nervously, and the attack would go. We'd look at each other. Are you going to chase? Nope. Are you? *Nein*. So, no points for either of us. I followed him everywhere, which must have been quite annoying for him. I felt that even if he stopped for a toilet break, I'd stop too. I wanted to know exactly where he was and what he was doing, from the start of the stage to the finish.

It was actually incredibly stressful and nerve-wracking. I wasn't enjoying it at all, and I knew that one mistake would finish it. There were only two stages where I'd realistically score any points: the 18th stage to Bourg-en-Bresse, and the final stage in Paris. The others were mountains and time trials. No chance.

But no chance for me didn't equate to no chance for Zabel. I had to kill myself to hang onto him up the climbs, just in case he made it over the top. He was renowned for nicking points here and there, and so I didn't take my eye off him once. I was going to sleep at night thinking about what might happen the next day, worrying about getting dropped and losing six points or worse.

But, in my favour, he'd only outsprinted me fair and square on two occasions in the whole Tour: stage one, and the stage that he won, in Alençon. Every other time, I'd had his measure. I'd probably beaten him about ten times, even if he'd been close behind me every time. And I couldn't rely on him making a mistake. Zabel didn't do mistakes.

Zabel was an enigma to me. He was very cold and calculating as a rider, and I never got more than a 'hey' from him in the morning. I couldn't talk with him – he didn't talk to his rivals. I never knew whether he was trying to psyche me out or he was like that the whole time.

In the Bourg-en-Bresse stage, the break had taken all the bonus points, which suited me fine, but there was a big climb in the middle of the stage, which Erik would normally drop me on. I'd got the lightest possible climbing bike the team could build, but I also actually climbed really well that day. It came down to the sprint, and Zabel and I were sprinting like mad for 11th place, as if it were for a win. I beat him again, and I went into the final day with a one-point lead. I considered myself superior to Zabel: I was faster than him. I'd beaten him from the front, from the back, from the side and upside down. But I still only had one point on him. He was incredible, really.

We came to the final stage into Paris, the scene of my triumph three years previously. I was wearing the green jersey, and between me and winning it outright there were two bonus sprints and the final sprint. I simply couldn't let Zabel beat me in a single one. Everybody else in the peloton was in a good mood, drinking champagne for the television cameras and relaxing because the race was virtually over. Meanwhile, I was highly strung and mentally exhausted.

Approaching the first intermediate sprint, outside Paris, Telekom lined the whole bunch out. But I had a plan. I told my team to get me to Zabel's wheel, at the back of the line, and I directed my Russian teammate Guennadi Mikhailov to sit in my wheel and, whatever I did, follow it. If I rode across the road, he was to do so too. If I jumped, he was to jump. I needed him behind me, to protect my back wheel from Zabel. He had Jan Ullrich, Rolf Aldag (Germany), Steffen Wesemann (Switzerland) and Gian Matteo Fagnini (Italy) – basically four of the strongest, fastest riders in the bunch – leading him out, on a downhill run towards the sprint. We were going well over 60 kilometres per hour.

And just around the side, I could see up ahead that the road went up a false flat to the sprint. My speciality.

I thought, *I am going to hit you like a ton of bricks.* I didn't want to wait for Fagnini to finish his leadout; I wanted to gap him.

I absolutely smashed my way out, jumping out of Zabel's wheel. I couldn't have gone any harder. Mikhailov tried to follow me, and he was immediately four or five lengths behind. Zabel saw what was happening and almost whacked Mikhailov into the gutter to get past him, but I was gone. He never got closer than about six metres.

That gave me a three-point lead. Still not enough. Still the stress.

And then, for the first time in that Tour, Zabel looked at me. Zabel never looked at me, and other riders who'd been up against him in the past told me that he never looked at them either. It was part of the method. I got absolutely nothing from him in three weeks of hammering each other, until after that first bonus sprint of the final stage.

We were just rolling out, after the sprint, waiting for the bunch to catch up again, and he came next to me and gave me a look, a kind of smile, as if to say 'I cannot beat you in a sprint'. He wasn't giving up – I think he was just saying 'You've got me covered, but I'm not giving this up yet'. It was a chink in the armour, the first I'd been aware of in seven years. *Gotcha*, I thought.

I glued myself to his back wheel again, and as we were riding on the Champs-Élysées I overheard him talking to Lance, in English. Lance was telling him, 'Look, Erik, don't go for the second bonus sprint, because, one-on-one, he's faster. He'll gain another two points and be five clear. And then you've got to beat him by two or three places at the end. Miss this one and, if you win the stage and he's second, you've won the green. If you're second and he's third, you've won the green.'

I could hear Zabel agreeing with him. That suited me just

fine – we'd let other riders take the points and I could rest up for the final sprint. It made me feel stronger and more confident. Lance was basically saying to him 'McEwen's faster than you'. I was thinking to myself, *Yep, I'm faster than him.*

Lance showing solidarity with Zabel was cycling's establishment resisting the newcomer. Cycling is a conservative sport – you have to earn your place at the front of the race. Lance and Zabel had won the yellow and green jerseys for the past three years, plus I'd had that run-in with Lance, so he was only too happy to support my rival.

I stuck to Zabel's wheel all the way to the Place de la Concorde before the final sprint. All I had to do was beat him and the green jersey was mine. But as the bunch reared like a snake preparing to strike, I realised I wanted more. My fellow Aussie Baden Cooke went, and suddenly the race was taking a different direction. I thought, *This is where I leave you*, and I took myself off Zabel's wheel. I didn't need him any more, and I followed Cookie. Suddenly, I wasn't sprinting just for the green jersey but for a stage win as well.

Blast-off. I gave it everything. One last sprint, and my aim was to empty myself. I didn't want to have enough energy left to pedal one metre past the finish line.

I could see it coming, and I was clear. Zabel, Cookie and all the rest didn't exist. I was dominating them. I hammered up the Champs-Élysées and won the stage. It was the holy grail of holy grails – the most important sprint in the world – and I'd won it wearing the green jersey.

I was dead. I geared myself up for the mother of all victory salutes, got my arms up to about horizontal . . . and they stopped there. I couldn't lift them any further, I was so completely wasted. The stress, the pressure, the relentless point-scoring and the calculating had drained me of emotional and physical energy. I both looked and felt like I'd been crucified. In 1999, I'd been punching the air and shouting. In 2002, I just wanted to lie down and go to sleep.

The first person to congratulate me was Zabel himself, who not only looked at me and smiled but gave me a big hug, which, considering what I'd just done to him, was very sporting of him. He may have been as cold as ice through the entire Tour, but now that the race was over he was generous in defeat. I really don't know if I could have done the same in his situation.

I couldn't make sense of what I'd done. Jef Braeckevelt, our team manager, was crying. I was just knackered. It was totally different from 1999, but in their two distinct ways those victories were the absolute pinnacles of my career.

I was battered after the Tour. I'd drained myself of physical, mental and emotional energy, and that was before we went out and hit Paris that evening.

I could have done with a rest from cycling after that, but instead I took part in as many criteriums and exhibition races through August as possible. Organisers were happy to pay through the nose to have the green-jersey winner show up at their race, and I was just as happy to oblige. In fact, considering I'd started the year earning a quarter of what I had done the year before, I was suddenly rolling in cash again. Lotto had quickly seen what they had, and after I'd won two stages at Paris–Nice, Sercu and Planckaert had come to me with a piece of paper.

'Sign here for 2003 and 2004, and we'll give you 260,000 euros a year,' they'd said. I'd bitten their hands off, but now that I'd won four Grand Tour stages plus the green jersey, I was beginning to fear that I'd undersold myself. However, 2002 must have been a lucky year, because there was a big change in the company management, and all the contracts had to be nullified and redone. Sercu and Planckaert came back to me after the Tour with 700,000 euros a year. Not only that, but they signed my best mate, Nick Gates, to ride on the team with me. I was right on track again.

2006 Tour de France green-jersey winner

Celebrating my third green jersey on the Paris podium.

2004 Giro d'Italia, stage five

Alessandro Petacchi dominated the 2004 Giro, with
nine stage wins. I managed to take one.

2005 Giro d'Italia, stage two

The first stage win in any Grand Tour feels good, but this one
also put me in the *maglia rosa*, the race-leader's jersey.

2005 Giro d'Italia, stage six

It felt like winning at will in the 2005 Giro. Henk Vogels (arm
raised) almost won but was caught just before the line.

(Graham Watson)

2005 Giro d'Italia, stage ten

Pipping Alessandro Petacchi. Beating riders commonly held to be the fastest in the world has been a theme of my whole career.

(Graham Watson)

2006 Giro d'Italia, stage two

The first of three stage wins in the 2006 Giro d'Italia.

2006 Giro d'Italia, stage four

Petacchi had crashed out of the race, and I was dominating the sprints.

2006 Giro d'Italia, stage six

Three stage wins: the same total as I'd win in the Tour de France that year.

2007 Giro d'Italia, stage two

I'd got over a very tough climb with the front group to put myself into contention for the win. Crossing the line first was the least I could do after that.

Cadel working for me at the Tour Down Under

Two strong Aussies on the same team, but we'd have
difficulty sharing resources at the Tour de France.

(Graham Watson)

Tour of Wallonia 2011, stage four

Life in the old dog yet! My first win in RadioShack colours.

(Graham Watson)

Chatting to Cav

Mark Cavendish is a very similar type of rider to me physically. It's like
riding against a younger version of myself with an exceptional team.

Nick Gates helps me to catch the bunch

My best mate, an exemplary teammate, top bloke and talented
cyclist: Nick Gates has helped me through many races, such as
here at the 2006 Worlds in Salzburg, where I finished fifth.

(Graham Watson)

15

Sprinting (II)

I'M NOT LIKE CIPOLLINI OR PETACCHI. They only really had one tactic, which was to ride on the back of a sprint train consisting of eight or so extremely strong meatheads who kept the pace extremely high in the final 15 kilometres or so of a race.

I have as many tactics as there are possible scenarios in a sprint, and I was much more able than them to improvise a win out of an unexpected situation, just because my sprinting instinct, developed from the age of eight, is one of my biggest weapons. I am fast, don't get me wrong – in the last 15 years, I'd say only Cipollini, Petacchi and Cavendish could match my speed in a straight line, and only Cavendish has had a jump equal to mine – but my sprint wasn't just in my legs; it was in my head.

I got a reputation as a rider who basically looked after himself in the sprints. This is only partially true. I had eight riders riding fully in support of me on many occasions, but their work was much less visible than in a team like Saeco for Cipollini or Columbia for Cavendish. Lotto didn't have the budget to sign eight riders capable of leading out a Tour de France sprint, so we allocated resources accordingly. I was able to handle myself in the sprints, as long as one or two of my teammates could just get me up to the back wheel of someone like Cipollini, because from there Cipollini's teammates were essentially working for me as well. If necessary, I'd get myself there. I see gaps where other riders don't, so slipping up the peloton and putting myself right in the sweet spot just behind the leadout train was a viable tactic for me.

Another reason people think I'm good at looking after myself is that I am. I have an advantage when sprints are chaotic and disorganised: my jump means that I can get up to speed faster than my competitors, and when sprints start from a lower speed it suits me just fine.

It sounds like I'm disparaging Cipollini and Petacchi by describing them as one-dimensional but I'm not, because it's exceptionally difficult to ride like they did. A sprint train doesn't just ride on the front of the bunch unchallenged – you'll get other trains trying to overtake, busting in on the line or otherwise trying to stop them from doing so. It can get pretty chaotic up there, and you really have to have some of the best riders in the world on your team to ride an effective and dominant sprint train. And even after that, you have to be able to sprint at 70 kilometres per hour.

A train works because if the pace is very high it does two things. It stops riders from being able to attack – being the best sprinter in the bunch doesn't count for anything if you're always going for second place. It also enables the strongest team to dictate the terms of the sprint in favour of their sprinter. Cipollini's teams – Saeco, then Domina Vacanze and Acqua e Sapone – could ride a virtual team time trial on the front of the bunch, holding the pace well above 50 kilometres per hour, accelerating gradually all the way to the finish, each man sacrificing everything before dropping away. By the time there was one man left in front of Cipollini, the speed would be over 60 kilometres per hour. That man, usually Gian Matteo Fagnini, would sprint at about 98 per cent of his top end until about 200 or 150 metres to go, and all Cipollini had to do was jump out at that point, accelerate to 70, and the race was won.

In spite of being exceptionally rare talents, Cipollini and Petacchi were still vulnerable. Since the idea behind their single tactic was to launch themselves off the back of their teammates' work, it stood to reason that whoever was in *their* wheels had every chance of an equally effective armchair ride to the sprint. Which meant that some of the biggest scraps I've ever been involved with were for that one place in the peloton. In late 2002, at the world championships, I'd have my second big battle of the year with Erik Zabel, for that very spot.

You can't just ride up and be the guy who sits in Cipollini's wheel. Sprinting is no different from any other walk of life that I've experienced, in that there's a very strictly defined hierarchy.

There are established stars, who may ride near the front of the bunch into a sprint, and there is a group of younger or less established sprinters, who may not, unless they are very brave or reckless. A big sprinter will allow another big sprinter into the line in front of him. In fact, Cipollini used to let Petacchi in front of him, then use him as an extra leadout man before jumping past him with 70 metres to go. But if some guy no one has heard of tries to muscle in, he's going to find himself on the receiving end of some verbal abuse, or being squeezed out of the line with the tried and trusted 'hips on handlebars' manoeuvre. You have to earn your place at the top table.

To earn your place at the front, you've basically got to keep bashing away until you get a run of results. There is also another way, which I wouldn't recommend. If you ride so dangerously and erratically that everybody's scared of going near you, that can work too. Danilo Napolitano, an Italian sprinter, fights very hard indeed for a wheel, and that's why he gets lots of results. He hasn't necessarily got the legs to win very often, but he'll put himself in an excellent position by sheer force of aggression. He's always left me alone, because he knows I'm established and don't take any of that behaviour, but I've seen him ride like a madman to get position.

The hardest thing is getting that run of wins. But when you do, it changes everything. When I'm sprinting well, riders know that it's my wheel that is the best one to follow. I noticed during 2002 that suddenly I was fighting a lot less for wheels, because the fight had moved back behind me. Riders were fighting each other for my wheel, while I cruised along ahead. Not having to fight saves a lot of energy.

Mario Cipollini was the overwhelming favourite at the world championships. The race, run using national teams rather than our professional trade teams, is usually held on a hilly circuit, but in 2002 it was almost dead flat, around the Zolder motor-racing circuit in Belgium. It was a once-in-a-lifetime opportunity for the sprinters. Cipollini was having an exceptional year, and the riders in the Italian team had been picked for one reason only: to lead him out. His last two men were Petacchi and Lombardi, which is about as close as you can get to guaranteeing victory before it actually happens. Everybody in the entire bunch knew that, apart from Cipollini, only one man would have a chance of winning if the race came down to a sprint: whoever was in his wheel 100 metres from the line. I intended that rider to be me. Cipollini wasn't the only rider having an exceptional year; I'd beaten everybody, including him, and I wanted to win a rainbow jersey. The winner of the world championships is awarded this special jersey – white with five coloured rings – and that rider has the honour of wearing it in all races for the next year.

Cipollini's wheel was a coveted spot, but it didn't always work out to be the best place to be. The week before the worlds, both of us were taking part in Paris–Tours. I knew he was on fire, so I followed him all the way through the finale. The trouble with Paris–Tours is that, while it's a relatively flat Classic, it's not a straightforward finish. That long, wide run-in through Tours is very hard to get position on. I really should have won it by now, but I'm fast running out of time.

In 2002, Cipollini was not far from the front as we came towards the sprint, but the extra distance had tired his team-mates, and they were incapable of imposing their will on the race. Normally, you'd want to do a sprint in a race like that – just before the worlds – to give yourself a confidence-booster, but Cipo got caught right out of position. Considering I had carefully chosen his wheel and spent a good few kilometres manoeuvring myself onto it, I was also out of position. We both ended up running well back.

While that one race wasn't a good time to have chosen his back wheel, the world championships a week later was.

It was probably not the most interesting race from the point of view of spectators and television viewers. The landscape was dull and the racing predictable. The Italians kept tight control all the way through. I think one small break got away, but not so that they were ever in with a chance of winning. However, for me, the less interesting the race, the better.

I was the protected rider in the Australian team, which was a pretty obvious tactic, and the boys did a good job of looking after me. I was the main man, but we had backup plans. We rode in little clusters. I had three guys, Stuey had a couple of guys, while the others fetched water bottles from the team car. But the plan was to ride just about the whole race on the back of the Italians, just like everybody else. Coming into the last kilometre, the Italians led, in a line, while the bulge of riders just behind them at the front of the bunch looked like a fight in a pub.

I wanted to be on Cipollini's wheel, *had* to be on it. The trouble was, Erik Zabel was already there. He'd hardly beaten me all season. I was faster than him. And I knew that he wouldn't have the speed to match Cipollini. Two lengths back was too far for me to come back from, so I had to get in Zabel's spot.

I got level with him, and we started shouldering each other. I got him off the wheel. Then, bang! Seven hundred metres to go, and Zabel hit me away from the wheel. There was a left-hand corner, then a straight. Bang! I hit him back. We were shoulder to shoulder, close to 60 kilometres per hour, pushing, shoving each other back and forth. I've never had to push that hard before or since to get somebody off a wheel. He was like a brick wall, but I wasn't prepared to give in. We had our full weight right on each other. I got my front wheel just in front of his, giving me the slightest advantage. My hip was level with Zabel's handlebars, and he had to back off, and suddenly I was in Cipo's wheel. You beauty.

And then, BANG! He'd swung out, swung back in again and

given me everything he had. But I gave it right back to him again. Zabel was strong, but I think I was more agile, because I managed to get my hip onto his handlebars again, and finally he was gone. I neither knew nor cared where he was.

But you can't expend that much energy at the end of a 260-kilometre race that has averaged 47 kilometres per hour and not expect to pay the consequences. By the time I had settled back into Cipollini's wheel, there were 300 metres to go and I was breathing heavily. I'd just had the biggest fight I'd ever had for position, and it seemed to me like it had taken forever. I don't blame Zabel for trying – one of us thought he was an unstoppable force, the other thought he was an immovable object. Unfortunately for him, he turned out to be movable.

The sprint happened pretty much the way I'd feared it would. Petacchi had peeled off over the drag at 500 metres to go at 60 kilometres per hour. Lombardi peeled off at 65 kilometres per hour with 200 to go. And Cipollini monstered us all in the sprint. I held him but couldn't pass him, and Zabel did the same behind me. Cipollini's worlds were won in that final 200 metres, but I'd lost mine between 700 and 300 metres from the end.

Zabel said in the press conference after the race, 'This is bike racing, not a boxing match, you know?' As if I cared. I felt like offering him 30 cents to call somebody who did care. I just told him that my hands had stayed on the bars all the way through. But it didn't matter. We'd both lost. My view was that he should have got out of my way because I was faster than him. He didn't want to be moved, and it lost the race for both of us. Except he'd have lost anyway, and I might have won.

You can see from the photographs of the medal ceremony that I didn't have my best face on. Erik had his podium smile on by then, but I didn't like losing the world championships any more than I liked losing any race.

I should have been happy, really – that podium was a snapshot of sprinting in the late 1990s and early 2000s. Cipo won 200 races in his career, Zabel had around 160 and I'd won 120. Count up the wins on that podium and you have nearly 500. I bet there's not been a podium to equal it before or since.

In retrospect, I don't think I lost the gold that day; I won the silver medal. I think I had the legs to do to Cipollini what I'd done to him at the Giro, when he'd had a perfect leadout, but I needed an undisturbed run-in to the finish. Later, I was extremely proud, but at the time I just had the shits. You don't stop having a winner's mentality, even when you lose.

16

How Much Is a
Green Jersey Worth?

DID I TELL YOU THE ONE about an Australian underdog challenging for the Tour de France green jersey against the defending champion, with the result going right down to the final sprint on the Champs-Élysées? How the plucky underdog snatched the green jersey right on the finish line?

The trouble is, I'm not talking about 2002 but 2003. I was expecting the experience of having won the green jersey to help me the following year, but it didn't. When I look back at the 2003 Tour, when I was riding for the Lotto-Domo team, it's as if some guy who looked like me was riding the event. It felt like I didn't even show up. I had another one of those mystery dips in form that affected me through much of the 1999 and 2000 races, and I struggled. Actually, that's not true – I was going neither well nor badly, just falling down the hole that lies between the two. I was mediocre.

Form is what lies between art and science in training. I'm

generally quite good at building it and bending it to my will, but I find it equally fascinating and frustrating that I can do identical training over the course of two years and end up riding out of my skin one season and like a bag of spanners the next.

That's almost what happened in 2003, although I was going okay for a bit. I was good but not great. I won races, and even took two Giro stages, beating Petacchi and Cipollini. But when I started the Tour in Paris, I simply wasn't on my game. In 2002, I rode the first few stages knowing it was a matter of when, not if I won a stage. In 2003, I just hoped something would come along. Hope never won anybody anything.

It didn't help that Alessandro Petacchi showed up to the Tour, told me he was in such bad shape that he'd get dropped climbing the stairs, then proceeded to absolutely roast everybody in the sprints in the first week. He won four stages, while I scrabbled around wondering if I should be going for bonus sprints or stage wins. The only other sprinter to win a stage in the first week was my fellow Australian Baden Cooke.

I'd actually been wearing the green jersey – I'd started chiselling out points right from the first bonus sprint of the first stage, which I'd won, before coming second on the stage. That was enough to give me the jersey that I'd worn in Paris the previous year. Second in the stage but picking up bonus points to put myself over the top. Bloody hell. I'd turned into Erik Zabel.

Consistent mediocrity somehow gave me a one-point lead over Petacchi even after he'd won three stages. But I wasn't around to see him win his fourth – Erik and I came around a right-hand bend about two kilometres before the finish in Lyon, and there was an oil patch on the road. We both went down like a sack of potatoes, and I ripped myself up a bit as I hit the deck.

With some crashes, you know what is going to happen and your body will prepare itself for the impact. Not this time. I hit the ground like a guided missile.

I started trying to get back up and onto my bike even before I'd stopped rolling. I swore blue bloody murder, put the chain back on and launched myself in pursuit of the bunch. Adrenalin and anger propelled me through the streets of Lyon. I was sprinting at almost full bore, just to give myself the chance to be near the front.

But my morale cracked when I only caught the back end of the bunch with a kilometre to go. Game over. I sat up – there was no way I was getting back to the front after that. Petacchi won again, Cookie was second and I was 164th, and while I got my wounds sorted out Petacchi was being presented with my green jersey.

It was a nightmare. I wasn't sprinting well, and now I'd crashed. I just wasn't moving that well on the bike.

It turned out that Petacchi wasn't lying about his climbing form, however. He climbed into his team car as soon as we started riding up the first mountain of the Tour. His manager, Giancarlo Ferretti, was ropeable, but Petacchi was like that – he'd got his four stage wins and he couldn't be arsed to ride over the mountains for three days to see if he could make it five.

Lucky him. I've always made a big point of not giving up in the mountain stages of the Tour de France. Apart from missed starts, I've only ever failed to finish the race once: in 2007, when I was bent out of shape after my crash on stage one. And even then, I got to the finish of the mountain stage at Tignes, though I was well outside the time limit.

I've been close to getting eliminated a few times. On the

climb to Courchevel, in the Alpine stages of the 1997 Tour de France, riding for Rabobank, I'd just about run out of energy and we'd passed the '20 kilometres to go' sign, so there was no more feeding from the team cars. I was delirious – I was going to get dropped, and the gruppetto were riding bloody hard, just to make sure of making the time cut. I went back to Adri Van Houwelingen in the team car and just about managed to communicate that I needed a Coke, and I needed it right now.

'I'm not allowed. You're in the last 20 kilometres,' he said.

'Give me the fucking Coke or I'm going home,' I rasped.

He gave me the Coke.

You have to do the mountains if you want to get to the end of the Tour. They're a necessary evil if you want to win the green jersey. While the climbers and yellow-jersey contenders love the big mountains, sprinters climb them for exactly the same reason as George Mallory: because they are there.

At best, I struggle over mountains. To be the best at sprinting, I work a lot on speed and power, not climbing. I've got quite a lot of upper-body muscle for my size, and it weighs me down, at the same time as making me strong in the sprints.

Some days at the Tour, I wake up and know I'll get through. It's the other days, when I feel like I'm nailed to the bed, that I can't really laugh about it. When I've been going for the green jersey, there's always been a rival who can climb well, like Erik Zabel, so I've not been able to risk getting dropped early. Ultimately, though, the mountains are pure survival for me.

In 2003, there were three days in the Alps. The race organisers must have really had it in for me when they laid out the route of the third, which went from Bourg d'Oisans to Gap. It went straight up at the start, over two huge mountains: the Col du

Lautaret and the Col d'Izoard. Then it was just undulating and grippy, with two more big climbs before the finish. Just getting out of bed for the Gap stage had caused my legs to burn with lactic-acid pain – that's the sensation you get after running up a couple of flights of stairs. Walking to breakfast was like running a mile. Lifting my breakfast plate was like doing a weights workout. I knew it was going to be a horrible, horrible day, and that I'd be in the hurtbag for the foreseeable future.

I got dropped after about eight kilometres, and we'd hardly started the climb. The Lautaret is a horrible, open, draggy ascent up the side of a long valley – it goes up and up for about 20 kilometres. The road is wider than most Tour climbs, which makes me feel exposed, for some reason. I was straight out the arse, in the middle of nowhere, climbing on my own, thinking, *Oh shit, I'm in trouble here.*

The last place you want to be in a mountain stage of the Tour is off the back of the gruppetto. In the 2000 Tour, I'd had one of the worst days of my cycling life on the 16th stage to Morzine. I'd made the elementary error of going for the first bonus sprint in Albertville. The route then went up a steep two-kilometre climb, then dragged up to the *bottom* of the Col des Saisies, the first of four mountains. I went out the back on the two-kilometre ramp after winning the sprint and was on my own for a long time after that. It took me three climbs to catch the gruppetto.

Getting dropped on the Lautaret in 2003 was worse – I went over the top in last place.

The only thing worse than climbing the Lautaret is descending it – the downhill on the east side is not steep enough to really save energy, and I found I was working far too hard. I caught Stefano Zanini, who looked as bad as I felt, and Pierrick Fédrigo, from France. We got off the descent and then had to turn sharp left and go straight up the Col d'Izoard, one of the hardest mountains in the Tour. It was a couple of kilometres up, then a flat section, and then 14 kilometres of pure steep climbing hell. Zanini wasn't stupid – he'd had enough and just climbed off his bike. Me and Fédrigo lost each other – I can't even remember who rode away from whom, because I was mainly looking down at the road as I ground my way up the climb.

And I punctuated every pedal stroke by saying, or at least thinking, *Shit, shit, shit, shit, shit.* I'd not won a stage, I was going badly and I was going to be out of the Tour by the evening at this rate. That's if I made it to Gap by the evening.

And then, about three-quarters of the way to the summit, I looked up and saw the most amazing sight. My best mate, Nick Gates, zigzagging across the road, looking back for me, waiting to help. What a legend. I could have bloody kissed him. He urged me to get cracking.

The team was having a shocker that day. Just towards the top, we came across Léon Van Bon, another teammate, who'd had a hunger flat and was experiencing a very bad moment. Suddenly, it was me encouraging him, but he was muttering about pulling out, he felt so bad.

This is the Tour de France that the television cameras and viewers don't see. The story of the race is always who's attacked whom at the front, who's winning, who's losing, all the intrigue of the yellow-jersey battle, and action-packed, exciting fast racing. But there are 180 riders in the Tour de France, and in the mountain stages there are 170 stories that are not told, as riders struggle to beat the time limit just so they can do it again the next day. Stories that nobody's interested in but are just as interesting as those of the race leaders, like those of Stefano Zanini, who'd been too beat to even carry on pedalling, or Léon, who was in his own personal, private hell when we caught him on the Izoard.

At the top of the Izoard, with 100 kilometres to go, we were 25 minutes behind the leaders. There was no chance we were going to make the finish in time – the Tour organisation eliminates riders who finish outside a certain percentage of the winner's time. There were three of us, against faster-moving, stronger, bigger, less totally knackered groups ahead. I could easily see us losing another half-hour by the finish. Big groups go faster than small groups – it's one of the elementary rules of cycling.

But Gat and I went into survival mode. The first job was to get Léon into good-enough shape to be useful, so we forced Extran down his throat and made him eat everything he could keep down. We were yelling at him, 'Eat! Drink!' all the way down the descent. We caught Sandy Casar, a good French rider who should have been a long way up the road – he must have been having a really bad day.

The four of us rode through the feed zone, and there was nothing there – no team cars, nobody left, just discarded bags, empty cans, wrappers and energy-gel packs, blowing around in the wind. It was eerily quiet.

I didn't have to notice which way the trash was blowing through the feed zone to know that we were facing a block headwind, which was going to make our lives even more difficult. Luckily, Léon had come around, and he started pulling huge turns at the front. He pulled for four kilometres, right into the wind. Then Nick would take over for a kilometre. Then Léon for another huge distance, and Nick. I just hung on, and I'd have started screaming with the pain in my legs if I'd had any breath left to do it. I didn't even have the breath to tell them to slow down, which I desperately wanted to do.

Nick and Léon towed me and Casar all the way to Gap, along windy valley roads and over the two climbs to the finish. I'd been going badly in the sprints, and I was getting dropped on every climb, but the boys still had enough faith in me to risk their own elimination, just to try to keep me in the race. We hammered across the line, and I glanced back at the clock that hangs on the gantry at the finish. Thirty-nine minutes. We'd only lost 14 minutes to the leaders of the Tour de France, over 100 hard, hilly kilometres. We were still in the race. And my immediate thought was, *Shit, I've got to do this again tomorrow.*

How much do you think a green jersey is worth? When I won it in 2002, I got the prize money, divided among the team, minus taxes. By the time all that maths had been done, I pretty much had no money left. But it still made my accountant very busy.

In terms of my contract, it helped Lotto decide to offer me a pay rise from 65,000 euros to 700,000 euros a year. A lot of that rise was owing to the 19 wins I'd got in 2002, but the green jersey certainly helped.

However, it's the post-Tour crits where being the Tour de France green-jersey winner really makes a difference. Tour de France stage winner Robbie McEwen used to earn a couple of thousand euros a go for showing up and taking part in an exhibition race. Green-jersey-winner Robbie McEwen was getting ten grand a pop. If I took part in 15, which was entirely possible as long as I was well organised with the logistics and didn't mind making myself even more tired, the green jersey earned me another 100,000 euros at least.

Which is why I found myself in conversation with my main rival for the competition in 2003, Baden Cooke, as we rode along during the third-last stage to St Maixent-l'École.

'How's it going, Cookie?' I asked.

'Good mate. You?'

'Yeah, good. Listen, I've been thinking . . .'

The day to Gap had been the low point of my Tour. After that, although I didn't exactly start feeling fresh or anything, I got a little bit of snap back in my legs. And, as we left the Alps, I was only ten points behind Cookie, who'd inherited Petacchi's green jersey, and I set about chipping away at his lead.

The situation was just like me and Zabel the year before. I beat Cookie in a bonus sprint, but then he just got his wheel in front of mine for tenth place in Marseille, behind a break. The next day, I repaid the favour – me ninth, him tenth. There was nothing between us. And, in another echo of the previous year, we each scored nothing through the Pyrenees. It was more relaxing racing Cookie than Zabel – he was one of the few riders in the field who were as bad as me at climbing, so at least I didn't have to worry about him taking bonus sprints in the mountains. That said, Zabel himself, who'd been having a pretty average Tour, got over the mountains in the final Pyrenean stage and got second place, putting him only five points behind me. I was all set for a very stressful final few days.

Cookie was sprinting really strongly, and he'd been getting very good leadouts from our fellow Aussie Brad McGee. But I kept on chipping away. Me 11th, him 13th into Bordeaux, and I thought, *Right, gotcha.*

Even better, Lance Armstrong and Jan Ullrich, first and second overall but very close to each other on time, started going for bonus sprints. In the run-up to the first sprint on stage 18, they started going at each other hammer and tongs, while Cookie sat on one of his teammates, not realising the danger. I railed it around a corner after them and hit over them both. Outsprinting them was like taking candy from a baby. I got six points, while Armstrong and Ullrich got second and third.

The difference between my battle with Zabel and my battle with Cookie was that at least Cookie and I were looking at each other and talking. We're not best mates or anything, but we kept it civil in that Tour, and we'd wish each other good luck in the mornings.

As the two of us rode along and chatted during stage 18, after I'd taken the six points in the bonus sprint, I decided to make him an offer that would benefit both of us. I said, 'Listen, Cookie. I've got the jersey by one point. I'll give you 50,000 euros not to sprint any more.'

I thought that was a pretty good deal. I'd got the upper hand in the competition, and it looked like I was faster. But it was better to be safe than sorry, so I thought a professional agreement might be a good idea. From my point of view, the green jersey would cost me 50 grand, but I'd make it all back up, and more, in criterium fees and future contract negotiations. From his, he'd have a guaranteed 50,000 euros instead of a possible green jersey.

I didn't really have the intention of doing a deal, but I wanted to play a mental game with Cookie. I wanted to see how much he wanted it, now that I'd pulled ahead. The green jersey is as much a mental war as a physical one, so I wanted to try to break his concentration – if he was considering it, it might take away some of his intensity.

He came straight back at me and said, 'I'll give you a hundred.'

That put an end to the game pretty quickly. 'Looks like we're going to sprint for it,' I replied.

So we did. And it didn't go well for me.

I did win the bunch sprint at the end of the stage, one place in front of Cookie, which meant I was in the lead by two points. There were two stages left: a time trial, with no chance of points, and the final stage into Paris.

I'd actually felt almost human since the Pyrenees. But something happened during the time trial on the penultimate day, which took place in filthy weather. I don't know what it was, but I'd put my back out, or twisted my hip riding the lower position on my time-trial bike through the cold rain and wind. I'm never comfortable on those bikes anyway, and I climbed off at the end, not even having ridden that hard, with my hamstrings and glutes feeling like tightly strung piano wires.

I didn't get any better overnight. As the last day started, I felt really crappy on the bike – I just couldn't get comfortable, with the lower-back pain. It wasn't ideal.

The two intermediate sprints were at the top of the Champs-Élysées, up the drag past the finish line, and Cookie's team, Française des Jeux, stitched me up good and proper. They set a trap, and I walked right into it.

They lined it out, going hard up the right-hand gutter. Their rider on the front, Frenchman Carlos Da Cruz, peeled off, but instead of freewheeling he carried on pedalling fairly hard, so he was drifting back slowly. Brad McGee surged through, pulling for Cookie, and he left a small gap on the barriers for Cookie to slip through. I was on Cookie's wheel, and my only route through was after him, because Da Cruz was on my left side, preventing me going that way. I could see it coming a mile off, but there was absolutely nothing I could do about it: Cookie got through, McGee shut the door, and by the time I'd extricated myself he'd got six points. I could only come second.

I was filthy with myself for screwing it up so badly. They'd out-clevered me, and I hate being out-clevered. We were level on points, and since Cookie had won a stage he'd be leading the classification.

Two laps later, they tried to pull the same trick again. Da Cruz swung off again, and I could see him coming back slowly.

There's a saying in Belgium: '*De ezel stuit zich geen tweede keer aan dezelfde steen*' – a donkey doesn't stub its toe on the same stone twice. I pre-empted their little manoeuvre, jumped out and easily gapped Cookie. Chalk two points back up for McEwen.

It was clear that whoever came highest in the final sprint would win the jersey. It was a chaotic lead-up to the finish, but McGee was leading Cookie up the final straight, with me right on his wheel. Perfect. *Gotcha*, I thought to myself.

Cookie hit out of McGee's wheel, and all I could hear as we went past was Brad shouting, 'GO! GO! GO! GO, COOKIE, GO!'

I attacked out of Cookie's slipstream, but I wasn't feeling myself. My sprinting style was like something in one of those dreams you have where things just aren't working the way they should, or you're cycling really hard and going about two miles an hour. My mind knew exactly what to do, but I just sensed that my body wasn't understanding the instructions properly.

It was a bad advert for road sprinting. I think we were both pretty wasted, and as I drew level we were all over the place. I was vaguely aware that somebody – it turned out to be France's Jean-Patrick Nazon – had already gone past us on the right. He was busy setting himself up for life as a French winner of the Champs-Élysées stage of the Tour, but Cookie and I only cared about each other. I had none of the focus or mental acuity of my normal sprint – I was just bloody going for it, with everything I had.

I've always had a tendency to get right into someone when I'm going past him in a sprint. Maybe it's a hangover from my BMX days, but I'm often close enough to touch elbows, and I find it intimidates opponents that I'm happy to be riding so close to them. A small amount of contact – a shoulder, elbow or a little lean against a rival – is standard in BMX, and I brought it to cycling with me when I needed it. It's actually good sprinting – you can gain a bit of slipstream by sheltering right inside your rival's personal space. Plus, if sprinting at close quarters puts them off, it might just distract them from putting 100 per cent into their own sprint. But Cookie's also that kind of sprinter, and so we were all over each other. It was very uncomfortable. And if I felt like I was floating over the setts when I'd first won here in 1999, this time I could feel my bike clattering over every single one.

We approached the line locked together. As my elbow came into him, he got himself forward, leaning into me, and I could sense he was a bee's dick in front. As our bodies banged against each other, he just managed to get his shoulder in front as we threw our bikes at the line. We were virtually holding each other upright.

It was messy. It was ridiculous. And as soon as we hit the line,

I knew he was in front. One metre beyond it, all I could think was, *What happened?*

Almost straight away, I said, 'Good on ya, Cookie.' He'd beaten me fair and square.

I hung around for long enough to see if the judges had any appetite for looking at the way Cookie had sprinted – there had been a touch before the line, which was where he'd got the edge on me, but they told me fairly quickly that the result would stand. It was fair enough – we'd been bumping and barging, sprinting all over each other for the best part of two weeks.

But I was devastated. It hurt that I lost the green jersey to someone I felt I was better than. But that's the Tour – I was average, and Cookie rode out of his skin. He also got a 30-point head start on me when I crashed, and he came second on stage five. If I'd sprinted that day, I'd have been comfortably in green from the moment Petacchi pulled out. Then again, there was one day Cookie got blocked in a sprint and almost knocked off, and I gained a handful of points on him, but it wasn't 30. It did occur to me that if I'd got my wheel in front of Cookie's, I'd have won the green jersey without winning a stage – it wouldn't have been a very green green jersey, but I'd still have taken it.

Cookie was never the same rider after that Tour. Maybe if he'd lost that battle, he'd have come back for more. But he won, and I lost, and it hadn't cost him a penny. And even though I was disappointed to lose, I never once thought, *I wish I'd taken the hundred-thousand euros.* Not once.

It wasn't just poor form that had cost me in 2003. Instead of prioritising stage wins and letting the green jersey come and find me as a natural consequence, I'd actively gone looking for it. I won the very first bonus sprint of the Tour, but going for bonus sprints in the first week tired my legs for the finishing sprints.

I'd learned my lesson. From now on, I'd win stages, and the green jersey would come to me.

17

Why I Am the Way I Am

A LOT OF PEOPLE SEEM to be able to go back to their past and pinpoint some miserable experience that they can use as a hook to hang their character on. Maybe their parents split up, and it's given them attachment or abandonment issues. Or their dad was an alcoholic, and it goes some way to explaining their own addictive or obsessive behaviour.

With me, sorry, but there's nothing there. I had a happy, well-adjusted childhood. My mother and father were supportive and hardworking. I got on well with my brothers. I was no great shakes at school, but neither did I find it particularly difficult. The biggest trauma in my childhood was having to choose between chocolate and strawberry milk.

But I am still my parents' son. There are all kinds of personality traits and tics that I've got straight from them.

My dad was a car salesman. He was very good at it, because he knew cars, he understands people and he is very smart. Dad was a proper boy racer when he was a young man – he rolled a souped-up Mini once. My dad and I spent a lot of time in the car when I was young – he drove me all over the place to race (without rolling the car). We talked a lot, sometimes about BMX, sometimes not.

My dad is one of those people who like to do things properly. We'd drive over a mountain to an event, and he'd explain how to take a line through a corner and then demonstrate it, accelerating through the apex. He took the technical side of things very seriously, and I think I got a big chunk of that from him.

I sometimes see riders who go through their careers with their eyes closed. They train hard, ride hard and race hard. But I can see they're not taking care of the small things. The level of detail with which I analyse everything possible makes me a tiny bit better, many times over. British Cycling have made a big thing of their Olympic success at cycling, that their unique approach – the accumulation of marginal gains – is what makes the difference between them and their rivals. But I can tell you now, I've been doing that stuff for close to two decades. Can I corner more smoothly, without losing speed? Can I relax more when I'm climbing and save energy? Can I keep my upper body more anchored when I'm sprinting? Can I ride closer to a wheel and get more draught from it?

When I was a young pro, I taught myself how to urinate off the bike – there's a surprising number of riders who can't do it. If you have to stop, you have to chase back on, and that takes extra energy. Once the bunch is going at 40 or 45 kilometres per hour, you want to be in it, not behind it, chasing. I do everything I possibly can to make myself better at winning races. It drives me crazy watching people not doing things properly, because I'm such a perfectionist about it.

My dad and I used to speak a lot about the tactics to use in

BMX races, as we drove to and from events. My dad didn't race, but he'd seen me enough times to have worked out what advice to give. He'd usually be right.

My dad is a quiet, unassuming, patient, well-mannered man. He's also very funny, and he's always ready with a smartarse comment or comeback. He didn't go to university, but if he had he would have excelled. He understands things very clearly and logically, he's very well read, and it's from him that I get my recall.

We both remember the most useless bloody facts about everything. I can remember just about every sprint I've ever done, for example. Not long before I wrote this chapter, I was at Paris–Tours, and the team and I went out for a spin in Chartres the day before the race. Coming back from the ride, about two kilometres from the hotel, I said to my teammates, 'Hang on a second, I've been up here before.' Before they could say, 'Shut up, Robbie,' I was telling them about the 2004 Tour de France. Stuey won the stage. Sweden's Magnus Bäckstedt pulled the sprint. I won the bunch sprint for sixth. All the details were in my head, and I was telling my teammates, some of whom hadn't even turned professional in 2004, exactly what had happened. Cipollini and Petacchi both crashed mid-stage. I could remember it as we rode along, even though they'd put in a couple of extra roundabouts that weren't there in 2004.

When I tell stories, I'm always digressing, which must be pretty annoying for people, because I have to get every single detail in. It pushes me off on tangents, because I've stockpiled all the information, ordered it in my mind and want to get it all out again. Ask me to tell you about a certain sprint, and I will. You'll also find out what the weather was like that day and probably hear a list of results attained by one or more of my rivals, plus what I think of them as people – to me, that's all part of the story.

I can't overstate how important my memory is to me as a sprinter. I've got a reputation as an instinctive rider, able to chop and change tactics even as events unfold before me, but really I'm not. I've got so many experiences in the memory bank, ready to be used when necessary, that it's not instinct but subconscious recall and my mind working out what to do according to a thousand events that I've experienced in the past. The way I see it, if I don't take in all this information to be stored for later use, I might lose a centimetre in a sprint some time. Stage finishes are like a movie in my mind. Instant recall is a big component in my weaponry, and I get it from my dad.

Where my dad and I differ, however, is that I'm an Aussie. He's been living here for over 40 years, but four decades in Australia haven't been able to take the Britishness out of the Brit, and he's pretty proud of his heritage. He's more or less lost the Queen's English accent, although he doesn't really sound like an Aussie either. But he fits in well over here. What you really need to know about him, though, is that everybody likes my dad, because he always makes a good impression. People say to me 'Your dad's a good bloke'. 'Funny bastard', they invariably add.

My mum never lost her British upbringing either. While I'm a typical Aussie who has no airs or graces and probably swears a little too much, Mum is much more refined. She's also the only person in the world who still calls me Robert – although, to be fair, it was only really in my late teens that everybody started calling me Robbie, to my mother's disgust. I was Robert or Rob for most of my childhood.

But she's no retiring flower. My mum can get fired up pretty well. If I get beaten, and she thinks it was unfair, she'll sit there for a bit, fume, and then go off on one. She'll say, 'That bloody Boonen, getting in front of you in the sprint. It wasn't fair.'

She'll stick up for herself as well, which is possibly something she had to do living in a house of four McEwen males, three of whom were doing dangerous boy-type stuff more or less on a daily basis. But maybe it's just the way she is.

That's something I've got from my mum. I'll stick up for myself, in the bunch, or in a sprint, or in a team meeting, or when I'm in a bar with my mates, or any time I think I need sticking up for. It happens more often than you'd think, but at least most riders know by now not to try to take my place in the line.

My mum's a real organiser, which she had to be in our household. It's no easy job keeping three young boys clothed, clean and going to school at the right time, and she ran a tight ship. She's also a very hard worker, and I've inherited her work ethic. She worked at the post office, doing the parcel run – she had to sort the parcels, load them into her car and deliver them to houses. And here's the best bit: she ran from the car to the house with the parcels. Then she ran back. I think I got my fast-twitch muscle fibres from my mum and my racing brain from my dad. It's quite a combination.

I'm not blind or deaf – I know what my reputation is among cycling fans. Sometimes, my directness, and the fact that I'll always stick up for myself, makes me look chippy.

Generally, I'm pretty relaxed. I don't like to get stressed about things, although there is a different kind of stress that I internalise and see as healthy. That internal stress is the pressure I put on myself to keep winning, and I find that it gets me sharp. When I'm going well, I'm very good at visualising victory, and that in itself makes me a little nervous, gives my system a shot of adrenalin. I internalise the feeling and add it to everything else – it's like mixing the ingredients for a bomb that I need to explode in the finishing straight.

Sometimes, before a race, I'll be that focused that it's not worth talking to me, because I'll only tell you to fuck off. It's not me being evil, it's me being focused and trying to do my job as best I can. I call it my race face, while my team manager at Lotto, Allan Peiper, calls it my angry mode. He's slightly wide of the mark, because it's not anger, it's focus. But it does make me look like I'm contemplating violence, which isn't strictly true.

It's probably true that I get into more altercations and arguments than most, simply because of the way I need to ride in order to get results. I've never had a full train working for me, so I have to go for gaps in the bunch to move up. Winning bike races is all about saving energy – I can't go the long way around into the wind, so I've sometimes had to shove guys out of the way. It's the way I sprint, too. I get right into people, just like I did with Cookie on the Champs-Élysées in 2003, and it makes them uncomfortable. That's usually an advantage for me, even if it didn't work with Cookie in Paris.

I ride in a way that exposes me to more risk, but cycling is a battle for position. I'm battling people to win races, and because I'm mainly doing it on my own I come into more situations where somebody (not me) is going to come off second best.

Generally, riders don't get in my way, because they know I won't back down. If somebody is causing me problems, I'll do the hip on the handlebars trick to just put them off balance, then tell them that next time they'll be on the ground. There was a late-season race in 2010 where I tried to get around a Skil rider, who switched me, crossing his back wheel in front of mine to make me swerve, because he thought I was chasing down his teammate. I patiently waited, got in front of him, then lifted my back wheel into the air and flicked it sideways so it hit his front wheel. Bang. I said, 'Switch me again and the next time it will be real.'

I'm not quick to allow an up-and-coming sprinter, or in fact anybody who doesn't belong at the front of the race, to drop in on me. My reasoning is fairly simple: you're not as fast as me, you're going to interfere with people who are capable of winning and there's no point trying to break into the line right near the front, only so you can come fifth rather than tenth. People trying too hard and getting in where they don't belong causes crashes.

I can be a bit of a hard bastard in the peloton, but, then again, I've had a 16-year professional career, and nobody messes around with me. I prefer to think of myself as firm but fair.

And all this, I stress, is when I'm on duty. It's what I have to do to maximise my chances of winning. When I'm not on duty, during the mountain stages of a Grand Tour, or when I'm not racing, I'm not that person – I don't have to be. Come round to my house of an afternoon and you'll find me building dirt jumps in the garden for me and Ewan to ride over, or just relaxing, talking to whoever's around and enjoying the company. If I'm out having a coffee and somebody comes up to have a chat or get an autograph – which happens pretty much every day in Belgium – I'm happy to oblige. My wife will tell you that I'm possibly too patient with people. I know other cyclists who just tell people to get stuffed. Most of the time, I'm Dr Jekyll. Mr Hyde only makes rare appearances, but unfortunately people judge him, not me.

18

The Most Important

Man in Cycling

THERE WERE TWO IMPORTANT things that had to happen in 2004. First, the team had to trust me to be able to continue to do things my own way, rather than start micro-managing me. And second, whatever I was doing in 2002, I needed to do that, rather than what I was doing in 2003. It's not even that 2003 was that bad – I won seven races, including beating Cipollini and Petacchi at the Giro d'Italia, and almost won a stage and the green jersey at the Tour. But it was still a let-down. I was only just off, but off nonetheless.

I've no idea what happened to me physically in 2003, but I probably went deeper into my reserves in 2002 than I realised. I was tired from the start of the season in 2003. If there are cracks in the foundations, the building won't stand up straight.

It stood to reason, I thought, that I should probably not try to win absolutely every race in 2004. I'd rather win one Giro stage, one Tour stage and the green jersey than any number of smaller races, although I still couldn't help myself at the Tour Down Under, where I took two stage wins and second overall. And I was going well enough to finish second overall at the Tour of Qatar. But I was very conscious that I didn't want to burn myself out before the Tour.

I found life difficult at the Giro. I was pissing into the wind there that year – there was nothing wrong with my form, and I was capable of winning more, on paper. But sprints aren't raced on paper, they're raced in the real world, where ambition and talent sometimes bump up against inconvenient truths. The fact is that Alessandro Petacchi was in probably his best ever form in 2004, and his Fassa Bortolo team were dominating everybody. It's very hard to ride against a team that can do that.

They hammered it on the front every single day, and there was such a fight for Petacchi's wheel that I was always shot by the time the sprint started. Petacchi won nine stages. I managed to win the fifth stage, when Fassa Bortolo lost their rhythm and it got a bit more chaotic.

I was quite right to be frightened of Petacchi at the Giro – he was at his peak, the course favoured him, with lots of flat stages, and his team were basically beating up the rest of us and stealing our lunch money. But at the Tour, I wasn't scared of anybody. The race started in Liège, in Belgium, so I was virtually on home ground. I was going to try to win stages and, once that had happened, start working towards the green jersey.

There's no race in the world like the Tour de France. From the outside, it probably looks like an exciting, fun place to be. It's a travelling circus – 200 riders, another 200 team staff, the Tour workers, press, television, the people who work on the publicity caravan, hangers-on and fans. But the view from the inside is a lot different. It's actually quite a stressful place to be.

The stress is everywhere – it's internal and external. I'm stressed because I haven't won a stage yet. The other sprinters are stressed because they haven't won yet. Teams who haven't won a stage, or got a contender for the yellow jersey, or maybe don't even have a sprinter, they're all stressed, from the management to the riders. It happened at Rabobank in 1999, and it got so bad in the second half of the race that they just gave up, except for me. The only real stress-reliever is a stage win, or the end of the race in Paris, when the GC race is more or less over the day before.

The stress can show in any number of ways, and the more tired everybody is, the worse it gets. Through the first week, you just sense a general narkiness in the bunch. Somebody will drop in on somebody else – something that happens every minute of every bike race I've ever been in. But the stress magnifies the effect. Words are exchanged. Sometimes, there's contact. I've seen riders whack other riders on the helmet or give them a shove. In rare cases, fist fights break out, either on the bikes or after the finish.

The Tour can be a real mood-enhancer. For the riders who've been winning, life is easy. You can never escape the tiredness, but a couple of stage wins can turn the second week into a holiday camp. If you've missed out, though, it can be a prison camp. The microphones and Dictaphones of the journalists at the stage finish feel like prodding, poking fingers, pointing at you, singling you out, asking why. Why haven't you won a stage yet? Why aren't you as fast as the others? Why? Why? It's not just the press. You start doubting yourself as well.

If you're not going well in the second week, the management

start to wear an air of pessimism, just like at Rabobank. At the team talks, the urgency to get a rider in the break becomes more desperate. Miss the break and it's going to be another long, grim, hot day in the saddle, and another long, grim, quiet team dinner at the hotel that evening.

By the third week, everybody's too tired to really get stressed. Fuses are shorter than ever, but you don't tend to see the energetic shouting and arguing you'd get in the first week. That doesn't mean the pressure has gone, however – everybody's getting angrier and angrier but just internalising it all. Add that to the fatigue and it's no wonder everybody looks about ten years older than they did when they started the race.

On the second evening of the 2004 race, following the Prologue time trial and first stage, the only people who weren't stressed were the two stage winners so far: Jaan Kirsipuu and Fabian Cancellara, and their teams. Plus, oddly, one more person: Robbie McEwen.

Kirsipuu beat me fair and square in the stage-one sprint. He was a bloody strong sprinter, and he got the jump on us all. I could sense that he was going to get it from a long way out, but the good news was that I was by far the best of the rest, and I really took a lot of distance out of Kirsipuu in the last 50 metres or so. Confidence can make a big difference in how your Tour will go, and what I learned in the sprint at the end of stage one was that I was the fastest rider in the Tour and that the other sprinters who'd normally worry me – Petacchi, Cipollini, Zabel, Stuey and Thor Hushovd – weren't going to be close.

Kirsipuu had handed out a tactical lesson to me, outwitting me by going early, but long-term I couldn't see him causing me trouble. He rode the Tour 12 times and never once finished it.

He was as strong as an ox and about as good at cycling up hills. He could barely climb the steps to the podium to get his winner's champagne, let alone the Alps and Pyrenees.

I knew that if I stayed calm and rode my normal race the next day, I'd be surprised if I got beaten again. Stage two finished in Namur, and it was one of those days where I was focused from start to finish. I did my homework carefully, memorising the maps of the last five kilometres in the Tour's route book. I put my boys on the front all day – I wanted to make sure the break came back. And I sat with my wingman Aart Vierhouten all day long. I talked to him non-stop through the finish – I wanted every detail to be perfect. Vierhouten would essentially be an extension of my own body. I needed him to get me up the bunch, shelter me, use the potential energy of the peloton to move us forwards, but still save energy himself, so that he could give me one really massive acceleration when I needed it.

My favourite kind of sprint is one where there's a corner quite close to the finish. For some reason, quite a lot of sprinters won't go until they can see a line to sprint for. I did my research, looked at the map, pointed at that corner and told myself that whoever was first into it would win the stage.

Me, in other words.

It was a good finish – classic Tour de France. Fabian Cancellara was leading the race overall, but he was Petacchi's teammate, so we had the yellow jersey on the front of the bunch leading out the sprint. Hushovd was there, I saw Cipollini, but I had better legs and a better plan than any of them. I'd jump at the sharpest point of the sweeping left-hand bend before the finish.

Aart dropped me off a few riders back from where I really wanted to be. But I felt in total control. I just waited until there was a gap on my right-hand side and burst forwards, absolutely full sprint. The others might have thought I was going too early, but after the bend would have been too late. I felt incredible, and as soon as I went I thought, *Yes – I'm on.* Through those first few pedal strokes of the sprint, I felt like I was the master of the Tour – I was bending the race to my will. I gave it everything, while the others were far too late. I didn't look back, but I knew that I'd gapped everybody – nobody was close. For the final 25 metres, I wasn't sprinting any more. I was cruising, just turning the pedals over and enjoying the feeling.

I wasn't the only one enjoying it. Lotto felt like they'd won the lottery. As a proudly Belgian team, winning a stage in Belgium was as good as it got, and the presentation ceremony featured the four most prominent people in the country at that particular moment, all together: King Albert, the prime minister, Eddy Merckx and me. One of the Aussie journos, John Trevorrow, who is a bit of a character, had taken the liberty of going up to the King, saying g'day and pinning a kangaroo badge to his lapel earlier in the day – he's pretty approachable as kings go. I've got a photograph from that day that is one of my favourite memories in cycling. I'm saying something to King Albert about the badge, and he's laughing his head off. Life truly was good – my Tour was already a success. Let the others feel the stress. I could get on with enjoying the race.

The main thing about winning that early stage in 2004 was that it confirmed in my mind that I was one of the best sprinters in the world. There'd be no more three-year waits between stages.

But it was going to get better. The next day, I'd started in second place in the green jersey and third place in the yellow jersey. Thor Hushovd led them both. I was pretty sure I could handle Hushovd for the green jersey – I was consistently faster than him. But what about the yellow? Back then, stage finishes and bonus sprints carried time bonuses – six, four and two seconds for the mid-stage sprints, and 20, 12 and eight seconds for the first three riders over the line at the finish. I was 17 seconds behind Hushovd and nine behind Cancellara. If I won the stage and Hushovd wasn't in the top three, or I could sneak some seconds in a bonus sprint, I had a chance. As it happened, Hushovd was far too clever to allow me to outwit him in the mid-stage sprints. We each gained a third place – deadlock.

The stage finished in Wasquehal, but it covered several cobbled sections. The cobbles are a feature of the Spring Classics. The Tour of Flanders and Paris–Roubaix are the most famous of these races, and their cobbles are incredibly difficult to ride on. Racing bikes are rigid, because the stiffer they are the more power can be transmitted into forward motion. But riding a racing bike over cobbles is like being beaten up with a cricket bat. There are crashes because the surface is so bad. And riders know that they can be dropped, or crash out, so everybody wants to be at the front, which makes it a dangerous and congested place to be.

What's more, in 2004, Lance Armstrong's US Postal team had decided to try to use the cobbled sectors to put a few of their rivals out of the race early on. They didn't particularly need to, but it was the kind of thing Lance liked to do, to establish and maintain psychological superiority.

I saw it happening and stayed as far up as I could, while a bunch of Spanish riders were bouncing all over the place – going out the back and crashing. A crash can instantly cut the peloton into two. In this case, the pressure at the front and the crashes further back broke it into several pieces. It was chaos – riders were drilling it at the front, not knowing for definite but sensing that the damage caused would be huge. I put my head down and hung on as we juddered, almost sprinting, over ridiculously bumpy cobbles, skidding on the gravel, hearing the shouts of riders around me as they tried to make sense of the situation. When the dust settled, US Postal, with Lance Armstrong, his countryman George Hincapie and my old teammate Ekimov, realised one of their main rivals – the Spaniard Iban Mayo – was behind. That was it – team time trial to the finish.

I was trying to conduct my own audit of the situation as well. It dawned on me that Hushovd wasn't there. Righto – US Postal weren't the only riders who were going to gain today. It felt like it was going at about 100 kilometres an hour through the last ten or 15 kilometres – a lot of riders were very keen to stop anybody who'd crashed from catching up.

My main target still was winning the stage and getting green-jersey points, but it got very chaotic, and I was playing it quite safe. I went way too early, just to guarantee that I'd be out of trouble. It wasn't enough to win. Kirsipuu gave Jean-Patrick Nazon a fantastic leadout, while I was more less on my own. I got my wheel in front, but Nazon kicked again and went back past me, while Zabel also pipped me on the line. Third. Good points. But what about yellow? I thought it might be on.

A couple of journalists came running up at the finish and con-gratulated me on having taken the yellow jersey, but I needed to be sure. The last thing I wanted was to claim the yellow before it was officially confirmed.

And then the news came through: McEwen leading the race;

Cancellara second by one second. It turned out that the two seconds I took in the first bonus sprint put me over the top after all.

The best thing was that my family had come to see the finish. Angélique had been on at me for years to get her one of the Crédit Lyonnais lions that the Tour gives out at the yellow-jersey presentation, and the organisation gave me a little one for Ewan as well. He was two at the time, and he was super proud of his dad because of all the interviews – both McEwens wearing yellow jerseys in the wrong size. I think he enjoyed the attention even more than I did.

Wearing the yellow jersey makes you the most important man in cycling. I've had prouder moments personally, simply because I was never a real contender for the overall classification of the Tour, but I still appreciate that not many riders get to spend even a single day in yellow through their whole careers. I've got it hung up in a bag at my house right now, but one day I'll get it framed and hang it in the basement. It's a reminder to me of how surprising cycling can be. When I look at my old green jerseys, I feel pride and vindication. When I look at that yellow jersey, I feel privileged that I had the opportunity to wear it.

But fate can shake you by the hand one day and slap you in the face the next. I wore my yellow jersey for precisely one hour, 17 minutes and 22 seconds. It's funny. Not many people even remember that I wore the yellow jersey, because the next day was the team time trial. Lotto were off mid-field, and we'd finished before the television cameras even started rolling. It was a filthy, cold, wet day, blowing like a hurricane, so hardly any spectators showed up to watch. I finished the day in 47th place overall. I was no longer the most important man in cycling. I'd have loved to have worn the yellow jersey for a proper road stage and to have had a chance to sprint wearing it, but the Tour de France had decided it wasn't to be.

19

Victor

I FIRST MET VICTOR POPOV when I was an amateur on the QAS program in 1992. He was a local physio in Brisbane, and somebody recommended I go to see him just to have a check-up. I thought he was good, and after he fixed a sore knee that I'd developed, we stayed in touch. He's been fixing me ever since.

Victor's parents are Russian, but he was born in Australia. He's a genius, really. He's the best physio I've ever worked with – he knows my body as well as I do. In fact, he's more than a physio – he's a natural caregiver. Victor approaches problems very analytically and laterally, and is always open to different ways of treating them. The moment I climbed off my time-trial bike on the second-last day of the 2003 Tour, I was thinking, *I wish Victor was here – he'd have me straight by dinnertime.*

Twenty years of cycling have left their mark on my body. I look after myself as best I can, but crashes and impacts have bashed and bent me out of shape. My shoulders are shot, one of my legs is stronger than the other, my collarbones sometimes look like they are about 90 degrees out of line and my back's not always quite straight. Victor's the guy who keeps it all hanging together.

When I lost the green jersey in 2003, the team weren't too annoyed with me. They'd seen me come within three or four centimetres of it, after three and a half thousand kilometres, and that was after I'd crashed and lost 30 points, and was suffering from mediocre form. But even after all that, what really made the difference was my sore back in the final stage. Luckily, they listened to me when I said, 'Let's not allow this to happen again.' I suggested that at the 2004 Tour it would be a good idea for Victor to spend the whole three weeks with the team. Funnily enough, Victor often works with Cookie as well, who's about as bent out of shape as I am.

I learned in 2002, during my battle with Erik Zabel, that you can't afford to have a single off-day in the green-jersey competition because it puts the result out of your hands. If you miss out on a sprint, you can gift 35 points to your opponents, whether it's because of a crash, a bad day, a disqualification or bad tactics. In 2002, I managed to avoid all of these. So did Zabel, which is why it was such a close, memorable and fair fight. The following year, the crash in Lyon cost me the jersey. Cookie gained 30 points on me that day.

That meant I was pretty angry with myself and with others for the next two days of the 2004 Tour after the team time trial. In Chartres, Stuey got into an escape, hoovered up the three bonus sprints and then won the stage – a perfect day for the green jersey – while I was only sixth, coming in at the front of the bunch. He gained 33 points for that. It was careless of me to allow that to happen.

But that was nothing compared with the next day.

The stage, into Angers, had 'bunch finish' written all over it in letters so big that we could virtually read them from the start, 196 kilometres away in Bonneval. I still had a lead of about 25 points in the green jersey. I felt like I was the fastest man in the race, and a win would probably have put me into green for good.

I was in a good position coming into the final kilometre – except for one thing: I was riding just behind René Haselbacher, an Austrian sprinter on the Gerolsteiner team. A journalist once told me that Haselbacher's nickname in the Tour press room was René 'Crashelbacher'. Haselbacher's problem was that he liked to get in at the front of the bunch for Tour sprints, but he just didn't have the horsepower to get anywhere near winning a stage. He was also quite rough and ready anyway, and when you're at your limit the first thing to go is your finesse, which meant that, going into the final kilometre, Haselbacher would be all over the shop. He was renowned for it. Sure enough, into Angers he was weaving from left to right and back again when he went down at the final kilometre marker. He said later that his bars snapped, but I think he must have ridden into the barrier.

I was in the second or third row of riders, somewhere in the first 20, and there was nowhere to go except down. The pile-up was massive. Anybody who wasn't in the first 15 riders in the bunch, or the last 15, hit the deck.

Bike-race crashes are horrible. They are all yelling, dull thumps and smacks as riders hit the deck, the scraping and snapping of metal on asphalt, the shredding of carbon fibre, blood, broken bones, torn flesh and a total lack of control over your destiny. And then comes the second wave of shouting and swearing as the pain hits. Riders land on their faces, elbows, shoulders, backs, legs, hips, knees – anywhere except the feet. You hit the deck, but it's not over, as you roll and slide, the asphalt grabbing, ripping and tearing at your cycling clothes and skin. And behind you, the wheels of riders going at 60 kilometres per hour have nowhere to go but right into you.

Coming into Angers, I was right at the bottom of the pile-up. I don't really know what happened – maybe somebody's knee or shoulder hit me, or maybe it was somebody's bike, but I got a huge impact in my back. The crash took off a horrible amount of skin. Skip this next bit if you are squeamish, but basically both arse cheeks were gone. I'd been ripped open.

But the burning-hot pain of lost skin was nothing compared with my back. The pain was absolutely excruciating.

I scraped myself up off the road and hobbled over to Haselbacher, who was half-lying against the barriers, with a bit of a bloody nose, not looking too pretty himself.

'You fucking idiot. You've done it again,' I said to him. There were reports I was trying to punch him, but if I'd really wanted to punch him I would have done. I turned around, managed to get myself over my bike and rode to the finish at about two kilometres per hour.

The immediate effect of the crash was that I'd lost the green jersey. Stuey was second and got another 30 points on me, going into the lead. I could have done without that.

But the second immediate effect was that I was in big trouble. My back was badly injured – I could tell it was extremely serious.

I got back to the hotel, and Victor knew he had his work cut out. The doctors had to clean and dress the wounds first – more excruciating agony. It was like a three-course meal of pain: a starter of crash, followed by a main course of wound-cleaning, and finally a dessert of Victor trying to work out what I'd done to myself.

Victor needed to feel around to try to ascertain the damage, but I was in such pain he couldn't even touch my back, let alone poke and prod it. He took me through a few movements, just to test which muscles were doing what, but I was in too much pain to complete many of them. Every time I moved, it felt like someone had stuck a knife into my lower back. I'm not one to complain about physical discomfort, but bloody hell I was in pain.

From his investigations, Victor reckoned he knew what I'd done. He was 99 per cent certain I had a fracture of the transverse process on my L1 or L2 vertebra. The transverse processes are the set of 'wings' that protrude on either side of the vertebrae. It's not necessary to fully understand their anatomy to realise that fracturing them wasn't going to help me ride faster on my bike.

Victor does a lot of work with the Brisbane Lions Aussie Rules football team, and it's actually a common fracture with football players, when they get a knee in the back. The transverse processes are surrounded by muscle, so even if they are broken, it's very difficult to actually displace them. You can't put them in a cast, so the only way to fix them is for them to heal over time. Plus plenty of rest.

The good news, Victor informed me, was that if I could put up with the pain, it would be possible to ride with it. It was, he added, going to hurt like hell.

At this point, I couldn't even sit down to eat my dinner. I had to sit on the edge of my chair, all crooked. Every time I moved, my back was killing me. Sneezing was unspeakable. Laughing probably would have been pretty painful, too, but I didn't find out – there was absolutely nothing to laugh about.

I couldn't lie in bed, because there was skin off everywhere. If you're lucky in a crash, you'll fall on one side, which means at least you don't have to lie on the grazes at night. I had a 360-degree loss of skin – I don't think there was a position I could sleep in that didn't involve me lying on an open wound. I was, in short, going to be losing sleep.

Victor's first priority was to get me straight and keep me straight. My injuries would likely tighten me up on one side or the other, which would leave me bent on the bike. Pedalling hard was going to exacerbate the imbalance, leaving me sore and out of line. He worked on me before the stages, sometimes on the team bus at the start, after the stage finish, then again after dinner. I can't begin to describe how painful the work was. He was doing his best to loosen the muscles around the part of my back that was black and blue from the bruising, just to get me straight. He needed to loosen my gluteus muscles as well, but the problem was there was no skin on them. There was a dressing on them, and there was nothing for it except for Victor to work on them through the dressing. He was sticking his thumbs into what was basically raw meat.

I had one aim: get through the next two stages to the rest day, then reassess.

I was seeing blue with the pain all day, but my body was allowing me to compete. I mostly drew a blank the next day, a horrible, hilly, wet day through Brittany. Luckily, a break stayed away and took most of the points – just as well, because Stuey and Hushovd both beat me in the sprint. I even managed to sprint for the win the next day – Hushovd won, but I got fourth.

But I'd had to go really deep, and I pulled my whole body out of whack.

And all the time, my knee was getting sorer and sorer. During the rest day, the team went for a spin, but I had to stop four times. An Australian television crew was filming me, because I'd worn both green and yellow, and I had to ask them to put my bike in the back of the car and drive me back to the hotel. I assumed that was my Tour over. If I couldn't finish a two-hour training spin, I wasn't going to be able to ride the next day.

I also wasn't confident of being able to compete in the green-jersey competition. I was somehow back in the lead, but there were three riders – Stuey, Zabel and Hushovd – within ten points of me.

But, miraculously, I won the next day. We left it very, very late to catch the break – in fact, I wasn't that keen on chasing, just because it would have saved me having to sprint so hard. Hushovd's teammate Julian Dean, from New Zealand, did a huge pull in the final couple of kilometres, and we could suddenly see two guys dangling just in front of us. I threw caution to the wind and noticed that the bunch was taking the long way round to the left of one of the escapees.

I hit out through the pain and aimed my wheel straight at the finish line, just squeezing through a small gap to the right of the final escapee and brushing him as I went past. Stuey was following me through the gaps. Hushovd was on the other side, pounding a very large gear, dead level with me. We were like that all the way to the line, which meant having to throw the bike across the finish.

I could virtually feel my muscles going into spasm as I crossed the line – neither of us knew who had won. I watched the replays on a small television monitor by the Lotto team bus, saw the photo finish, shouted 'Yeah!' as it became clear I'd won, threw my hands in the air, then collapsed in agony as the shooting pains travelled up and down my back. I don't think I've ever had a less enjoyable win in my life.

It turned out that I won a cow – of all things – for winning the stage that day. It was a prize Charolais. I considered bringing it home to put in the field out the back of our house, although my wife very quickly banned me from doing that. My old team-mate Serge Baguet had won a cow in the 2001 Tour, and he'd decided to keep it. It was the worst decision he ever made, he gravely informed me. The cow was a real stubborn, nasty piece of work that used to break through the fence into the back yard and terrorise his family. I ended up selling my cow to former Tour de France winner Bernard Hinault, who owns a farm in his native Brittany. He gave me a thousand euros for it. That's not the strangest prize I've won at a bike race either. I once had to figure out what to do with my own bodyweight in sweets, which I won at the Classic Haribo in 2002 for being the most aggressive rider.

Victor was still working on me three or four times daily. At the same time, we weren't letting on to the Lotto management how bad my injuries were. We hadn't bothered with an X-ray, since it wouldn't have told us anything we didn't know. I also didn't want my rivals to know. Although I was sprinting fast, they could have made life more difficult for me by trying to put me under more pressure in the bonus sprints in the mountain stages.

The Tour spent the best part of a week in the mountains, which suited me well, because none of my rivals for the green jersey was picking up points. I could just ride tempo, with no violent accelerations to pull me out of shape. I was getting out-sprinted at the finishes when there were points on offer, simply because my back was so stiff. Every time I sprinted, it still felt like somebody was kicking me really hard in the back.

I also knew that Hushovd was the most dangerous of my rivals for the green jersey. He outsprinted me a couple of times in the second half of the Tour and was only 11 points behind going into Paris.

I didn't care about the stage victory on the final day. I was going to spot weld myself to Hushovd's back wheel. I was dead, anyway – riding the Tour injured had taken so much out of me that my only real aim was to finish the race in the green jersey. In the end, Hushovd stuffed up the sprint, and I got fourth, just by putting my head down and basically hammering down the finishing straight over those bumpy cobbles, saying 'Ow' every time I put a pedal down.

I've experienced such a broad range of emotions on the Champs-Élysées: pure joy, pure relief, and this time it was dif-ferent again. It was almost pure gratification that I didn't have to hurt myself any more. The fact that I was also wearing a green jersey was nice, but I just wanted the pain to stop. I'd spent two and a half weeks waking up in the morning groaning and wondering if it was worth it.

It was. Just.

But I was still a bit of an idiot. I needed rest and a couple of weeks off the bike while my back slowly forgave me for the violence I had inflicted on it. Instead, I rode some criteriums. I thought, *Well, the damage is done, and if I'm going to be in pain, I might as well be in pain and significantly richer.* It wasn't until the

Wednesday after the Tour that I had a day off, so I went to the hospital to have an X-ray and see what they thought.

The radiologist called me into his office, shook his head at me and asked, 'You rode the Tour de France with this?'

I'd told him my physio had suspected a fractured transverse process.

'You don't have a fractured transverse process,' he said. 'You have two.'

One of them had cracked right through. He said most people would be six weeks in bed with an injury like that.

I went home, then rode a criterium the very next day.

20

Aussie Rules

I'M A PROUD AUSTRALIAN. Being Australian is very important to me – I love my country.

When I was a kid, we'd sing the national anthem every day. Compare that with Belgium, where people maybe know the first and second line of the national anthem, after which they start mumbling. I got the impression at school that it was important to the country to learn how to be a good Australian.

You can't reduce an entire nation to a list of adjectives, but when I compare what I think about myself to what I think about Australia, there's so much overlap. Aussies are battlers and underdogs. We roll up our sleeves, get stuck in and do what we have to do. Being Australian means being prepared to fight and work hard for the good cause. Living in Belgium, as I do, I'm not far from the cemeteries where thousands of Australian and New Zealand soldiers are buried. As a nation, we had a good excuse for not going to fight a war on the other side of the world, but we did go, and it says a lot about the Aussie character.

When Ewan's old enough, I'm going to take him down to the cemeteries to show him. He's grown up mainly in Belgium, and that's part of his childhood. But he's an Aussie, and it's important for him to see.

But we're lucky, too, we Australians. We live in a beautiful country that has managed, for the most part, to maintain the balance between having a very strong national identity and being seen as a welcoming, warm place for outsiders. Australia's built on immigration – including my own parents' – and I'll never forget that.

As cyclists, the Aussies are different. The Europeans are born into cycle racing, while we have the additional stress of transplanting ourselves around the world to take part. Many of my European teammates go home after a race, back to their parents' house, where their mother washes their clothes and their dad sorts their bikes and takes them out motorpacing. I've never had the option to nip home for a bit – the Aussie pros are in Europe from January to October, and it's a real sacrifice. Even the North Americans, who tend to cluster in the same areas in Europe, often go home during the season. These days, they've got the Tour of California in May, which means they can be back for the best part of a month. I'd love to have a month at home midway through the season.

For that reason, there's quite a lot of solidarity among the Aussie pros in the peloton. We've managed to understand that we're cut from similar cloth and have been through very similar experiences. Most importantly, we don't see why we can't be mates with everybody while still maintaining a very strong competitive spirit. Some of my biggest fights have been against fellow Aussies, like Cookie or Stuey, and while we're not bosom buddies we'll say 'g'day' in the morning and 'good on ya' when one of us has come out on top.

Maybe for the younger riders, it's not such a big deal to come to Europe any more. There are a lot more of us, for one thing, which means the support network, while not perfect, is a bit better. But the world's a smaller place anyway. When I came to Europe in the mid-1990s, there was no internet, and I was writing my parents a letter once a week and faxing it through. I remember my first mobile phone – it virtually needed its own suitcase, and it cost me an arm and a leg in roaming charges. Usually, I'd be paying for journalists calling me up and asking me why I hadn't won.

Now, there are lots of Aussies in the peloton. At most big races, you'll see a dozen or 15 of us – that's almost ten per cent of the field. I used to have to search other Aussies out to say g'day at the start of a race, but now it's hard to make sure you've seen everybody.

The Australian Cycling Federation takes the national team very seriously, because though we ride most of the season for our professional teams, we ride as a nation at the world champion-ships, Olympic Games and Commonwealth Games. At regular intervals through the season, irrespective of which team we ride for, we'll have a get-together organised by the Federation. It keeps us feeling that even if we don't make the squad for a cham-pionships, we are still part of the team. We do it a lot, much more than most other countries, and it gives us a real advantage in terms of team spirit and knowing how to work with each other.

I love representing Australia, but most of all I love represent-ing Australia at the Olympic Games.

Following my back injury in the 2004 Tour, I should probably have taken a very long break from cycling, possibly even for the rest of the season. But that would have meant missing out on the Athens Olympics.

Victor had gone home the day after the Tour, so I couldn't rely on him to get me back into shape, but the Australian physios did a good job of looking after me. I had a couple of quiet weeks, then built up and actually started going quite well.

Athens was a hard, hard race. I don't think I've raced on many hotter days. We had to start right under the midday sun to suit the broadcasters, which probably made the race look quite nice, but it was like riding with a giant hairdryer blowing on us.

We didn't come away with a medal. However, we raced well as a team – I got Stuey into a strong break at one point. A few riders had just attacked up the hill. I pulled up the early part, then gave Stuey a handsling up the road, which was good preparation for the Madison event on the track, a two-man relay, in which he won the gold medal with Graeme Brown. The break came back, then Paolo Bettini got away with Portugal's Sérgio Paulinho. There were only 40 guys left in the race by this point, so chasing was more or less impossible. Then Axel Merckx went away for the bronze.

We were sprinting for nothing. However, I wanted to give it everything to finish as high up as possible, even if medals were out of the question. But it was a difficult sprint. Stuey gave it everything out of the last corner, leading me out, but he started cramping. Then, when I sprinted, I started cramping as well. With all the good work Stuey had put in with Cookie, Michael Rogers and Matt White for the team, I wasn't going to stop sprinting just for some cramps.

189

It was bloody painful — I felt like I was tearing my muscles apart. I was all over the place, just trying to get to the line as fast as I could, while my legs were seizing up. I was 11th in the end. I'd have liked to have been top five, or top ten, but when you're not sprinting for a medal it doesn't really matter much beyond personal pride and wanting to reward teammates for their hard work.

However, my season pretty much ended there. The best possible work I could do for the Aussie team in the world championships a month later was not to ride. It was on a very hilly circuit, which didn't suit me, and I wouldn't have lasted long enough to do anything useful. But it had been a good year — I'd won eight races, including two Tour stages, a Giro stage and two stages at the Tour of Switzerland. And I'd regained my green jersey. In my mind, I was one of the fastest, if not the fastest, sprinters in the world. Petacchi had dominated the Giro; I had dominated the Tour. And the Tour is the biggest, most important bike race in the world.

During the off-season, I also pulled some strings to make Lotto a little bit more Australian. I got them to sign my old teammate Henk Vogels, and also Cadel Evans, who had huge potential for riding for the yellow jersey but had suffered poor luck over the years. I said to Marc Sergeant, our team manager, that Cadel was a real talent. He'd ridden for the Telekom team, but they'd been doing his head in for years, and he'd gone through a phase of breaking collarbones. Nobody had seen his potential since he came from nowhere to lead the 2002 Giro d'Italia. And most had written him off since then. Sergeant was looking for suggestions for team managers as well, so I said he should give my fellow Aussie Allan Peiper a go.

I should tell you about Allan, as he has been one of the most positive influences on my career. Allan was a professional cyclist himself, one of the pioneers of Australian cycling in the 1980s, along with Phil Anderson. He'd graduated from the school of hard knocks. There was no AIS in those days, so he just went to Europe with a bike and a couple of hundred bucks in his back pocket, and painfully carved out a good career for himself.

I remember seeing him on television riding the 1991 Tour, being interviewed on the move by a guy on a motorbike. He retired in 1992 and drifted away from the sport, although he always continued riding, come rain, hail or shine. He's one of those guys who loves riding his bike.

Allan is one of the most empathetic managers in the sport. He has never forgotten what suffering is, not just because he was a hardworking domestique himself, but because he's done some hard yards in his life. He ran a hamburger van for a while and got separated from his wife. He had some wilderness years, although that's not to say he was wasting time. He went on pilgrimages to find himself, visited India, studied philosophy. And it's one of his biggest skills as a manager that he is entirely open to all new ideas. He'll never pre-judge anything anybody suggests. He'll try an idea, and if it goes wrong he doesn't get angry, he just re-evaluates, tweaks and adds it to his knowledge bank, just like he did while he was wandering around the world, finding himself. He listens to riders – in fact, when Allan is in the team car it's like having an extra rider. He's everybody's big brother but also a very smart manager.

As well as getting Allan on board, I made the team a little bit more sprint-friendly. We'd kept Aart Vierhouten, Henk would be good for me, and we also signed the sprinter Fred Rodriguez, who'd be my final leadout. I couldn't have been happier. We had a good, settled team, with plenty of Aussies and plenty of willing workers for the sprints.

I liked working with Aart Vierhouten. He wasn't just an excellent leadout man, but he was also a great motivator for the team, always encouraging us and geeing us up. We rode together for four years at Rabobank before being reunited at Lotto in 2002. Aart's always been a real battler. He was one of those kids at school with spectacles on, but the difference with Aart is that he always fought back. Anybody who thought he was a soft touch would be in for a surprise. He would usually be covered in scabs from one crash or another – he got into scrapes so that I didn't have to.

Team harmony was one thing, but in cycling you never seem to be far from big egos wanting to pitch in with ideas. There'd been a change of sponsors – Lotto continued, while Domo pulled out. Marc Coucke, who owned the Omega Pharma company, wanted in. Davitamon, the vitamin company under the umbrella of Omega, already sponsored Quick Step (run by Patrick Lefevre), but they'd had a disagreement. What further complicated the matter was that Coucke also had a small team in Spain: Relax-Bodysol.

When the dust settled, we had become Davitamon-Lotto, having taken a few riders from Relax-Bodysol as part of the deal. Marc Sergeant stayed as team manager, which I was happy about, but Coucke was very hands-on, and, since he was putting a lot of money in, he often decided to listen to himself first and the people he'd employed to do a job second. Later on, he was pushing very hard for the team to support Cadel Evans in the Tour de France, to the detriment of my sprinting chances. He was also very hands-on in signing riders, and, being such a gifted self-publicist, he sometimes hired riders more for the column inches they might gain than because of their results.

I've always felt that team owners should leave decisions about team selection and tactics, and especially critiques about team performance, to the managers they've employed. It rubs everyone up the wrong way and leaves the team open to criticism.

Things started very well in 2005, however. Cadel and I got away with two other riders at the Australian national championships. Normally, they'd be very good odds, but I wanted to make sure that I would be in a position to win – the four of us were 20 seconds clear of a group containing Matt White, Stuey, Simon Gerrans and several others. They were far too dangerous to be allowed back on, so I offered the two other riders, Robert McLachlan and Paul Crake, money just to make sure they contributed to us staying away.

McLachlan turned me down, saying he had to race for the win. I told him fine, race for the win, but let's just make sure it's the four of us, not ten of us, sprinting for the win. I was that confident of winning that I was willing to give up the prize money plus a little bit to get some extra effort from the others. As it was, Cadel was riding hard enough for us to stay clear, and I won the sprint. I was national champ again, with the added bonus that I felt the team spirit within Davitamon-Lotto had moved to a new level. Cadel had helped to engineer my victory, and at the jersey-presentation ceremony I could see Allan Peiper had a tear in his eye. It was very emotional. To be able to wear the Australian champion's jersey for a whole season, representing Australian cycling to the world, means a great deal to me.

And then something happened at the Tour of Qatar the following month that gave me even more confidence in myself and my team. Even in 2004, after nine years as a sprinter – nine years of winning races – I was still looking after myself in sprints. This was partly down to the team's budget. If we'd had countless millions of euros, I'd have got the management to hire the eight best leadout men in the world. But we didn't, so I had to do whatever I could to win races. The team always did its best, and I'd relied on Aart Vierhouten, who knows his way around a sprint, to look after me and pilot me into position.

At the Tour of Qatar in 2005, many of the big sprinters were present, including Tom Boonen and Mario Cipollini, and they were riding bloody well. Boonen won two stages, Cipollini won one, and a breakaway had taken the other. The last stage finished along the Corniche road in the capital city, Doha. It was flat, wide and smooth, curving gently around the harbour past a city that was half shiny glass-fronted skyscrapers, half dusty building site.

Even before the start, I sat down with the team and dictated the one plan for the day. No getting into breaks. No panicking. We would stick together like glue for the whole stage – all eight of us. I didn't want a single rider from another team to get in among us.

It's normal to split up a little bit during a race, just because of the dynamics of the peloton. A team leader will ride with a couple of teammates, and the closer you all are together the more able you are to deal with a situation – a puncture or crash. But, generally, it's not a panic if you lose sight of each other. This time, we stayed together. I told them to sit together towards the finish, and, when I gave the order, we'd attack out of the bunch all together. We'd create a leadout train of our own and go straight past the rest. I told them to hold nothing back when it was time.

From one kilometre out, we went, from about 20th position. The riders at the front were already doing 60 kilometres per hour, because of the tailwind, but we just pulled out to the left and roared past them. We had one guy after another doing almost a full sprint then peeling off and dropping back. We were doing a good five kilometres per hour faster than the peloton. I looked across at Boonen and Cipollini, and I almost had time to wave and smile. Cipo's face at that moment, looking at me with his mouth hanging open in shock, was something I'll treasure for the rest of my life. He'd spent many years making it very difficult for me to outsprint him, and now I was leaving him for dead, even before I'd started sprinting.

Freddie Rodriguez was my last man, and he launched me into an unbeatable sprint. I didn't win by much, because the Belarusian Alexandre Usov had seen what was up and followed me and my teammates up the finishing straight before riding my wheel pretty much all the way to the line. But I'd dominated Boonen and Cipollini, and that didn't happen very often. In fact, we didn't just dominate them, we ripped them apart.

Finally, I had a team.

21

Surfing the Peloton

THE TOUR DE FRANCE has always been the most important race of the season for me. Good Tour = good season. Bad Tour = bad season. This has been true right back through every year of my professional career – apart, perhaps, from the very first, when I was probably too young to ride the race anyway and had a pretty good season.

The Tour is the pinnacle of road cycling. If I win everywhere else but not in France, it feels like I've qualified for the World Cup but not won the finals. No matter how exciting the other two Grand Tours, of Italy and Spain, the fact is that at those two events you'll get only a few of the top sprinters going well. At the Tour, everybody is in top form, everybody wants to win. It might be that the form and talent that won somebody a Giro stage might only be good enough for fifth in a Tour stage. The quality is higher, the level is higher. To win a sprint at the Tour means you are the best, no question, and I've always hated it when I haven't won there.

Take 2003, for instance. I won two stages of the Giro d'Italia, a stage of the Tour of Switzerland (not an easy thing to do – it's an extremely mountainous race, and I'm lucky if more than one stage ends in a sprint), plus a fair few other races. But I didn't win any stages at the Tour, and I fluffed the green-jersey competition.

It was, in other words, a bad season, even though many riders would love to finish a year with seven wins, including two Grand Tour stages.

But while the Tour is by far my biggest target, the Giro is probably my second-favourite race. It's an event that has been good to me. Oddly, I often seem to win the same number of stages at the Giro and the Tour every season. In 2002, I won two stages at each. In 2005 and 2006, I won three at each, and in 2007, one apiece. I don't like to draw attention to 2000, 2008 and 2010, when I won zero in each race. The only discrepancies have been 1999, when I didn't do the Giro, 2003, as described above, and 2004, when I took two Tour stages but only one at the Giro, thanks to Petacchi's dominance. It still counts as a very successful season, however.

One race has nothing to do with the other, but put it this way: the more stages I win at the Giro, the better mood I'm in on the start ramp of the Tour de France.

I've also never finished a Giro. For my form to be sharp at the Tour, the final week of the Giro is too much for me, especially as it tends to be mostly mountain stages anyway. The cumulative fatigue of three weeks of racing takes me a while to recover from, so I've always pulled out after about two weeks. It seems to set me up perfectly to be sharp from day one of the Tour.

Some of my best ever wins have happened at the Giro. Outsprinting Cipollini in Strasbourg in 2002 was one of my all-time favourites. I beat the best sprinter in the world in his best year, fair and square, off the back of him being given a full leadout. The following year, I won a stage using a combination of my racing brain and my bike-handling skills, into San Dona.

I'm better than most pros at handling my bike. It comes from my BMX background. From the age of eight, I've been throwing bikes around and bouncing off other riders. Cycling's not a contact sport, but there can be contact. I love pushing the bike into corners and railing it around, leaning far over. I ride around corners faster than most. My centre of gravity is low, so I can tuck in, fly around and be much more stable than a taller rider. I'm also less prone to skidding off in the wet, which is perhaps because I got used to racing around dirt circuits with hardly any grip on my BMX.

In San Dona in 2003, it was a flat stage with a technical finish circuit, and when some huge black clouds moved over and dumped about an inch of standing water on the roads, most people were mentally out of the race. That's exactly what sharpens me up.

The race organisers had put the finish line about 150 metres after a sharp corner, and as we came around it for the second-last time, I just rode normally around it, turned around and saw everybody else about ten lengths behind. *Right*, I thought. *I know exactly what my tactic will be: my favourite — first into the corner and first over the line.* On the last lap, Acqua e Sapone were leading out for Cipollini. Coming up to the corner, I attacked up the inside, was first into the corner and went round as if it were in the dry. Cipollini went round the corner in the wheel of the Spanish rider Isaac Gálvez, and they both slid out into the barriers on the other side. I didn't even need to pedal from there to the finish. In the photos, Petacchi is second, but he's really just an out-of-focus blur in the background, he was so far behind.

And once I came over the line, through the photographers and team helpers, I grabbed a handful of back brake and did a massive powerslide. It's what anyone would have done in the same situation.

In 2005, the team had settled into the shape it would have through my peak years, give or take a rider or two, and at the Giro I had Henk, Gat and the Belgian rider Christophe Brandt looking after me in the sprints. We had managed to put together a team in which the riders were extremely good at their jobs, plus we were great mates, and we went in determined to win stages.

We had this technique of riding that Gat and I had worked out. We called it surfing the peloton. It was a tactic for moving up and holding our place near the front of a fast peloton without expending extra energy, and it was especially useful to a team such as ours because we didn't have a committed train.

You can't pull up the windward side of a peloton and try to ride all the way up – it's too energy-consuming. We worked out that we had to use the energy of the bunch, just like surfers use the energy of a wave. Aussies understand it best because we all surf – don't use your own power to get to the front, use that of the bunch.

When you surf, the wave comes underneath you, picks you up and you've got to be in that one very powerful spot where the wave is breaking, so you get its full momentum behind you. If you are behind the breaking spot, in the white water, you're getting thrown around. If you're too far ahead of it, you're going to run out of wave and power – there's nothing pushing you along. You have to stay right in the sweet spot. The wave moves, but you move with it, that steep part of the wave moving you along the whole time. The important thing is that it doesn't take a huge amount of energy to do this – it's all minor adjustments, just to keep the power going through the surfboard.

The area behind the front of the bunch is just like that. There's a line of riders in front, and the spot just behind them is where everyone wants to be. But only one rider can be there at any one time. You can't ride through that rider to take his spot, so the only way is to go up the outside of the bunch, then drop into the spot from ahead of it. There's a constant rotation of riders going up, around, in and back down the peloton as more take their place. Surfing the peloton means sitting dead still in the middle of that eddy of riders. You can use the power of the riders coming up the outside from behind, shelter behind them as they come around, then drop in again as they move forwards, to be replaced by another.

All around me, when I'm surfing the peloton, riders are coming up around the outside and back down again, and each time they do it they're burning up energy. On the other hand, they're sheltering me, and I'm moving neither forwards nor backwards in the bunch, so my energy output is steady, and less than theirs. Sprinting up the outside of the bunch is extremely tiring, and some of the effort of the riders who are doing it is going towards my sprint.

When things went really fast, Henk and Nick would surf me all the way to the head of the bunch, then we'd drop in just behind the arrowhead of the lead riders. Because we were so good at it, they'd still have the energy to give me an extra half kilometre if I needed it.

We loved it. A bunch of Aussie beach boys just surfing all day long in the multicoloured waves of the Giro peloton. Me, Henk and Gat.

There isn't a single rider who knows me better than Gatesy does. We met in 1993 and rode together at the AIS in 1994 and 1995, and though our paths through cycling took us well apart, then back together again at Lotto from 2003, we've been training partners for 14 summers on the Gold Coast.

Without Gat's help, it's safe to say I wouldn't have won as many Giro stages as I have, nor done as well in the world championships, nor won any number of smaller races. He's a bloody good teammate and a bloody good mate.

Gat's my motivator, and I listen to him a lot more than I need to listen to most people because he's got a ton of charisma. During big blocks of training, the last thing I actually want to be doing is training, because I'm so tired, but Gat's got this way of making me listen to him when he suggests yet more riding. We'll get to the end of the 140-kilometre Gold Coast hinterland lap, then he'll make me do another 60 kilometres through the northern suburbs. If it was anybody else, it would piss me off, but he likes to wind it up at the end of those 200-kilometre days in 35-degree heat yelling, 'This is where it's won and lost!'

I liked having Gat around at Lotto because, when we were on duty, he was a hard worker, never shirked his responsibility, always put me before himself and could read a race like a book. When we were off duty, he'd have us all in stitches with his deadpan humour and impersonations of cycling commentators.

You never know in cycling who your lifelong friends are going to be and who you'll never see again. But Gat and I are still the best of mates, and we get together whenever we can: me, him, our wives and our seven children. And he's still the biggest kid of the lot of us.

In 2005, we hit the Giro like a train. I don't usually hit the Giro in peak form compared with the Tour, but in 2005 I felt good. I just missed out on stage one, on a filthy uphill finish in Tropea, where Paolo Bettini got away. Second on the stage, second overall by 12 seconds, within one time bonus of taking the pink leader's jersey.

I must have been keen to add the pink jersey to the yellow one I'd worn at the Tour de France the year before, because coming into the finish of stage two I found myself in an extremely good position. Jaan Kirsipuu was getting an extremely promising-looking leadout from Julian Dean, so I tagged along after them. We ambushed Petacchi, then I came off Kirsipuu, went past the lot of them, won the stage and took the race lead. A stage win and the pink jersey – I could have gone straight home, but I wanted to have some more fun.

There are times in cycling when everything's going so well that you can start gifting stage wins to teammates. I wasn't concerned whether I won one, two or three stages at the Giro in 2005. I love winning, but to be able to help a teammate win after all his hard work for me is the least I can do.

On the sixth stage to Marina di Grosseto, Petacchi's Fassa Bortolo team were throwing their weight around as usual, keeping the pace high on the run-in to the finish. I was confident I had Petacchi's measure, having beaten him already, but with two kilometres to go they went around a 90-degree corner at a speed even I wouldn't have dared try. Virtually the entire team wiped out, leaving the rest of us scratching our heads and wondering what was going to happen. Davitamon-Lotto took responsibility for leading the final kilometres to the sprint, and with no Petacchi I was confident.

I'd noticed on the previous circuits that there were two right-handers onto the finishing straight, and as Henk led into them I let his wheel go. Henk's a smart rider; I knew he'd know what to do. He got the gap and quickly understood. It would be up to others to come around me and chase him, but in doing so they'd give me an armchair ride to the finish. So there was hesitation, while Henk was 50 metres up the road giving it absolutely everything.

I was convinced he was going to win. The others were all looking at me because I was the favourite for the sprint, but what did they expect? That was my teammate up the road. Tricked you all!

But our fellow Aussie Brett Lancaster went around us and closed the gap. He was riding for the Panaria team, whose sprinter Paride Grillo, from Italy, wasn't ever going to get close to winning a stage, but their actions still caused Henk to lose. That's bike racing. But what's also bike racing is that once I saw Henk was going to be caught, I came off Kirsipuu, who'd led me all the way up the finishing straight, went past and won. The win was still Davitamon's, but I wish it could have been Henk's.

It was a good plan, and it shows how confidently and strongly we were riding. We were improvising, playing. We had a cast-iron plan A, switched to plan B more or less for the fun of it, and when it didn't come off we went right back to plan A and won the stage.

And I took one more stage off Petacchi a few days later in Rossano Veneto. I out-psyched him, which was especially satisfying. Fassa had given him an excellent leadout, but he knew exactly where I was – about two centimetres from his back wheel, ready to come around him. He was also wise to my tactic of jumping first if there was a bend before the finish. However, this time I didn't. He panicked, jumped too early and just ran out of gas with about ten metres to go. I won it by centimetres, but beating Petacchi at 70 kilometres per hour after he'd had a good leadout is not something many riders can boast having done, especially between 2003 and 2005, when he was at his best. Three stage wins in a Grand Tour – my best ever. And at the back of my mind was the thought, *If I'm this good at the Giro, how good am I going to be at the Tour?*

The answer was: very good indeed, which made it very frustrating that, after three days of the race, with two bunch sprints so far, I'd been third and 186th – third last.

I'd arrived at the Tour start in the Vendée in excellent form, having won a stage at the Tour of Switzerland again. I floated through the first stage in France, gathering myself for the sprint. It was routine: the break was caught, and I was in a great position coming into the finish.

I've mentioned before that the first road stage of the Tour is one of the most difficult sprints of the year to get right. In 2004, I left it too late and couldn't catch Kirsipuu. In 2005, I hit out way too early. We got to 250 metres to go, and I thought, *This will do me, I'm just going to go.* Tom Boonen got my wheel and just swept past me as I started to blow. Hushovd passed me too. I remember coming to a stop, totally out of breath – which is normal after a Tour stage – sitting over my handlebars, thinking, *That was crap.* I was so desperate to get the first win that I'd ridden like an idiot. I was thinking about the second road-stage victory before I got the first one. Third place, good legs and a mistake. Still, I was optimistic that if I took the mistake out of the equation, a stage win would be a formality and I could start thinking about the green jersey. Unfortunately, instead of winning the next day, I got into a bit of a ruck with Stuey.

22

Stuey

MY HEAD SHOULDN'T HAVE BEEN anywhere near Stuart O'Grady's head when we came into the final 100 metres of the third stage of the 2005 Tour into the city of Tours. But I'd mistimed my sprint, putting myself in the melee, when I should have been well out of it, up the road.

Instead of charging towards the finish line in first place, like I'd anticipated, I was tangled up with Stuey, about five seconds from finishing third, and probably about five and a half seconds from being relegated to last place in the bunch. The photographs of the sprint, with my head well across in Stuey's face, looked bad. But they don't tell the whole story.

I'd gone too early the day before, and I wasn't going to make that mistake again. I sat in Freddie's wheel coming into the finish, and I was just about to tell him to go when Boonen anticipated it and went just before me. He rode incredibly intelligently. He came up alongside me on my left, and as I noticed Stuey coming up on my right I instantly realised I had nowhere to go – he'd boxed me in behind my own teammate.

I had to wait for Boonen to go past, which cost me a little bit of momentum, and by then there was no time for me to take a run – he had a gap and was going bloody fast. It was becoming an emergency. On the right, Stuey had gone. I jumped out of Freddie's wheel, with the aim of getting into Boonen's slipstream, then rolling him from there. Trouble was, Stuey was swinging in from the right to take that same spot.

He was just in front of me and defending his position, sticking his left elbow out.

He's bloody clever, Stuey. He is one of the best followers of a wheel I've ever encountered, and, from his track background, he is very good at getting position. He wasn't as fast as me, though, and I felt I deserved Boonen's wheel more than he did – I'd use it for something useful, like winning the stage. He'd probably follow it in for second place.

Stuey's arm was absolutely rigid, and as I came up alongside him he got his elbow on top of my right arm, then pushed down, either deliberately or not. It put me completely off balance, and I still don't know how I didn't go down. As soon as contact was made, however, I knew the stage win had gone. When you get into that kind of situation, your sprinting becomes 50 per cent getting to the line first and 50 per cent self-preservation. Braking would have meant coming fifth, sixth or seventh, so I didn't back down, but it cost me momentum.

I get fired up in situations like this. My attitude was, 'I'm coming through; I'm faster than you; you're on me; get off me.' The only thing in my mind was getting him off me so I could sprint.

That's why I had to use my head.

If I'd taken my hands off the bars, I'd have gone flying, or at best lost all my speed, and I certainly couldn't push back – we'd have both come down, along with the next 50 riders behind us. I didn't fancy another three weeks with a broken back. So I pushed back with the only thing I had that I wasn't using to keep my bike upright: my head.

There was no power behind it; it was just me trying to balance and get him off my arm. When you consider the mechanics of the situation, his elbow pressing down on my arm was forcing my handlebars to the right. To compensate for that, I had to let my arm go down but twist my body and drop my right shoulder. And, to move him off, I had to tap him with my head. In the end, I managed to wriggle out from underneath him, get ahead of him, as I'd expected, and finish third.

The Tour race jury didn't give a crap about watching the incident properly, though. They saw the footage of the head coming across, deduced that it had taken place in a vacuum and disqualified me. I found out on the team bus back to the hotel, and I was absolutely ropeable. They told me that whatever the merits of my reasons, it was too spectacular to ignore. Two days into the race and I was looking at a 44-point deficit in the green-jersey competition. Game over.

My career and Stuey's have run parallel, and they've often intertwined. We first met when I had my short-lived spell at the AIS track program in 1992.

I was the rough and ready outsider, who was really still learning how to race a bike. Stuey and Brett Aitken were the golden boys, winning Olympic medals and world medals.

But while we'd met, raced and trained together, we didn't come through the ranks together. I was back in Queensland by the time he won his world team-pursuit title, and we hardly saw each other again until we'd all turned professional.

Stuey and Henk turned pro in 1995, and me the next year. From 1996, we were sprinting against each other, and that created tension.

We actually did a series of criteriums in and around Perth in 1997, with me, Henk Vogels and Stuey in a team. We all wanted to win, so we basically divided up the first three between us. I won, Henk won, and in the third race it was Stuey's turn to win. We were away together, the two of us, and while we hammered it up in the sprint, he was always going to win.

The problem came in the fourth and final race, which was in Perth, Henk's home town. Henk got away with another guy, with another three riders between him and the bunch. That was going to give him the overall, which was fine by me – I remember thinking, *Henk's going to be happy with that*.

Then Stuey attacked out of the bunch to catch the other three. I think deep down he just wanted to race me flat out. I was up for that, so I went across and we battled it out over the closing laps while Henk was up front winning the stage and taking enough points to win the overall. Well, enough points if Stuey and I weren't racing flat out behind and catching the three guys Henk needed to finish in front of us to win the GC. I rolled Stuey in the sprint for third – big deal.

Unfortunately, this meant that I'd won the overall, which wasn't my intention at all. Stuey had a big go at me, but I replied that if neither of us had gone, Henk would have won. One of those schoolyard 'he started it' scenarios. I won, but I didn't feel very good about it. Minor incidents fuel rivalries, and when the press get a whiff of it they're looking for anything combustible to throw on the fire.

The thing about Stuey is he's not a super-fast sprinter, but his positioning is about the best in the world. He's also very strong and resilient – he can get good results in sprints because he's strong enough to hold a very high speed. This makes him an excellent rider to come off in a sprint. He's also an incredible trainer – he'll put together three back-to-back weeks of 1000 kilometres in the run-up to the Classics.

Stuey and I have got in each other's way from time to time. We've always been trying to do the same thing at the same time in cycling – two young, up-and-coming pros who happened to be from the same country and share similar ambitions. It was unavoidable that we were going to get in each other's way, and neither of us is particularly fond of having people in the way.

The press like a rivalry and often reported that we were always battling, didn't like each other and didn't talk. But we got on okay. It's just that we've got the same competitive nature and both of us despise losing, particularly to a fellow countryman. When you want to be the best in the world, the last thing you want is to not even be the best in Australia. We were fishing in the same waters, and sometimes our lines got tangled.

We never really went head to head for the green jersey, however. Stuey was trying his hardest to win it from around 1999 to 2001, and he came pretty close in 2001, when Zabel basically did to him what I did to Zabel the following year. At that time, I was still working on trying to win stages regularly, or at least get selected by my team to start in the race. By the time I started winning the green jersey, Stuey had diversified, although he had a decent crack in 2004 and 2005. Stuey was always ahead of me results wise when we were younger and had much more experience. But eventually I caught up and overtook him. At sprinting, that is.

Stuey's true calling is as a Classics rider. He stopped trying to win bunch sprints in the Tour and started winning Classics, such as Hamburg and Paris–Roubaix. He also got on the podium of Milan–San Remo – something I've still never managed. When he won Roubaix, I was in my front room cheering and shouting for him. He's won an Olympic gold in the madison on the track, and now he's seen as one of the road captains of the world. Versatile is an understatement. Stuey is a class bike rider.

We get on better these days. Maybe we've mellowed, or just learned to appreciate each other better.

There were two people I wanted to speak to the day after my disqualification in Tours: Stuey and the chief commissaire. I hadn't managed to speak to Stuey after the stage – he'd been interviewed by Australian television, and his version of events differed slightly from mine.

So I found him the next day and asked, 'Whaddya reckon?'

We had to talk about it. I was still pissed off. I said my piece, which was that I felt my head had gone towards him in an effort to keep balance, and that I wouldn't have had to do it if he hadn't leaned on my arm first. He said that I'd come across the road at him.

We agreed to differ and moved on. It wasn't a big blue or anything. We didn't have a big argument or sulk for the rest of the race. We talked, we each gave our version of events and we both felt hard done by.

It smouldered a bit after that. Relations were a bit tense for a while, but it doesn't come up any more. I let it go. There's a lot of water under the bridge in cycling – sometimes, it's best if it just flows away. Now that we're older and wiser, I've got a great deal of respect for Stuey, who's been a worthy adversary, even if we've had our moments. When we're done, we'll crack open a few beers and have a good laugh about it all.

I was more blunt with the chief commissaire, to put my side of the story over. It was bullshit, I informed him. We showed them photographs, which backed me up. I was a little bit annoyed with Stuey – his actions had cost me third place, 26 points and likely the green jersey. But I was extremely irritated with the commissaires. They'd never been riders; they had no idea how things worked. But the chief commissaire was in no mood for going back on the decision.

'Forget it. It stands,' he said.

Boonen was now on two stages out of two, and the Belgian media were loving it. Every time I opened a newspaper, all I saw were stories about him. The general tone was that the new man had arrived. Even the adverts were all about Boonen. One of his Quick Step team's other sponsors, Innergetic, made a range of latex mattresses, and they ran an advert showing me and Boonen. They had an arrow pointing to him, with the caption 'Well rested', while the arrow pointing to me said 'Bad night's sleep'. I had a good laugh at that with one of their representatives, while making it very clear that they owed me a mattress at the end of the Tour. (I'm still sleeping on it to this day.)

Like Stuey, Tom Boonen isn't a sprinter. That might sound ridiculous, but he's not. He's not like Cipollini, or Petacchi, or me – we have very fast jumps. Boonen's a Classics rider who happens to be so incredibly strong that he can hold a very high top speed at the end of a race. He was still difficult to beat, however.

But the headlines were 'Boonen unbeatable'. I thought, *I will show the whole fucking lot of you*. I was already filthy that I wasn't going to win the green jersey, which Boonen had more or less wrapped up after three days, but I was going to bloody well win some stages, starting in Montargis the day after the team time trial. It was eating away at me that I hadn't won a stage yet.

But it turned out to be easy, really. About 100 metres from the finish in Montargis, I said to myself, *I'm winning today.* Boonen was leading up the drag, riding very powerfully, but I drew up next to him. I could sense myself just coming over the top of him, but he didn't give much – he was virtually ripping his bike in half. Sometimes, he stays still when he sprints, and that's when he does his best rides. Other days, he's all over the shop, and it costs a lot in efficiency. He was really hammering it, but I was edging clear. I was so aggressive that I wanted to crunch the finish line down into the bitumen and rip the handlebars off my bike as I sprinted. I got it by three-quarters of a wheel.

Then I sat up. I didn't feel relief. I didn't feel happiness. There was very little in my mind at all, apart from a feeling that I wanted to say two words to the whole world: 'Told ya.'

Instead of raising my hands in victory, I pointed at myself. I was the best sprinter in the Tour. I had the form. In the Belgian media especially, it had been 'Boonen this' and 'Boonen that'. Unbeatable, invincible, indestructible Boonen. My gesture meant this: not him, me; and only me.

I was away. The stress left me. I'd been suffering from the normal Tour pressure – slightly shorter fuse, a little prickly with people, but I did try to stay calm.

You can ride in one of two ways. The first is with anger and frustration, and if you channel them properly they can actually help you to win. But I prefer the second way, which is to be riding with that winning feeling you get when you are on a roll. The tricky thing about that is winning the first one.

But once the duck has been broken, I can almost feel it getting easier. It's still hard physically, but the first win unblocks me. I see gaps better, I feel more in charge of my own destiny, I worry less about what others are doing. Two days later, I won again in Karlsrühe, in spite of the fact that the sprint was chaos. Perhaps having the clearest head among the disorganisation in the sprint made the difference.

The finish was on a wide road, and there was an absolute wall of riders pelting to the finish. I was calm. I told myself, *Just wait, have one plan: wait for it to open up, and when it does go through with everything you've got.* Even though I got horribly boxed in, I didn't panic, which I probably would have done if I'd not won a stage yet. Somebody tried to lead out on one side and somebody on the other, and, as riders fanned out for the finish, there it was – the gap. The others could do what they wanted; it was as if the pathway to my destiny had just opened up right in front of me. I got through the gap just as it was closing up again and gave it everything. Two up for McEwen – the new man had arrived!

23

My Boys

AT LOTTO, WE WEREN'T THE kind of team that went to dinner, ate, left the table, went to our rooms and lay on the bed. Dinner always took a while. We talked. Sometimes, we went for a stroll outside or just hung around at the table talking and laughing.

There's one hotel at the Tour de France where we always stay on the rest day in the Pyrenees. It's called the Hotel des Pyrénées, on the D817 main road, which heads east out of Pau, near the village of Ousse. As soon as the Tour route was announced every year, we used to look to see if there would be a rest day in Pau, and if there was we knew where we'd be staying.

It's a dusty, stuffy old place with poky rooms and low ceilings – you expect to see suits of armour standing around. But it was a good hotel because it was very open, like a big house, and out the back there was a big grass area. The rooms were small, so we didn't really want to spend too much time in them, apart from one with a small balcony that backed onto the grass area.

One year at the Tour, Wim Vansevenant was in that room. We'd been in the mountains a couple of days, so everybody was stuffed. It was a lovely warm evening, so after dinner we congregated on Sevi's balcony out in the open air, sitting on chairs, talking and hearing the occasional car go past on the main road out the front.

We called the woman who ran the hotel and ordered one round of beers. It was relaxation time on the Tour, probably the first time since we'd started the race. The Tour never feels like a holiday, except in these few snatched moments. It's the only time we felt like human beings. Me, Sevi, Mario Aerts, Johan Vansummeren, a few others – my Belgian boys, who rode their arses off for me all year round.

We had a nice easy beer, talked about who was a real bastard in the bunch or who was doing stupid things. And we talked about stuff that was nothing to do with cycling, laughed at people, laughed at each other and took the piss but were completely united by the tiredness we all shared.

A couple of the Belgians had a *snus* tucked under their lips – like a tea bag, only full of tobacco. It's a Swedish thing, but it seems to be quite popular in the peloton. Sevi had a beer and a cigarette. Mario and Summie were sitting there with a *snus* under their lips, having a beer and shooting the breeze.

I've got a huge number of memories of being a professional cyclist. People like to categorise my career into the wins or the moments of controversy, but it's snapshots like that evening in the Hotel des Pyrénées that make me remember the camaraderie and friendship I had with my teammates at Lotto.

I've got especially good memories of the quartet of Belgians I called my four musketeers at Lotto.

Wim Vansevenant: he's the quintessential team worker. Sevi's a no-nonsense guy, from a no-nonsense farming background in

West Flanders. He's never been afraid to get his hands dirty, and for him life is best when it is simple. He would ride his guts out during the stage and enjoy a cold beer in the evening.

During spring, Sevi was Peter Van Petegem's domestique at the Classics, and he was so good at it because he was rock solid. When it was time to ride, Sevi would go to the front, grit his teeth and keep on going, and going, and going. If somebody attacked, he brought them back.

At the Tour, he was one of the riders who did the hard work in bringing back breaks. If there's a break up the road, the sprinters' teams want to bring it back, so each will donate two or three men to the cause to work together in a temporary alliance to ensure a sprint actually happens. Sevi had been a pro for a long time, knocking around in small teams from 1995 onwards. He hadn't been given a chance to ride for a big team because for a long time they thought he couldn't stay with the bunch to the end, but people overlooked his qualities. Sevi's talent was doing exactly what the team leader needed, when he needed it. He would really go through the fire, as they say in Flemish – *hij zou door het vuur gaan* – for the team leader, whoever it was, with a total disregard for himself. He didn't care how much it hurt, how much tomorrow was going to hurt, or even whether it would put him out of the race. You get the same spectrum of selfish and unselfish people in cycling as you do in the general world. I have to ride selfishly to ensure I've got a chance of winning. Sevi rides totally unselfishly for the same aim.

Sevi thought it was nothing, but really it was everything. He rode on the front of the bunch from the moment the break went to the moment the break was caught, most of which never got broadcast on television.

And Johan Vansummeren. He's like my two-metre-tall little brother. Summie's pretty much the opposite of me in every single way. He's tall, I'm short. I'm relaxed, he's emotional and highly strung. I keep life simple, he likes it complicated, because he thinks too much. Because of all this, Lotto used to have us room together – I think they thought that putting two opposites in with each other would balance us out.

Summie was another diesel, but he was more than a domestique. He won Paris–Roubaix in 2011, after a career of service to others. He's the kind of rider who can sit on the front of the bunch for two hours or more.

Summie's first Tour was 2005, and I talked him pretty much all the way through it. He's pretty ambitious and goes uphill pretty well, but when I got to our bedroom in Courchevel, the first mountain stage that year, he was crying because he'd been dropped early.

The problem was he didn't even realise what an incredible ride he'd been doing. You can't drag around the entire peloton for a week, pulling back breaks, then expect to dance up mountains with the Tour leaders. Between Summie, Sevi and a couple of others, they'd dictated the average speed of the whole Tour. They'd ridden 1200 kilometres on the front. No wonder he wasn't going to finish near the leaders at Courchevel. In fact, just like me, the further back one of my domestiques finishes on a mountain stage, the better for the team. It will save energy that would be better used chasing down a break.

Summie can go deep. The day in the 2006 Tour when Floyd Landis lost the yellow jersey at La Toussuire in the Alps, I was one of the last in, but I still got back to my room before Summie, who'd finished in a right state. They carried him in, a gibbering, shaking mess, really pale. I had to help him into a warm bath, and they had to put him on a sugar drip that evening. But then again, he'd ridden the entire Tour up to that point on the front of the peloton.

It's funny how you can have two guys like Sevi and Summie on a team – complete opposites, but it seems to work. Sevi flat-lined his way through the whole Tour de France while Summie was very susceptible to the fatigue and stress and excitement.

And then there's Mario Aerts, who is possibly even more laid-back than Sevi. He's Valium personified, and when Cadel Evans joined the team, they put Mario in to room with him. Cadel's highly strung, so Mario was the perfect foil. And I think Cadel liked having him there – it was like having the room to himself, only with somebody to talk at. It was like putting a donkey in a field with a racehorse: it just calmed things down a bit.

Mario was also Mr Dependable on the road. I rarely needed to explain to him what needed to be done; he already knew. He's yet another diesel. Diesels aren't the most exciting riders to watch, but I've got a real soft spot for having them on my team, because without them doing their job there's no way I'd be able to do mine. Mario was a great help to me in the mountains as well. I'd be on the limit, just as things were accelerating at the front, and a clever little push, just a nudge, at the right moment could make the difference between being dropped and surviving. That tiny instant of respite was enough to enable me to hang on, and Mario had a sixth sense about when I needed it.

But Mario was a bloody good rider as well, as long as nobody needed him to make big flashy attacks. He won Flèche Wallonne in 2002, the year I joined Lotto. It wasn't just me getting good results for the team. A bunch of us were driving up to Holland for another race, and we were losing radio reception as we got further from Belgium. We pulled over to the side of the highway to listen to the finish, and we were shouting, punching the air and dancing around by the side of the road when he won. I've won a fair bit, and I'll never get bored of winning, but I get as much pleasure from one of my boys winning as I do from winning myself.

And there's Christophe Brandt, who is the firiest character of the four. He's like I am when I sprint, only it's 24 hours a day. Brandtje's always getting into fights. He's been the red-haired freckled kid his whole life, and he's had to fight for every centimetre. He's chippy, and he'll knock your head off. That's why I like him.

We call him 'the Crab' because of his riding style – he's kind of crooked on his bike, as if he were riding sideways, because he broke his arm once and he can't straighten his elbow. It makes him look even more determined and feisty on the bike. He's a real battler, though. Very strong, and one of those guys who could ride all day on the front of the bunch.

Those four guys were with me through my best years. Brandtje was at Lotto when I arrived and stayed after I left. Mario joined when I did, left, and then came back again in 2005, which is when Summie joined. Sevi was there from 2003 to 2008. It's quite rare that you get a core of guys who stay together and ride together that long in cycling. It's a transient sport. Two-year contracts are the norm, and there's a lot of movement as teams come and go. Unlike football, rugby or almost every other sport, the sponsors and teams tend to exist on a temporary level, so when tight groups form that stay together over a period of years, it's a precious thing. When a group of riders know each other that well and can work together with the success we did, it's worth hanging on to.

But I still thought Mario and Sevi had spent too long in the sun when they told me they were going to start chasing down the break on the 13th stage of the 2005 Tour, to Montpellier.

Any Tour de France goes through distinct phases, depending on the overall route. The first week tends to be flat and frenetic. Then there's a mountain range, either the Alps or the Pyrenees, during which I spend most of my time in the hurtbag. There's another mountain range afterwards, then a final couple of days to Paris. But between the two mountain ranges, there are always a strange few days that are described as 'transition stages'.

On the whole, these are flattish, although sometimes the Tour organisers make us go through the Massif Central, which is France's third mountain range. Those are the hardest Tours of all.

Luckily, 2005 had a flattish set of transition stages. But that's not to say they were likely to end in a sprint. During the first week, when everybody is fresh and the sprinters are all desperate to win a stage, breaks are usually chased down easily. However, breaks tend to stay away during transition stages. It's half unwritten rule – to give the riders who aren't sprinters or climbers a chance to win a stage – and half tiredness. Nobody wants to spend all day chasing a break when we're ten days into the Tour de France.

I had assumed that stage 13 to Montpellier would go that way. I'd won two stages, and we'd survived the Alps, but I was happy to let the break go. It was a very hot day, with a slight crosswind all the way, and after a very fast start five guys got away. I assumed that would be it.

But, oddly, Lampre started riding after the break. It turned out they were being punished by their team manager for having missed it and not really having done much since the start of the Tour. They'd had no stage wins, nobody had got into any breaks and they had nobody anywhere near the yellow jersey, so the managers had finally flipped and made them do something.

Somebody from Gerolsteiner asked one of our boys if we were going to ride after it and told him that they'd help if we did. Hendrik Redant, the manager in the team car, asked, 'What do you reckon, guys? Shall we ride and see what happens?'

I thought they were mad, and I told them so. And that's when Mario and Sevi said, 'Yeah, we'll ride.' I tried to tell them there was no need. We could rest up, get through the Pyrenees and then come out all guns blazing for the final few days of the race. When that didn't work, I told them to give up if it looked too hard, or if the break wasn't coming back. But they assured me they were going to catch it. And there was something about their demeanour that made me believe every word they were saying.

There were 100 kilometres to go. The gap was nine minutes. And in the break there were Spain's Juan Antonio Flecha, France's Thomas Voeckler, Ludovic Turpin and Carlos Da Cruz, and my future teammate Chris Horner. If you could choose five hard nuts to ride all day in a break and stay away, these five would probably be them. It was going to be hard work to bring them back. The general rule, in a small break of one, two or three blokes, is that you can give away a lead of one minute per ten kilometres remaining. And that's with a fresh bunch and lots of teams involved in the chase. We were right on the limit of what the wisdom said was doable, and there was only us to chase.

Lampre weren't much help. They spent about ten kilometres riding absolutely as hard as they could, at about 55 kilometres per hour, before blowing themselves up so they didn't have to ride any more. But my boys had started, and I knew they wouldn't stop until they'd caught the break or died trying. Mario, Brandtje, Sevi and Summie held about 45 kilometres per hour for a long, long time, which was a very fast pace given that we had spent half the day riding up draggy hills in burning heat. It was just a kilometre or two per hour faster than comfortable, into a crosswind, so everybody was lined out against the gutter, and quite a lot of riders weren't very happy about it. Guys started saying to me 'Just let them go, have the day off'.

Lance Armstrong was pretty happy about it, however. Horner was about a quarter of an hour behind him overall, which meant his Discovery team would have had to take responsibility for chasing if we hadn't. We'd given his team a day off.

My teammates eroded the lead steadily, but it was really taking its toll. It all went wrong at 20 kilometres to go when Quick Step started attacking and all my boys got dropped, except for me and Freddie, plus Cadel, who was hanging around just outside the top ten overall at that point. That was a problem – I had nobody left to lead the chase. The French rider Sylvain Chavanel attacked us, bridged to the remainder of the break, then went away again with Horner. It looked good for them.

I was devastated – we'd been in sight of the front, but I knew that we wouldn't catch Chavanel. All the other teams started looking at each other, and I was stuck, floating near the front of the slowing peloton as I watched the leaders going away. Chavanel was too strong, and Horner too savvy to get caught. We'd wasted all that effort.

But others in the bunch weren't willing to have spent the entire day suffering not to have a go at winning themselves. Liquigas came hammering through, and I shouted to Freddie to get on them. And ahead, I could see Chavanel and Horner starting to mess around – neither wanted to lead through the final kilometre, in case the other outsprinted them from behind. It looked like we might catch them.

I wonder how many other sprinters in the field had studied the route book as closely as I had. Even though I'd assumed it would be a day off, I still looked in detail at the final kilometre, and what I had seen made me happy. There was a sweeping corner about 400 metres before the finish – too early for me to jump, but I still had Freddie with me. I told him to jump before the corner and make sure that he was the first through and out the other side.

I had the rush of adrenalin I get when I'm sprinting for first, even though Horner and Chavanel were *still* away. Ahead of the corner, Freddie railed it so fast that only one guy was able to follow us: Stuey. Just as we passed Horner and Chavanel at 150 metres to go, I went off Freddie and shouted at him to carry on sprinting. I wanted him to be first across the line, as a symbol of how much teamwork had gone into today's stage. But Stuey had other ideas. I could see his wheel coming up, so I had to go again. As I was going clear, I gave him just the slightest little switch. It was nothing, really – just my way of saying 'Ha!'.

The team loved it. We got to the hotel – a really nice golf resort – but we were so tired after the day we'd had. Coucke had invited a load of VIPs and sponsors to the hotel – they all wanted to party the night away. We were dead on our feet, in no fit state to party. We left them to it.

That wasn't the end of the Tour for Lotto. Cadel rode extremely well in the Pyrenees and moved up to eighth overall. I was also disappointed not to win the final stage. I won the bunch sprint in Paris, but unfortunately Alexandre Vinokourov had got away with Brad McGee, with Fabian Cancellara also away, and we just failed to catch them in time. I'd also lost the green jersey by 16 points to Thor Hushovd, who'd won it without taking a stage. In fact, he'd only had a second and a third, but he'd consistently been scoring decent points all through the race.

I was more frustrated that my disqualification had cost me 26 points. Just as in 2003, events outside my control had cost me winning the green jersey. But I'd won three stages to add to my three at the Giro, and in the Aussie champion's jersey. I was coming to the zenith of my powers. I didn't need the green jersey to prove I'd been the best sprinter in the Tour – anybody with eyes could see that was the case.

I've got a reputation for doing things alone, just because I never had the leadout train like Cipollini or Petacchi, or Cavendish now, but Lotto were functioning so well on every level through 2005 and 2006 that I wouldn't have swapped. What the boys did for me in Montpellier was the equal of anything Cipollini's team did for him. And while I had my eye on the world championships, on a course reputed to be good for sprinters in Madrid later in the year, for now we were going to have some fun.

I rode Paris–Brussels – one of my favourite races – and was given such a good leadout by Peter Van Petegem that I couldn't lose. He led for an entire kilometre, rolling a huge gear while everybody was in a line behind him. We all piled into the team car after the race to get to our hotel for the Grand Prix Fourmies the next day.

We had a celebratory glass of champagne at the hotel. Then another. Then another. Between me, Belgium's Nico Mattan, Sevi, Henk and Brandtje, we drank the entire hotel bar dry of beer. It was a proper end-of-season blowout, except it wasn't the end of the season yet – we were racing the next day.

We crawled out of bed in the morning, and maybe Nico Mattan was still drunk, because he was on the startline, geeing us all up very loudly. I was thinking, *It's either going to be a very long day or a very short day.* Nico carried on revving us up all through the race, and for some reason we thought it would be funny to get on the front. We started controlling the race, riding along on the front, but all laughing and yelling at each other. Nico was actually riding incredibly well, and Henk, too. They led me out, I sprinted and I won for the second day in a row, even with a gutful the night before. Better still, my form was coming up nicely for the world championships. I already had my silver medal from 2002, and I went to Madrid with big ambitions to win.

But the circuit turned out to be harder than I'd hoped. It split on the last climb, and I was caught in the second group. There was a small group off the front, containing Paolo Bettini and my old Rabobank teammate Michael Boogerd, and it was Mario Aerts and Peter Van Petegem – my Lotto teammates, who were riding for the Belgian team at the worlds – who chased it down. But I'll always remember that on the climb, as my group tried and failed to get back on, Peter and Mario were sitting at the back of the group, looking back and *waiting for me.*

That's how strong our team spirit was. They knew they had time to close the gap to the group at the front but were just seeing if I could get back on before they did it. We couldn't quite get back on, and the lead group went away from us. Mario and Van Petegem chased the lead group and were instrumental in their Belgian teammate Tom Boonen winning the race, but they were still hoping for me to come back on. You keep the world-champion's jersey in the trade team if you can.

24

My Best Victory (Salute) Ever

MY AIMS FOR 2006 were similar to those of 2005, with one extra goal: win some Giro stages; win some Tour stages (and the green jersey); win the worlds; have a baby.

Angélique was due to give birth to our second child in mid-February. However, the rhythms of life are rarely in sync with the rhythms of the professional cyclist's season, and the chances were that the birth was going to clash with Het Volk.

At least Het Volk was in Belgium. Ewan, our first child, was born in May 2002, just on the eve of the start of the Giro d'Italia, which was being held in Holland. That time, Lotto showed what a family-orientated team they were. He was due at the end of May, which I'd thought would be perfect – I could do ten or 12 days of the Giro as planned, then be home for the birth. But Ewan was in a real rush, just like his dad. I was training on the Prologue course the day before the race started when I got the call from Angélique.

'It's happening now. You've got to come,' she said.

My first reaction was, *Shit.*

I grabbed Walter Planckaert, we jumped in the car and drove halfway to the hotel to meet a soigneur, who'd brought me some clothes. I changed, jumped in the soigneur's car – a Fiat Maria – and drove it 450 kilometres to Zottegem, getting there just in time for Ewan's birth.

I slept that night in the hospital room with my wife and son.

I'd had to organise special permission from the International Cycling Union and the Giro organisers to get back on Saturday in time for my Prologue ride. Lotto came through, and via one of their sponsors they organised a private jet from Belgium to Holland. Me, two pilots, croissants, coffee and orange juice. Back to the Giro to win two stages. It was the best year ever.

My daughter Elena's birth, in February 2006, should have been a bit easier, but she was also in a rush. At 8 pm on the 24th, the evening before Het Volk, my phone rang while I was eating dinner at the team hotel in Ghent.

'You've got to come – she's not going to wait,' Angélique said.

I ran out, jumped into the car and did the 25-minute drive from Ghent to Zottegem in 17 minutes. Elena was born at 9 pm. We had what they call in Flemish the *koningsdroom* – the king's dream – a son and a daughter. I was such a proud dad.

I raced Het Volk and called Angélique the next afternoon, looking forward to hearing our daughter crying down the phone.

Angélique sounded like death. She whispered the story of what had happened since I left the hospital, and it left me extremely shaken. She'd lost a lot of blood when a piece of placenta attached to the womb tore off. Her body thought everything was still attached, so she had bled for some time before they realised what was up. They'd also snipped through a vein that didn't get closed off properly.

They had to take her into surgery twice, put her under three times and give her a heap of blood. The doctors had wanted to ring me because they were extremely worried she wouldn't make it through, but she'd told them not to because I had a big race the next day. And all the time, I'd been sleeping and then taking part in a bike race. I should have been there. I was overcome with anger and fear that I could have lost my wife; at the same time, I was experiencing the overwhelming relief of everything being fine.

The doctors told us after Elena was born that what Angélique had been through would probably prevent her having any more children. This made it a big surprise when she got pregnant with our third child, Claudia, who was born in June 2010. Claudia considerately made her appearance a few days before the Tour of Switzerland – at least I was at home for that one.

I've attended the births of all three of my children. It's not something that all professional cyclists are able to say, and it's something that was very important to me. Bike racing's just a hobby I happen to be very good at. It's not a matter of life and death.

I won at least one race every month from January through to May in 2006. I was able to hit form and keep it rolling on. The team were stronger. We'd brought in Chris Horner to help Cadel in the mountains, while one of our younger riders, Gert Steegmans, from Belgium, was about to add an extra dimension to our sprints. At the Giro, I won as easy a hat-trick of victories as I ever have. I was helped by the fact that Alessandro Petacchi crashed out in stage three, although I'd already beaten him once by then. Petacchi's decapitated Milram team still took it upon themselves to control the sprints during the flat stages, inadvertently giving me some of the best leadouts I've ever had, and I won stages two, four and six. I started the Tour de France in my best ever form with my best ever team.

I did continue my incredible run of non-wins in the opening sprint of the Tour, however. In four seasons of riding the Tour with Lotto, starting in 2002, I'd finished third, second, second and third in the first sprint of the race. And in 2006, I cocked it up again, finishing second to French rider Jimmy Casper in Strasbourg. I'd been outwitted by somebody different every year for five years. The worst thing is that the chaos of the first-stage sprint should suit me down to the ground. I'm not one to suffer from nerves. But you can't always pick and choose your wins.

And while I spent all those years very conspicuously not winning the opening stage of the Tour, the other common theme, with the exception of 2003, was that I felt like I had great legs and a very positive mindset. Each year, I've known it was a matter of waiting impatiently before the stage wins came.

In Luxembourg the next day, all the sprinters were present: O'Grady, Freire, Hushovd, Zabel and Boonen, who didn't seem to be going as well as the previous year. Freddie dropped me off in Zabel's wheel. It was a hard end to the stage, and I knew he'd go for an early one. As soon as he did, I responded, overlapped him almost immediately and thought I might as well go for it.

There was a big curve towards the finish line. I got the inside line, then rode in a straight line from the exit to the finish. Hushovd and Boonen tried to come on my left, but it was the long way around, and Hushovd ended up hitting my foot with his front wheel, which made him pull his foot out of his pedal. I might have given him the tiniest switch, probably just three centimetres, but enough for him to hit me. He was very angry about that, but the winner is always right. And the best thing was that a bunch of my mates from the Gold Coast were over to see me win and take the green jersey.

I'd also pre-empted the Belgian media this time. They'd talked up Boonen and predicted he would win many stages in his world champion's jersey. Unfortunately for him, the only group sprint he did win – up the Cauberg climb the day after my first stage win – was for second place. I'd noticed him fighting his bike again in the sprints, wasting energy, and even though he was wearing the yellow jersey for a few days I wasn't worried about him at all. In fact, I wasn't worried about anybody, except Óscar Freire, who was sprinting very fast.

I felt invincible, but cycling is a sport that specialises in quickly eroding feelings of invincibility. As we raced through Belgium during the third stage, we were coming down a very fast down-hill. It was normal – everybody riding at 60 or 70 kilometres per hour – and I was just cruising down the right-hand side when I heard shouts. It's part of the social glue that keeps the peloton together that riders in front point out potholes or traffic islands to riders behind them. A day in the bunch is a constant series of gestures, shouts and small adjustments in the flow of riders as hazards are avoided. But at 60 kilometres per hour, the warnings can't possibly travel as fast as the riders are going.

As I descended, I noticed a huge, square-cut hole, half a foot deep, left over from some roadworks right in the middle of the road. I hadn't even seen it until I was level with it, even though I'd heard a yell. There wasn't even time to shout myself before I heard somebody behind me hit the hole. Freddie can't even have seen it before his front wheel was suddenly half a foot below the level of the road and he was pitching towards the ground at 60 kilometres per hour. My leadout man left the race in an ambulance, with a smashed-up shoulder, as did Erik Dekker, who'd also been swallowed up by the hole.

The good thing about Freddie being my leadout man was that he was a very experienced sprinter himself – he had the race knowledge, nous and speed to do exactly what I needed him to do, and now I'd be sprinting without him. It was time for plan B: Gert Steegmans.

We called Gert 'Steggles', after the frozen-chicken company. He's a very big, very strong lad, who'd been winning occasional races for us through 2004 and 2005. Steggles was a force of nature – he was bloody powerful, but he hadn't quite learned to properly channel that power. When things went right, and he started sprints from the right place, there weren't many riders who could beat him. Trouble was, he needed looking after and directing. I've seen it on television a few times that hammer throwers in track and field sometimes mistime their release, and the hammer goes flying into the fence around the athlete. Steggles's sprints were sometimes like that. He'd be putting out twice as many watts as the next man, but in the wrong way or at the wrong time. But when he did it right, he could really pulverise people. He was also mentally fragile, with a tendency to think too much and let the pressure get to him.

We weren't even sure about taking Steggles to the Tour in 2006 because we didn't know if he'd be able to take the pressure, but I reckoned I could harness his power to replace Freddie. All he had to do, I told him, was listen to me and do exactly what I said. I told him that if I said move up the bunch, then he was to move up the bunch. If I said jump on the right, I'd not want to finish the sentence before he'd gone for it. If I told him to ride along with no hands on the bars, singing the Belgian national anthem, he was to do it. If I directed him, and he did exactly what I told him, then it would be my fault and my responsibility if it went wrong. Beyond that, I didn't say much to him. I didn't want him sitting on his bike, thinking about it until his head started to explode, so I didn't let him know what our expectations were.

Steggles's main role throughout the day was to be the go-between for me and the team car. I hardly ever race with a radio, so when I needed something, I'd ask Steggles to contact Herman Frison, our team manager.

'Herman, Robbie needs some toilet paper,' Steggles informed him.

My teammates have come to learn that when Robbie needs to stop during a race, Robbie needs to stop.

There are some questions that every professional cyclist has to answer again and again and again. Such as, if you won three stages, how come you haven't won the yellow jersey? (It's done on cumulative time.) Or, are you all on drugs? (No, apart from a few idiots.) And the most common of all, what happens if you need to go to the toilet?

The answer to that one? It depends.

The peloton will often call a truce early in a stage for everybody to stop and irrigate the grass verges. Later in a race, it's going so fast that if you stop you're toast, so riders just go off the bike, maybe with a teammate pushing. It's remarkably easy.

But circumstances aren't always that straightforward. Our stomachs get pretty shot during a stage race, with all the food we're shovelling through, and it can lead to unpredictable timing with regard to digestive processes. In short, sometimes you need to go for a poo, right in the middle of a bike race.

It's not convenient, but it sometimes happens, so you've got to be organised about it. And on that stage to Saint Quentin, I needed to be organised. The race was quite brisk at that point, maybe 45 or 46 kilometres per hour. But you can't explain things logically to your bowels.

While I cruised along, I got my bib and braces off under my jersey, looking for a good place to stop. The trouble is, it was the Tour de France, and there were spectators everywhere.

I saw a spot with a parked car and no people around, and thought, *You beauty, that's me*. With Steggles waiting around the other side, I ducked down behind the car and did what I had to do. Suddenly, a man appeared from nowhere to ask for a souvenir water bottle, with his camera ready for a photograph. I looked at him. He looked at me. And there was a moment of silence during which his mind processed the visual information his eyes were sending it.

But I was done. No time for an apology. Shorts up, back on the bike, and I was up and running even before the convoy had finished going past. Steggles paced me back to the peloton.

Then I started talking to him. I said, 'Listen, I'm going to stay in your wheel, and you have to start circling up the bunch, but only ever in somebody's wheel. No need to thunder up the side of the peloton in the wind. Just move up with guys as they move up, and then stay still, near the edge, when they get absorbed back into the bunch and drop backwards down the middle.' I was teaching Steggles to surf the peloton.

And all the time, I kept up my instructions. Move up. Follow him. Stay here. Move up on that guy's wheel.

I told him that when we came to the last kilometre, we wanted to be in the first 20. There would be a false flat up, then a little bend, and we wouldn't see the finish until we got around the bend, with 200 metres to go.

'Go when I tell you. Start your sprint at exactly 400 metres to go,' I said.

I knew how strong he was. My plan was similar to what the whole team had done at the 2004 Tour of Qatar, only it would just be Steggles in front of me. We'd go whoosh, up past the side of the bunch, and motor past everybody.

Steggles was so eager, though, I really had to hold him back. From 800 metres to go, I was telling him wait, wait, wait . . . Wait. Wait . . .

At 410 metres, I shouted, 'GO!' and he accelerated so hard that they all missed my wheel. Steggles is 1.9 metres tall and weighs about 88 kilos – he's a monster of a bike rider – and I sat in his slipstream and got pulled right along. Steggles passed a dozen guys, who were doing the leadout as fast as they could. I glanced across and could see the riders in the line looking at us haring past them, and they knew they were watching the winning rider.

Steggles had us wound up to a good speed going up the false flat, and I jumped around him, taking the shortest line through the corner and taking lengths out of everybody, who just looked flat-footed in comparison. I was miles ahead across the line, just laughing at how well it had gone.

I was over the moon. I had *the* leadout man of the Tour, and we'd won because he did everything I asked, to the letter. Everybody was congratulating him and patting him on the back.

But I think it went to his head a little. He got much too excited the next day in Caen and went 100 metres too soon, into a headwind. I guess he felt that he was good, he was strong and it would be easy to do it again, but we got swamped because we went way too early, and I ran fifth. I was filthy angry, mainly because I always am when I lose, but also because we'd not made the most of ourselves.

Steggles is a sensitive, quite fragile guy, and he doesn't respond well to bollockings, so I just sat him down that evening and explained – never make your own tactics, use mine, like we had the day before, and we'd win.

I've never been one for bollocking people. Even when I've lost a race and mistakes have been made by me or anybody else, I've always tended first to just go into the bus and be quiet. I'll be angry, or frustrated, but I've found it's best to wait until I've calmed down a little and thought about it before wondering aloud who is to blame. You can make a useful lesson out of it that way, rather than shouting obscenities at people. In spite of my reputation, I've also never been one for throwing my bike and helmet around after I've lost a race. I've always taken time to try to sit and think about it. I'll still be angry, but the aim is to turn the anger into something positive, preferably a win, and the sooner the better.

My best ever victory salute was the American rider Levi Leipheimer's idea. We'd been riding in the bunch together at Tirreno–Adriatico earlier in the season, just chatting and messing around. On a downhill section, he'd come flying past me with his hands off the bars, pumping his arms back and forth like Jim Carrey in *Dumb and Dumber*, shouting, 'It feels like you're running really fast!'

About 20 or 30 kilometres from the end of stage six in Vitré, I had a quick chat wih Levi, and we were laughing again about the *Dumb and Dumber* scene. He said, 'If you win today, that's your victory salute. I dare you.'

'See you at the finish,' I said.

Steggles was very aware of having gone wrong the day before, so he was extra attentive to my instructions. The main thing was that we should just hang back and stay on the periphery of the bunch – we couldn't risk getting swamped again.

But I needn't have worried; it was perfect. At 400 metres to go, we were tenth or 12th wheel, and I gave him the go-ahead to light up the afterburners. It was even better than two days previously. We hammered right past Boonen, Bennati, Hushovd, Zabel, all the sprinters, about five kilometres per hour faster than they were going. He took me to 200 metres to go, nobody could hold my wheel, and I felt like I was barely touching the pedals, even at 65 or so kilometres per hour. I hadn't even started trying yet, and I remember thinking, *This is ridiculous.*

I went. Boonen was already banging on his handlebars. Nobody could get close to me – the others weren't even in the same photograph. Steggles had realised that nobody was anywhere near me, so he rode the last 150 metres pretty much freewheeling, with his arms in the air, and he still came ninth. That's how far ahead we were.

And as I crossed the line with my arms aloft, I remembered Levi's dare. I started pumping my arms. He watched it on television that night and loved it. He told me it was the best thing he'd ever seen.

It might also have been the best-executed sprint I ever did.

I'm not a big believer in superstition, but there was an incredible symmetry to my Giro and Tour stage wins in 2006. In both races, I won stages two, four and six. At the Tour, there were still four or five flat stages until the finish, but I started playing safe with the green jersey. Boonen and Freire were very close to me through the Pyrenees, and I had to keep a close eye on them. In the end, they both pulled out in the Alps, so for the second half of the race my lead over Erik Zabel, in second place, was about 80 points.

I wanted to win the final stage in the green jersey, just like I had in 2002, but somehow I went about 200 metres too early and gave Thor Hushovd the best leadout he's ever had, all the way up the final straight of the Champs-Élysées. I didn't win the stage, but it had been a bloody good Tour. Three stage wins. Green jersey. Bring on the crits!

But talk about snatching defeat from the jaws of victory. I'd just established a working partnership with one of the strongest leadout men I'd ever encountered, and Lotto managed to cock it up.

If Gert Steegmans had stayed at the team after 2006, I'd have won a heap more races than I actually did after that. I'd turned him from a big strong guy who wasn't doing anything useful with all that power into a winning machine. Before I started using him as my leadout at the Tour, he'd had a few wins, but he blew hot or cold and nobody really had a clue what was coming when.

Steggles runs on confidence and trust, possibly more than any other rider I've ever met. By directing him, and showing him how much I was relying on him and trusting him, we got the best out of him. The other thing about Steggles is that he is stubborn and hard-headed. Once he's made up his mind, you will not change it.

Lotto offered him something like 115,000 or 120,000 euros a

year to stay with the team through 2007. Steggles wanted a little bit more – he requested 130,000 euros. They tried to beat him down, and that was their big mistake. If I'd been them, I'd have given the extra money to him right there and then, in cash. He was worth his weight in gold, all 90 kilos of him.

Steggles was really offended that they'd wanted to haggle with him over ten grand, especially when he was obviously a real asset to the team, both for his own wins and for helping me. The managers thought they were playing hardball, but all they did was piss him off.

So Steggles went to Quick Step, who were only too happy to take him off our hands. The worst thing was that Lotto saw he was going to Quick Step, scrambled back and said he could have the extra money. 'Too late', was Steggles's reply. Like I said, once he's made his mind up, it's not going to be changed.

Quick Step wasn't a good place for Steggles. He's a quirky guy, a bit of a square peg in a round hole, and you've got to know how to manage him. The Quick Step riders probably just laughed at him, although when he outsprinted his own team leader Tom Boonen at the Tour de France in 2007, when leading him out, I probably found it funnier than they did. I'd obviously taught him a bit too well.

Things changed with Freddie in 2006 too, although that was his own fault. I had ambitions for the world road championships in Salzburg, which was on a similar course to Madrid the year before. Shorter and steeper climbs, but it was a circuit on which the sprinters could hope to survive. My form was so good in 2006 that I thought, *If I do survive, I'm winning that race.*

The worlds is a race that rewards smart riders. It's the only major event held on a circuit, and the good thing about circuits is that each time the bunch comes around, a smart rider will learn a little bit more and ride the next lap just a little bit better. I wanted to expend as little energy as possible, so I used my method of drifting on the hills. I started the climbs near the front of the bunch, drifted back through the peloton, sat on the back over the top, then eased through the peloton to be near the front again when the next climb started.

It really paid off because by the final part of the race I was drifting less – the Italians were going faster and faster, and the more I drifted the riskier it was for me to get caught behind a split. But I'd conserved so much energy in the first ten laps or so that I was capable of climbing nearer the front. I was exactly where I wanted to be, and there was nobody around me whom I feared in a sprint.

I was still in it with ten kilometres to go, with five kilometres to go, and three kilometres to go. Normally, put me at the front of a race with three kilometres to go and I'm more or less guaranteed to win. But I wasn't the only rider trying to use my head that day. The Spanish team ambushed us all through a sharp corner. They had the first three riders in the bunch: Sammy Sánchez, Alejandro Valverde and Xavier Florencio. It was elementary tactics – the first two dive-bombed the corner, while Florencio stalled a little and took the rest of us wide, giving Sánchez and Valverde a gap. I saw Bettini and Zabel just squeezing through and catching the Sánchez–Valverde train. Trouble.

There was the smallest gap, and, ahead, Sánchez was burying himself to get the group away. I couldn't react – I'd been caught wide.

Freddie was next to me.

I saw the race going away from me, and in an instant I said to

Freddie, 'Go. Close it.' Somebody had to react immediately or it would all be over.

I was riding for Australia, and Freddie for the USA. But just a year before, Van Petegem and Mario Aerts had tried to wait for me, their teammate, even though we were different nationalities and teams that day.

Freddie thought about it for a split second and said, 'No.'

And that was it. The gap tripled in size, just from that one hesitation. And then British rider David Millar came through, with Stuey on his wheel, yelling at him, 'GO! GO! GO! GO!'

Dave tried to close the gap, Stuey behind him, and me in Stuey's wheel. But it was too late. I cleaned everybody up in the bunch sprint, but I could see Paolo Bettini, 40 metres in front of me, winning the world title.

I'd had fantastic legs and I'd felt really good. I was dejected after the race – it's times like that when I see just how hard a sport cycling is. In a way, I was closer to winning the world title in 2006 than I had been in 2002, when I won the silver medal. In Zolder, beating Cipollini was such a huge job, and given the fight I'd had with Zabel I was never realistically going to get around him. In Salzburg, I won the bunch sprint. If we'd not allowed the Bettini group to get away, I'd have been the world champion.

Had Freddie done the team thing, he'd have been richly rewarded for his work. I was very disappointed in him. The rest of the team, management and riders, weren't ecstatic either – they'd seen a golden opportunity to have a world champion in the team. Freddie had ridden for himself, which was his right, but he'd come 11th in the bunch sprint, 15th in the race.

Freddie's contract wasn't renewed when it ran out at the end of 2007. He'd had a poor season in 2006 anyway, having crashed out of the Tour. He could have completely redeemed himself for that at the worlds. But he didn't. I let it pass, but others on the team were a lot less reasonable about it than I was.

25

Mini-Me

MY PEAK YEARS: 2004 TO 2006. Three seasons in which I think the results and facts supported my claim to be the best sprinter in the world. I won fewer races than Petacchi and got fewer headlines than Tom Boonen during these years, but I was consistently winning more Tour de France stages than anybody else. I took eight in those three Tours, twice as many as any other sprinter over the same period.

The statistics of 2007 don't make me look like the fastest sprinter in the world – my only Tour stage win was the one I took in Canterbury. But I'd argue I was as good that year as I was for the previous three. It's just that circumstances took away a lot of opportunities.

There was nothing wrong with my form as 2007 began, with the team now called Predictor-Lotto, after Omega Pharma's pregnancy-testing brand. I won a stage at the Tour Down Under for the sixth year in a row. And I even rode well in March, which never normally happened.

At Tirreno–Adriatico, there was a stage based on a circuit

with the start and finish in the same place. So while the rest of the bunch hung around their hotels, Freddie and I went to check out the final kilometre. There was a right–left combination of bends, almost a chicane: 90 degrees right, 90 degrees left, then 300 or so metres to the finish. The plan was simple: I'd hit the corners first, Freddie second, he'd let my wheel go, and I'd be 30 metres clear by the time anybody realised what was up.

It turned out I got it wrong. I was more like 50 metres clear at the finish line. I railed it so fast around the corner that I almost ran over the lead motorbike.

I like winning races when I'm the strongest and fastest – it's a source of great satisfaction for me. But I also enjoy winning races when I've been the cleverest, although I hate being on the receiving end of it.

Early April coincides with my first break of the season. I tend to back off, to allow my body to rebuild itself for the push through to the Giro d'Italia. My first race back is usually Scheldeprijs in mid-April. It's a flat race that ends in a sprint, although I tend not to enjoy it. It's the first sprint after not making a big effort for two weeks, and I can hardly walk the day after.

In 2007, I was surprised even to be in the lead group. Then even more surprised to find myself hitting out with about 300 metres to go. As I led into the final 200 metres, I thought that at least I'd guaranteed myself a top five, which became top three when I got to 100 metres to go and was still in front.

Holy crap, I'm going to win, was my final thought with about 50 metres to the line. And then, out of nowhere, a shadow appeared beside me. Some little fat guy in pink just rolled me in the last few metres.

I knew who it was: Mark Cavendish, getting his first

professional win. He was over the moon, punching the air, screaming, shouting. Good on him. He was the first new young sprinter I'd seen in many years whom I'd describe as a really fast guy. Not many come along in their first year with such good speed. You get guys who come along and they are strong or take risks. They might fluke a couple of good results, but real sprinters only come along every so often.

Heiko Salzwedel had told me about him a while back. Heiko had been working with the British track team, and he'd told me there was a young guy on the program who was another version of me. Not only that, but he apparently modelled his riding on mine. I was his sprinting idol, and he constantly mined Heiko for information about me. Heiko had also said he was seriously fast. I'd been looking forward to sprinting against him, and when I did it was like coming up against a younger version of myself. I still tease Cav about the fact I was his idol, even though he doesn't like to admit it any more.

My 2007 Tour de France stage win at Canterbury was possibly my greatest ever victory. It's hard to differentiate, but it's exactly what I mean when I say that miracle wins are more entertaining than predictable wins. Sport is supposed to be entertaining, and that is something people in cycling sometimes lose sight of.

I once did an interview where I talked about my ten greatest victories, which included my first pro win at the 1996 Tour of Murcia and winning in the green jersey on the Champs-Élysées. I could say that beating Cipollini at his peak was worth more than the others. My third stage win in the 2006 Tour, in Vitré, where Steggles catapulted me about ten metres clear of second place, was my most dominant. But Canterbury was the best. Ninety-nine per cent of professional cyclists, who are themselves the very elite of the elite, will not have a single exploit like that in their entire careers.

I knew I was going to win there, and even the most challenging circumstances possible couldn't prevent me from doing so. I don't believe in destiny, or that anything beyond physical ability, good fitness, circumstances and tactical decisions can affect a rider's results, but it was all very symmetrical in 2007, both for the fact that I'd really targeted Canterbury and because I'd won a single stage at the Giro – I was continuing my odd run of coincidental numbers of stage wins in Italy and France.

My Giro d'Italia stage win, on the second day of the race, almost made my top ten, purely because I had to get over a good-sized mountain to even be in the sprint. It was classic Giro d'Italia – supposed to be a flat stage but with a 600-metre-high hill about 50 kilometres from the finish, then a four-kilometre climb eight kilometres out. It wasn't Robbie McEwen territory.

It didn't help that the climbers such as Italy's Danilo Di Luca and Davide Rebellin were getting perky on that final climb and a lot of the sprinters were getting shelled, but I saw something that gave me heart – Alessandro Petacchi, surrounded by a group of his teammates, just ahead of me over the top. I made sure that I got to him as quickly as possible, because I knew that as soon as we got off the descent there would be a group of Milram riders making a beeline for the finish, and I needed to be on the back of it. Anybody who wasn't on board when that happened wasn't going to see the front of the race again.

In retrospect, it looks like my form dropped off in 2007 when compared with 2006 and 2005. After all, I'd won 12 Grand Tour stages over those two seasons, compared with two in 2007. But circumstances had a lot to do with it – I was possibly even faster in 2007, because when I came off Petacchi's wheel I absolutely trounced him. I was well clear when I crossed the line. I'll never get bored of winning Grand Tour stages, especially that early in the race. The goal's achieved, thanks for coming. And, of course, given that my career was becoming increasingly symmetrical, my Canterbury win came on the second day of the Tour, just as my Giro win had done.

I've rarely experienced the intensity of professional cycling more strongly than after the finishing line at Canterbury. I was shouting and yelling after I'd won – the euphoria was incredible, much more so than normal, because of the circumstances. My wrist was killing me where I'd fallen on it, which wasn't pleasant at all, but it magnified the sensory overload. And when my teammates rode in, I was thanking them, hugging them, in spite of the horrible pain in my wrist. Predictor-Lotto – still the best team in the world. My boys had other duties as well as looking after me, but they still pulled me to my best ever win.

I knew I'd damaged myself, though. My wrist was uncomfortable, although bearable. But I'd done something to my knee, which was getting more and more painful every day. Victor wasn't on the Tour, so I wasn't able to get the necessary work to make it better. Every extra day I rode, the tendons tightened up some more. I got sorer and sorer, and then it started pulling me skewiff on the bike, which meant I was putting less power down.

I could hardly keep up the next day in Ghent, where I'd scouted out the finish and would have been a dead cert if I'd been fit. As it was, that's where Steggles outsprinted his own team leader, Boonen, by giving him a leadout that was a little bit too good.

I got worse and worse in that Tour. My placings went first, sixth, seventh, 16th, then 151st. In the last sprint before the Alps, won by Boonen, I scraped myself into 13th place, but the writing was on the wall. The first Alpine stage only went over one mountain, the Col de la Colombière, but I crawled over it, with a few of my teammates hanging back for me. I was bad.

The next day crossed three increasingly difficult climbs in the first half of the stage, before three first-category mountains in the second half. I got dropped after one kilometre, along with Danilo Napolitano, Cav and a French guy called Cédric Hervé. Cav pulled out pretty soon – he was a young guy in his first Tour, and he'd gone about as far as he could. The three of us continued, but I knew early on that this time the cavalry was not coming. There was too much flat in between the mountains, with the wind blowing down the valleys in our faces. I went so slowly up the final climb to Tignes that I was almost glad I'd soon be put out of my misery. I was well over an hour behind the stage winner, Denmark's Michael Rasmussen, at the finish and was eliminated.

I didn't give up, though. It was the first and only time I've ever left a Tour before the finish, but at least I didn't climb into a car. I'd toughed it out. It wasn't my decision to stop; it was the race's.

There's nothing you can do if you've damaged your knee in a stage race. Knees are tricky things – to sort out injuries there it takes rest and lots of work by a physio. Riding 200 kilometres through the mountains every day is never going to fix a knee.

I didn't waste that last day, however. I spent a large amount of time daydreaming about where I was going to go on holiday as soon as practicably possible once I'd got home from Tignes. The family and I, plus my parents, booked a last-minute deal to the south of Barcelona. I'd never had a bonus holiday in the middle of the European summer before – it was just what I needed to take my mind off the Tour, where I was convinced I'd have won more if I hadn't been injured.

The team were happy with the Tour, however. As well as my stage win, Cadel came second in the GC by 23 seconds to Spain's Alberto Contador, and that was including 20 seconds' worth of time bonus that Contador took over him.

Apart from a holiday, only one other thing was going to make up for having to pull out of the Tour, and that was winning myself some money. In 2006, as well as sorting myself out with a hefty pay rise, I'd had my contract adjusted to include a clause concerning win bonuses. There were bonuses for winning Tour stages, the green jersey and Giro stages. But I also had a general bonus written in, where I'd get 100,000 euros if I won five high-level races outside the Tour de France, not including the Eneco Tour or Tour of Poland (both races are generous to sprinters, and the quality of field is not quite so high). That left me Tirreno–Adriatico or Paris–Nice, the Tour of Romandy, the Tour of Switzerland, Milan–San Remo, Het Volk (now Het Nieuwsblad), Paris–Brussels and Paris–Tours, plus Giro stages.

It's actually harder than it might sound. Het Volk is a real tough-man's Classic, while the Tours of Romandy and Switzerland are mostly mountainous. At best, there'd be three, possibly four, chances over the entire two races, and both come in the run-up to a Grand Tour, which means I'm just short of my best form. Paris–Tours and Milan–San Remo were long Classics with complicated finales. And I rarely went well at Tirreno or Paris–Nice because my fitness was always bad in March. Over the whole season, I probably had a maximum of 20 sprints that would count towards my bonus, of which I had to win five. Winning one in four sprints, spread out over the entire season, isn't easy.

In 2007, I needed Paris–Brussels to guarantee my money. It's got a tough route and a complicated finale, but I won it ahead of Cookie and Britain's Jeremy Hunt. You can see in the photograph that I've got two arms up: one for the victory, the other to represent the predominant thought in my mind, which was, *Kerching!*

26

Cadel

I WASN'T JUST seeing my leadout disintegrating towards the end of 2006, through 2007 and into 2008. I could also feel the ground beginning to shift beneath my feet in the team. Lotto were over the moon after the 2006 Tour de France, and it wasn't just my three stage wins and green jersey that were making them happy. Cadel had finished fifth overall, soon to be bumped up to fourth when Floyd Landis tested positive and got stripped of the win.

The team were in a great position. They'd won multiple stages for four years out of five, along with three green jerseys. And now they had a guy just short of the podium. I think the management got either complacent or spoiled – they didn't realise what they had and got greedy for more.

Their attitude was it's great that we can get green jerseys and stage wins, so now that we can guarantee that let's also have a crack at the yellow jersey. We can do both. The plan is to bring in a couple more climbers to help Cadel, and, by the way, we're not really going to ride for the sprints because Robbie can look after himself.

I could sense the focus changing around me. I didn't begrudge Cadel his ambitions – he was a genuine contender for winning the Tour de France, which he finally proved by becoming the first Aussie to win the yellow jersey in 2011. But the team certainly thought that Tour stage wins would still come flowing, in spite of all the invisible work the team had to do for me to get them. Putting resources into Cadel's ambitions was going to weaken us in the sprints. Sprints don't begin 200 metres out; they begin on the start line, when a sprinter's team paces the bunch, then chases down the attack, then spends 30 kilometres manoeuvring the sprinter into position.

I've been my own worst enemy by getting lots of wins and seemingly getting them on my own, because my teammates do a lot of invisible work. When a duck swims on the water, it looks easy, but the important action is happening under the surface. I'd have liked to go into the Giro and Tour on the back of an eight-man leadout and hit the race like a Sherman tank. That said, those wins aren't as inspirational nor as televisual as the miracle wins. But even the miracle wins don't come without a serious amount of unglamorous graft having gone on.

Cadel is quite high maintenance anyway – he likes to have the full support of his team. Coming fourth after he'd already come eighth made him higher maintenance and more demanding on team resources. And then he came second. By 2008, when the team had changed its name again to Silence-Lotto, he was the leader, and I was a spare part, charged with getting victories however I could without being a drain on resources. It's no coincidence that I stopped winning so many races that year. In the whole of 2008, I took five wins, although I was choosy about where I won – they all qualified me for my fat annual win bonus.

The team quite rightly thought they could win the Tour with Cadel in 2008, and for the first time they made it the single target. I was told that I could come to the Tour but that I'd be on my own. There'd be no Silence-Lotto riders on the front for the flat stages, and the other seven riders apart from me and Cadel were there to protect him and him only.

To be fair, it nearly paid off. And it was also fair of the team to make a decision and concentrate fully on it – it showed they really believed in Cadel's chances of winning the Tour. Lance Armstrong's team never took a sprinter to the Tour, but Lotto with Cadel wasn't yet at that level.

But there were a couple of issues that were brushed under the carpet. The first was that the team was no more capable of supporting Cadel in the high mountains than it was of giving me a full eight-man leadout between 2004 and 2006. Team selection basically hinged around the management asking who the next-best climbers were. But they weren't climbers who could really help in the Tour de France – they were climbers who'd be five minutes behind Cadel when the real action kicked off, rather than 15 minutes behind. Some of them were even climbing in my group by the end of the Tour. And if they weren't actually making a difference to Cadel's riding in the mountains, my opinion was that they should have given me somebody, just to keep me out of the wind and take me up the bunch to get position at the right time. I felt I'd given the team enough success and stayed loyal long enough to justify being given a domestique to help me at a few chosen moments.

But Cadel is very different from me. He needs reassurance that everybody is behind him, and the management giving him seven domestiques was the kind of signal he needed. I just go out there and get on with it.

Cav won four stages that year. It was the first time since 2003 that I hadn't won one, and it showed just how difficult it is when you are isolated. I was relying on luck and trying to use other riders to get to the front, but it was too haphazard, and I was usually exhausted by the time the sprints started.

I still felt very quick in 2008, and I'd had some good wins earlier in the year. But Cavendish had the full support of Columbia. They had Gerald Ciolek – a hugely powerful young German sprinter – leading him out, and the effect was similar to when Steggles and I were working together in 2006. I was as fast as I was in 2005 and 2006 but didn't get a chance to prove it. In Nîmes, where Cav won his fourth stage, I'd jumped and got level with him, but he still had shelter from his team. He jumped and stayed a length or two clear of me all the way to the line. We actually sprinted at the same speed, but I'd gone from way behind, without the benefit of a leadout. I'd been getting boxed by all the other teams supporting their sprinters, and it cost a lot of energy.

The second issue that the team didn't address properly was that Cadel, while one of the strongest riders in the world in a Grand Tour, was wasting energy. I'm a rider who has been obsessively parsimonious with energy expenditure at every possible moment throughout his career, so watching somebody else waste it was driving me up the wall.

Cadel ran second to Carlos Sastre that year, but I'm convinced he was a far superior rider. Cadel had had a crash, which gave the physio a lot of work to do and blocked him up a bit, but he started the last long time trial only one and a half minutes behind Sastre. That should have been easy for him, but he was flat-out exhausted.

And the reason he was exhausted was the energy wastage. At the time, Cadel was very nervous in a bunch, and he refused to ride in the middle, where you can virtually freewheel along in the slipstream of 40 or 50 riders. Instead, he tended to sit on the outside of the bunch with his head cocked out, making 150 small accelerations from mid-bunch up to the front every day. He rode halfway out into the wind because he didn't like to sit in the wheel, although he's much better at it these days.

Over the course of three and a half thousand kilometres, all this adds up to a hell of a lot of energy. The Tour, whether you are the winner or the lanterne rouge – the rider in last place – is about saving energy.

I told him one day to stop doing that and do what I did, to follow me and compare how much easier it was. I took him all the way to the front of the bunch, surfing off other people, out of the wind. Then I told him to hold his position in the first 25 riders. He didn't have to be in the first dozen, which is unnecessarily tiring, but we stayed near the front without wasting energy. It was better for him. I sacrificed a chance at one or two stage wins by actively riding for Cadel.

In that Tour, Cadel had hugely experienced riders such as Mario and Sevi spending a lot of effort trying to get him to save energy and remain calm – a difficult, if not an impossible, job. We stayed at our usual rest-day accommodation in Pau that year: the Hotel des Pyrénées in Ousse. The team were in a good mood because Cadel was in yellow, even though he was in a bit of discomfort from his crash. At dinner after the stage, the general consensus of the team was that we should sleep in the next morning, have a bit of a leisurely breakfast, then head out for a spin at 11 o'clock. We told Cadel, and he ummed and aahed before telling us we'd need to go earlier, say 10.30, because he needed to do some motorpacing. I checked with the others – sure, we can do 10.30.

We all got up half an hour earlier for breakfast and were all there on the dot at 10.30, ready to leave.

Except there was no Cadel.

Five minutes passed. That's fairly standard, unless you have some seriously anal riding partners – most rides leave five minutes late. Then ten minutes, then 15. Still no Cadel. I sent in Herman Frison, our team manager, to find out where Cadel was.

Herman came out again. Twenty minutes. Still no Cadel. I said, 'Righto, this is officially bullshit. You don't do this to eight guys who've been riding their arses off for you.'

Finally, at 11 o'clock, Cadel walked out and greeted us with a cheery, 'Morning!'

He'd done some physio. No worries – he's the yellow jersey and his injuries need some work. But they also wanted him to pose with some journalist at a table with breakfast all set up – orange juice, bunch of flowers, copy of *L'Equipe* – for a nice picture in the yellow jersey.

I said to him, 'That was way over the top. We're out of here.' The management were panicking because there were press around, but I told them he needed to have a bit more respect for his teammates.

I told him to his face that it wasn't on, that I didn't care who wanted to take his picture and what jersey he had on if it meant that he got his teammates up early before standing them up. I was really angry. I'd been in that situation before – in the green jersey at the 2004 Tour – but I would never have done that to my teammates. It was incredibly un-Australian of him.

The mental stress had got to Cadel, and I think it lost him the Tour. But fast-forward to 2011 – he didn't make a single mistake, and he was a deserving winner of the yellow jersey. Things that used to get to him didn't, and it showed he learned some lessons.

To be a good team leader, you have to understand that your teammates are not slaves. You can't be self-indulgent and self-absorbed, because if you lose the dressing room you've lost your support.

I'm very self-reliant and low-maintenance as a rider and as a person. The only advice I listen to is the advice that I agree with anyway. I listen to opinions, but I'm at my best when I'm making decisions and using people to help me carry out those decisions. It's my way or beat it. This could be interpreted as arrogance or stubbornness, but what you've also got to take into account is that I'm often right.

I went to the Vattenfall Cyclassics in Hamburg in September 2008 with good form. The team manager for Silence-Lotto was Roberto Damiani, who'd also been at the Deutschland Tour with us the week before.

I'd struggled through Germany and had pulled out with two days to go. My form was good, but I was a bit tired. I felt the extra two days' rest would benefit me in the one-day race.

There was a 20-rider breakaway in Hamburg, and I said we needed to ride to bring it back. I nominated two Belgian riders: Jurgen Van Den Broeck and Wim Van Huffel. Van Den Broeck had finished the Deutschland Tour and had told me he was tired and felt flat. I figured – and he'd agree – that the most useful impact he could have on the race was to ride early on, give what he had and maybe contribute to the team winning, rather than try to save energy, then get dropped anyway when the race heated up.

The problem was that Damiani had Van Den Broeck on a pedestal. Van Den Broeck had finished seventh in the Giro d'Italia that year, and Damiani had been hovering around him ever since. I've noticed that Italian team managers do like to attach themselves to their team leaders. Damiani was outraged that I was instructing Jurgen Van Den Broeck – seventh in the Giro! – to perform the duties of a lowly domestique. It didn't bother me – I don't race with a radio. If a rider needs a radio to communicate with me, he's too far away from me to help anyway. But without a radio, Damiani had no way of telling me what to do, and I'd have ignored him anyway.

Wim and Jurgen brought the break back, then Mario and Gat did the work. Mario did an incredible ride. He stayed with me to the last two kilometres and used up his final bit of energy dropping me into a perfect position just behind the leaders. I slotted in, bided my time, and bang! I won the sprint. Funnily enough, the podium was all-Australian, with Mark Renshaw second and Allan Davis third.

The plan had worked exactly how I'd wanted it to – it was a real team victory, led by me. Everybody was ecstatic. Except for Damiani, who had a face like a slapped backside that evening. We'd just won a ProTour race – it was my biggest ever one-day race win – and he couldn't even bring himself to offer congratulations. Gat wanted to flatten him. He told Damiani he should be ashamed of himself.

Damiani took it very personally, but what he didn't understand was that I didn't put Jurgen Van Den Broeck on the front to annoy him; I did it because it was the right thing to do. We needed to win a race, I knew how, and Damiani should have given me more respect than to assume he could call all the shots.

September got even better when I won my fifth Paris–Brussels and cheered myself up with my annual win bonus.

But it would be my last with Silence-Lotto. I'd decided my time at the team was at an end. I'd enjoyed a superb end to the season, with great support from the boys, but I couldn't allow myself to get isolated at the Tour de France again. I'd given Lotto a great deal of success, but they'd contrived to lessen my chances of having more. It was time for a new adventure.

27

Katusha

I NEVER THOUGHT I'd end up riding for the greater glory of Russian cycling. I needed a change at the end of 2008, however. I'd spent 13 professional seasons riding for Belgian or Dutch teams, and it was time for something new. So when an opportunity came up to join a Russian team in 2009, I was immediately interested.

There were no hard feelings when I left Silence-Lotto. We'd drifted apart in the last couple of years, and the spark was gone. Rather than drift aimlessly into a bad-tempered old age together, I thought both the team and I would be better off apart. At least the separation wasn't too painful – I had decided a long time before the end of the season that I'd be leaving.

I'd first met Oleg Tinkoff a couple of years earlier. Tinkoff was a Russian millionaire who'd made his money in the restaurant and brewing business. He was a keen cyclist himself and was spending some of his leftover money on a bike team that was also publicising his new line of business: credit cards. The Tinkoff Credit Systems team was at a good level – they'd got entries in the Giro d'Italia and won two stages there in 2008, which was more than I'd managed.

Tinkoff was a sprinter himself back in the day, which is why I think he was keen on me. He was a bit eccentric: a really intense, self-made, competitive guy with a genuine love for the sport.

We hit it off, and we chatted whenever we saw each other at races. Every time I spoke to him, he told me he was going to make his team much bigger one day, and that I'd have to come and ride for him. I assumed it would never happen, but during that 2008 Giro he said his team was going to get much bigger for the following season, with very big ambitions. I was pretty excited about it, because it sounded like such a fresh experience for me. Plus, I had direct contact with the boss, who was clearly keen on having a respected sprinter in the team.

We talked some more, and I signed a contract with Tinkoff for 800,000 euros – my biggest ever. He kept me up to date on the development of the team, which was going to be called Katusha. The backbone and backing of the team was Russian, although the riders came from many different countries, while the infrastructure was as Italian and Belgian as it was Russian. Tinkoff was cooperating with Igor Makarov, another former rider. Makarov was now the president of a Russian oil and gas company called Itera, Katusha's big backer.

But some time in the middle of 2008, things started changing. My old Lotto teammate Andrei Tchmil was suddenly involved. My main memory of him in 2002 was that he was extremely strong, nobody wanted to room with him and he said about two words to me all year.

Suddenly, it wasn't just Tinkoff in charge; it was Tinkoff

and Tchmil. But I sensed there was infighting going on. It wasn't long before I got an email from Tinkoff saying he'd been manoeuvred out. Tchmil and Makarov had known each other for some years, and now Tchmil was the general manager of Katusha – or, as he preferred to be called, president. He loves a title, does Tchmil. He also loved to remind us all that Premier Putin and President Medvedev were involved.

Apart from my reservations about Tchmil, and the way Oleg Tinkoff had been squeezed out, the team looked extremely well organised. Excellent bikes, Mercedes C-Class team cars and a very strong set of riders.

The boys came out for the Tour Down Under, and I was keen to make a good impression on the new team. What better way than winning the team's first ever race? At the Cancer Council Classic – the criterium warm-up for the Tour Down Under – after a nice leadout from my old teammate Gert Steegmans, who had also joined, I took Katusha's first race win. I'd been pleased to see Steggles come to the team, and I was really happy to have taken Katusha's first ever victory. For a team just starting out, winning in its very first race makes a very positive impression on the cycling world.

In our first European race, the Tour of Mallorca, which is a series of five one-day races, Steggles and I were dominant. In the Trofeo Mallorca, he pulled the sprint for me. I was just coming off him when I saw that nobody was anywhere near us, so I stopped pedalling, pulled my front wheel back and let him win. He did such a good job, he deserved it. The next day, in the Trofeo Cala Millor, I won the bunch sprint. And two days after that, our teammate Toni Colom, from Spain, won the Trofeo Bunyola. Katusha? More like Kat-whoosh-a!

It was too good to be true – we were winning all over the place.

And then it all went wrong. Colom had been riding incredibly strongly that spring – he won a stage and came fifth overall in Paris–Nice. We found out why when he tested positive. Toni's a nice guy, and I'd assumed he was riding better because he hadn't always been that serious about his job in the past – so maybe now he'd just started training properly. But what I've learned about cycling is that sometimes even nice guys dope.

That led to something that really changed the team dynamic. Tchmil decided that a big gesture would be the only way to keep us onside with the cycling authorities and the media, so he announced that all riders were to sign an anti-doping statement that would involve us repaying five times our annual salary if anybody tested positive. It was widely reported in the media, which is exactly what Tchmil wanted.

There was a lot of talk among the riders about the legality of it. Some went straight ahead and signed it. I looked at it much more closely – I wasn't sure if it was enforceable, which made it meaningless. Furthermore, somebody on 500,000 euros could eat the wrong food supplement, test positive for something he didn't even know he'd eaten (even though we are strictly responsible for anything that appears in our bodies) and end up with a 2,500,000 euro fine.

To my mind, it was full of holes – the contract essentially made it financially beneficial for Katusha if one of their riders tested positive, and there was no talk of what would happen to the money.

Then our Austrian teammate Christian Pfannberger tested positive, and Tchmil's reaction was that everybody absolutely had to sign the contract or it would look like they had something to hide. The atmosphere in the team was toxic by this point – Tchmil was going crazy over his anti-doping contract, while the riders were demoralised by the two positives.

I signed it eventually. It wasn't really legally enforceable, but not to sign was more trouble than it was worth. However, Katusha hadn't reckoned on Steggles's stubbornness. Tchmil fancied himself as a tough negotiator, but he'd never encountered Gert Steegmans once he'd dug his heels in.

Steggles refused outright to sign Tchmil's piece of paper. He rightly pointed out that they were changing his contract without notice or negotiation. Tchmil's attitude was sign or you're not racing.

So Steggles didn't race. They left him out of the Tour de France. In the end, he left the team, but he didn't race again for the whole season. They tried to make an example of him, but, just as with Lotto, he'd drawn a line and informed Katusha that it would not be crossed. He probably laughed last, however. He took Tchmil to court and won, and Katusha had to pay him his whole year's salary.

In spite of my good start, I felt like I was riding into a constant headwind with some of the staff at Katusha. I got exactly the same feelings from team manager Serge Parsani as I had from Roberto Damiani at Silence-Lotto.

Parsani has no appreciation of sprinters and what they do. He was Paolo Bettini's manager when Bettini was one of the best, if not the best, Classics rider in the world. And when Bettini retired, Parsani had latched on to the Italian Classics rider Filippo Pozzato, who'd also come to Katusha in 2009.

For Parsani, sprinters were the natural enemy of riders such as

Bettini and Pozzato, and I got the impression that, even though I was on Pozzato's team, Parsani felt I was preventing him from being the rightful leader. In fact, Parsani's attitude was just like Silence-Lotto's in 2008. At team meetings, he'd always have big plans for riders to get in breaks, and to get people up there in the GC. And, as an afterthought, he'd add 'Well, if there's a sprint, there's always Robbie'. I felt like plan B. It never even occurred to Parsani that the team could ride together to look after me and then set me up for a sprint.

Things came to a head at the Tour of Romandy. I'd crashed a couple of weeks beforehand at the Scheldeprijs. It was quite a heavy crash, but funnily enough I actually felt physically fantastic after it – it was almost as if I'd cracked something back into place. But on the other hand I was covered in grazes – arms, hips, knee and ankle – and had to go to the hospital to have them cleaned and dressed.

Coming into Romandy, I started feeling really flat. Even walking to dinner was making me tired. I'd also noticed that I had a small bright-pink graze on my ankle that really hurt, far out of proportion to the size of the wound. It felt hot to the touch, and when the masseur poked it, it was absolute agony.

I got dropped on both the next two days, I was going so badly, and the fourth stage was a team time trial. The route went flat for a couple of kilometres, then straight up a huge hill. I told the boys that I was absolutely finished, and I knew I wouldn't get over the hill with them, unless they waited for me and lost a lot of time. So I told them I'd lead up to the hill and give it everything. Then I'd swing off and say goodbye. That was the best possible contribution I could give to the team. I duly gave it everything, then, as they turned left and started going up the hill, I did a U-turn and trundled back to the team bus.

There was no point in continuing – the last two stages were mountainous and I really needed to sort out whatever was making me feel so flat. I phoned my doctor in Belgium and explained the symptoms. He said, straight out, 'You've got a staph infection – take antibiotics.' After two days on the pills, I felt absolutely fantastic again.

And then they told me I wasn't going to the Giro d'Italia.

In my opinion, that was one of the worst decisions I've ever known by a team manager – right up there with Patrick Lefevre not taking me to the Tour de France in 2001. Parsani's big plan was that Katusha should take a team of strong time-trialists because the first stage was a team time trial and he really wanted Pozzato to take the pink jersey. If Katusha were in the first few teams, Pozzato could maybe take the pink jersey in a sprint. Fat chance.

It was ridiculous. They were going to the Giro d'Italia without a sprinter, all because of an unrealistic plan to win a team time trial against some very good teams. After the time trial, there were still another 20 days of the race, but Parsani couldn't see past that first day. He was so convinced Pozzato was going to wear the pink jersey that he didn't even consider what would happen if he didn't. And even if he did, there were still eight or nine flat stages that might end in a bunch sprint. In the end, Katusha ran sixth in the team time trial and won no stages. It gives me no satisfaction to point out that if they'd taken a sprinter, they might have done.

Instead of the Giro, the team sent me to the Tour of Picardy and the Tour of Belgium. I used the good form that would have made me a definite favourite for a Giro stage win by taking a stage in Picardy. Belgium started well, also. My teammate Serguei Ivanov, from Russia, won the first stage. But the next day, not riding the Giro d'Italia suddenly became the very least of my worries. I started the stage thinking I had a good chance of winning it. I ended it thinking my career was over.

28

Rehab

THE FIRST BONE I ever broke was my right collarbone, when I was practising BMX on my local track at the age of 15. It wasn't even a race; I was just trying a new jump and the ground was wet. I didn't quite make it, went over the handlebars and landed with a big smack on my shoulder.

I didn't quite knock myself out, but I was quite groggy. The first words I heard were my dad's. 'You idiot,' he said.

He was dead right.

My body is like a stone tablet into which has been carved a list of injuries, breakages, scars and damage. I've done both collarbones. I've bust both acromioclavicular joints (that's the junction between the shoulder and the collarbone) – all the ligaments are gone on both sides. You'll remember the fractures of the transverse processes of vertebrae L1 and L2 at the 2004 Tour de France – at least those ones didn't keep me off the bike.

I broke a rib when I crashed with Matti Breschel at the Three Days of West Flanders in 2006. He came off worse in that one, breaking a vertebra. I scraped myself up, got in the car and went on to Tirreno–Adriatico, where I was in agony. Every time I breathed, it felt like someone was stabbing me. The rib wasn't just cracked, it was broken in two, so I had two sharp ends sticking into me. Ironically, when I was really trying hard, and breathing deeply, it hurt the least. Sneezing and laughing, on the other hand, were the worst. Even to this day, there's a tight spot where the ribcage doesn't quite expand as well as it used to.

My body's also covered in scars – every season leaves tattoos of lost skin and grazes, and the tan is never quite as even as I'd like it to be. In short, I'm a wreck.

But all of these injuries paled into insignificance when compared with what I did to my left knee in the second stage of the 2009 Tour of Belgium, which finished in Knokke-Heist. I fancied my chances of winning, and I'd put the team on the front – the bunch was together going into a finishing circuit.

I got separated from my team on the final lap, so I went around the bunch and started coming up the left-hand side. There was a fast left-hand bend approaching, and I reckoned if I went into it with enough speed I'd make up ten or 12 positions in the bunch.

As I came through, the guy on my outside cut in on me. Markus Zberg, the younger brother of Beat Zberg, also adjusted his line to cut the corner more finely. The trouble was, he came into my path, and I was forced to adjust and lean further in on the inside. I put my knee out to counterbalance myself.

Just on the inside of the bend, past the apex, there was one of those large red and white plastic road barriers. They fill them with water or sand, and they can be clipped together to form a long line – they're more or less immovable objects. It stuck out over the road. I was coming towards it, no space to move out, trying to make myself narrower to avoid hitting it, realising that it was in my way.

I thought I might miss it, but I heard a dull thud. There was enough forward momentum, enough surface area on my knee being jammed into it, to wrench my whole leg sideways. My foot stayed clipped to the pedal, and I didn't even fall off.

But something was wrong. In one second, I realised I couldn't pedal any more, couldn't move my leg. And that one second of shock was all the time I got before the pain overflowed into my world. I looked down at my leg, and a shudder went right through my body.

In 1996, I saw the Belgian sprinter Wilfried Nelissen end his career when we rode Ghent–Wevelgem. He smashed his leg on a wooden post, with me just a few riders behind. I looked as I went past, saw his leg open, saw the blood and the bone, and I knew he'd never ride again.

Now, looking down at my own leg, feeling sick with the pain and the sight of it, I thought I'd done exactly the same thing.

Then came the screaming and shouting. I had to stop. Get off the bike. Sit down. Get an ambulance. I pulled over and got my right foot out of the pedal, but I couldn't get the other one out. I lowered myself to the ground and called to a sign man who'd been directing traffic and was standing nearby to help me get my left foot out of the pedal. He started, but it was excruciating. I told him to leave it alone. Big roars of pain. Almost crying.

My team manager Bart Leysen pulled up in a car, and I could see the look on his face. He looked like he was going to spew. I begged him to loosen my shoe so I could untangle my leg from the bike.

I was taken away in an ambulance. All I was thinking was that it was all over. No comeback from this one.

I had expanded my collection of broken bones quite spectacularly. My shinbone was bust, I'd broken the tibia on the outside, I'd lost a few fragments of bone from the outside edge of the shin, but these, although serious, were the least of my injuries. They were easily mended – they opened me up, put the bone fragments back into place and fixed it all together with screws as big as your finger. That was very stable right away. I could put weight on it after a couple of days and it was not a worry. But the patellar tendon looked like the biggest problem.

The tendon had been the point of impact, and the first diagnosis was that I'd snapped it. Never mind my career being over – if my tendon had snapped, I'd be looking at not being able to walk properly, let alone cycle. My final thought as I went under in the operating room was that this time I was really stuffed.

Life doesn't easily get to me – I experience the same highs and lows as anybody, but I'm not one to dwell on negative feelings. But at that moment, more than anything else, I was sad, and I didn't like it. I was thinking, *I'm not going to race again. Can't be fixed.* I wasn't even wondering what else I could do with my life. I got no further than thinking that I'd spent the best part of 30 years really enjoying bike racing, and that it had come to an abrupt and incontrovertible halt.

I'm a lucky bugger, though. The anaesthetist came in after the operation and said that they'd had a proper look and the tendon was intact.

It was like 20 grand pianos playing a sustained C-major chord in my head – suddenly, my total mindset changed. The sadness lifted, and I instantly thought, *Right, I am back in business.*

I am a cyclist. I've got a lot of other things in my life – I'm a father and husband, a man who likes his mates and having fun. But the way the world sees me, and the way I see myself, is as a cyclist. I can't even describe the relief I felt when I realised that I still was one. From that moment, all I was thinking of was rehab. And getting back on my bike to race. It's not like I got straight down and put out 20 press-ups or anything, but I was already planning for the future. I knew that the leg was still pretty damaged; my tendon, though intact, had taken a heavy impact. It was as if I'd been hit with a hammer. Tendons are normally about three millimetres thick. Mine had blown up to one and a half centimetres.

I was still in the hospital when my rehabilitation began, using a CPM (constant passive movement) machine. You just strap your leg in and it flexes it to keep it mobile. It didn't even hurt that badly. The only real pain happened when a surgeon came to have a look. Surgeons aren't renowned for being sensitive, and he basically took my leg and bent it to a full flex, saying, 'Okay, everything seems fine,' while I'd just about passed out from the pain. Still, it proved my leg still worked, to a point.

Luckily, Victor was at the Tour of Belgium with me, so we started work immediately. He even advised me to use a crutch on the opposite arm from the injured leg, so that my pelvis stayed straight. I'd sit in my living room with the CPM machine flexing my leg while I hooked myself up to an altitude mask set at 3000 or 4000 metres. That stimulates the body to recover faster.

Every day, everything I did was geared to rehab. It was a full-time job. I was far busier being injured than being a healthy rider.

I probably wasn't very easy to live with at this point. I was stuck at home, sitting in the lounge, driving myself nuts and driving Angélique nuts too. She had two small children to look after, plus another one sitting on the sofa getting cabin fever. I couldn't sit there and fake happiness. I was in a filthy mood because I wasn't going to be at the Tour, which was coming up soon, and I didn't know if I'd get back to my former level. I was really struggling.

Nine days in, and I was on the exercise bike for ten minutes once a day. Then I moved up to ten minutes twice a day. I got on my own bike on a home trainer after another week and rode for 30 minutes in one go. The next day, I did an hour. By the end of June, one month after the accident, I got back out on the road. That day felt like Christmas – it was a huge step to be able to ride on the road. I felt like a cyclist again, even though I was just going for short little twiddles along the canal paths and getting overtaken by just about everybody who was out cycling.

Katusha were very supportive. They basically told me to have the year off, that there was no rush to come back. Better to come back fully healthy at the start of 2010 than try to race in 2009 and risk overdoing it and compromising the next season.

I went to the start of the Tour de France, which was in Monaco, and after the Prologue I went for dinner with Tchmil, Makarov and some other guys from Itera. Makarov's yacht was parked up in the port at Monaco – everything that could be gold was gold, down to the doorknobs and taps.

By the end of July, I was able to get a 140-kilometre training ride in, and in August I entered some post-Tour crits. It was good publicity for the organisers – they were being billed as my comeback races, and I got through them fine. I'd been on television being interviewed about my accident and recovery, so there was a fair bit of public interest in my appearances. The races were really good for me – they're nowhere near as hard as riding the Tour, but they were good hour-long workouts with sprints and decent speeds. The team were less excited about that – they were worried I was invalidating my insurance by taking part in criteriums. But for me, I can't stress enough how important it was for me to be racing my bike at high speed, with a group of my peers.

I was more worried about occasional shooting pains in my knee, which were being caused by the sharp thread of the screw that was holding my bones together catching on my flesh from time to time. After what I'd been through, it was nothing, but I wanted the screws out.

They were taken out on 25 August, three months after the accident, and I really was thinking that the problem was solved. I was still working very closely with Victor – he was loosening me up, keeping me straight, while every ride was spent focusing really hard on applying equal effort with both legs. There were no enjoyable, easy bike rides – you can't enjoy the sensations of bike riding when you have to concentrate hard on every single pedal stroke. This was work, not pleasure.

After the accident, my left leg was wasted compared with my right, and the danger was that I'd end up riding sideways in the saddle, causing more injuries. But I was still getting tendon pain when I rode hard uphill or used big gears.

Luckily, Victor's an absolute genius. He theorised that I had what he described as a neovascularisation of the tendon. After the trauma, new blood vessels had formed within the tendon. I would need, Victor suggested, a tendon scraping, and there was only one place I could get it done: Sweden, by a specialist called

Håkan Alfredson. He made room for me in his schedule, and I flew up to within 500 kilometres of the Arctic Circle, to a town called Umeå.

I did some more scans, and Dr Alfredson told me there was quite a lot of blood flow inside the tendon, so he'd need to do the scraping. Would 45 minutes' time be okay? That was absolutely fine by me. He put a local anaesthetic in and started to work.

I'm fascinated by the human body, and I'm not particularly squeamish, so I had a great opportunity to learn more about the human knee, using myself as the textbook. Dr Alfredson opened up my knee and removed a whole load of scar tissue that the tendon had been rubbing against. It was incredible to watch. You should be able to basically put your finger under a tendon and lift it up like a strap, but mine was so shot from scar tissue that it was stuck down. Scar tissue from a trauma can be fairly gnarly, and he had lots of work to do. He cut it all away, scraped the tendon, and I was left with a beautiful pinky-white, smooth, flat tendon, just how it was meant to be. I said to him, 'You are a genius.' I could have kissed him.

That was 16 September 2009, and I felt that the recovery should be smooth from there. No more racing, just slowly building up, lots of physio and my normal southern-hemisphere summer break. I bought a ticket and flew to Australia on 7 October.

Unfortunately, ten days later I found out I had a compulsory team meeting in Italy, with non-attendance punishable by firing. Good old uncompromising Tchmil.

I didn't need another round trip to Europe, but I diligently went, and the team informed me that one of their doctors would decide my status. It didn't matter that Victor's opinion was that I was fine; Katusha had decided that they wanted a knee specialist in Brescia to look at me and assess my fitness. The specialist said my knee was fine. I'd probably never play football again but cycling would cause me no trouble.

My impression was that if it hadn't gone well, it was contract termination time, although this was never explicitly stated. Tchmil, for all his idiosyncrasies, had been supportive all the way through my rehabilitation, in spite of the team's loss on their investment, but I had a feeling that Parsani had wanted to get rid of me.

But the way I saw it, if he'd picked me for the Giro like he should have done, I wouldn't have broken my leg, damaged my knee, missed the entire second half of the season and jeopardised my whole career. He also didn't take into account that I'd had great success over many years at a very high level on a very specific program of riding two weeks of the Giro, then the Tour. By tinkering with that, he was willing to risk that success. It wasn't his fault I crashed, but I believe his poor decision-making contributed to it happening.

I owed the team a great deal, and I'd start my payback at the Tour Down Under in January. But I owed Parsani nothing.

29

Tour Down Under

I WANTED 2010 to be a blank slate. A cyclist can afford to take six months off once in his or her career, and I'd used up my allocation. It was time for my comeback.

Tchmil made me laugh, however. He told me to come back slowly, no pressure – and, by the way, the team needed me to ride for the GC in the Tour Down Under in January.

The Tour Down Under is the first international race of the season, and it is a ProTour (now World Tour) event. The ProTour has a ranking, depending on points scored through the season's counting events, which has made the Tour Down Under an important event, especially for Aussies, since it's the only race on home soil. But it is also a very important event to team managers – the results dictate team-car order in subsequent events, which means that a good result at the Tour Down Under can give a team a prominent car position right through the Spring Classics. A team car that is close to the front of the convoy will be able to help a rider with a problem much more quickly than the car in 20th position. Tchmil was relying on me.

But the Tour Down Under was a big deal for me personally, as well. It was my comeback race. I'd gone well in training, but in training I could back off when I was getting tired or if my knee was sore. The Tour Down Under would be a week of intense, high-level racing, and I had no idea how I would go. I was desperate for it to go well.

It's often the small things that get you in life. I once heard a story about a professional footballer whose career was threatened by a niggling injury, which a smart physiotherapist traced to being caused by the way he got in and out of his car. And just before the Aussie national championships, which were a week before the Tour Down Under, one of the small things got me. I was doing a load of laundry at the hotel, dropped a sock, bent down to pick it up, and in doing so banged my left knee (the interesting one) on a tiled corner. Right on the scar.

It bloody hurt, but after the initial shock it seemed to subside. However, once I got back to my room I noticed the knee was filling up with fluid. The next day, at the criterium championships, it was extremely sore, and I had to pull out. Great. After seven months of pain, rehab and doubt, a stupid accident involving a dropped sock had jeopardised everything.

I didn't even start the road race but went back home and into full recovery mode. Everything I could possibly do that was legal and anti-inflammatory, I did. It meant I couldn't tweak my form, but I'd rather hit the race with a good knee and slightly sub-par fitness than roaring fit but with a bad knee and having to pull out halfway through. I raced the Cancer Council Helpline Classic – the pre-race criterium – and got through, finishing fourth. At the same time, Victor was working on me every day, keeping me straight and balanced. I'd got away with it.

And in the Tour Down Under, I finally unblocked myself. I didn't win a stage – André Greipel was sprinting extremely well, and he cleaned up – but I got a third and a second in the first four stages, and didn't lose any time. The race is often decided on time bonuses, and I was in second place going into the crucial stage – the fifth one to Willunga. It was the only stage with a decent hill: Old Willunga, which came not far before the finish. Attacks on the climb can stick, although it's always a close-run thing.

For European cycling fans, Old Willunga could be compared with the Cipressa or Poggio in Milan–San Remo. It takes a similar effort to get over both, and Willunga is made a little tougher by the fact that the race doesn't descend immediately but stays up on the ridge, where there always seems to be a crosswind. It's a time trial from the top, every man for himself, and the sprinters' teams have their work cut out to organise and chase in time for the finish.

I was determined to hang on to my high position in GC, and I had my teammates with me the whole way up the climb. One of them – I'm not sure who – got overexcited and gave me a little push, and I know that New Zealand's Greg Henderson, from the Sky team and who was third overall, wasn't overly happy about that. I could hear Hendy shouting, 'Oi!'

I was getting over the climb okay anyway, but a dangerous group including my old teammate Cadel Evans, who was fresh from winning the world championships, and Alejandro Valverde had put daylight between themselves and the sprinters' group. I could see them ahead – four extremely strong riders nailing it. It was trouble.

Hendy, Greipel and I, the top three, were in the group behind, but Greipel was low on teammates, and the two he did have weren't making an impression on the leaders. I got my boys to ride as hard as they could on the front. We didn't quite catch them, but we were so close at the finish that the race had been rescued. I was down to fifth, but it was nothing a few sprint bonuses couldn't sort out.

In the final stage, Hendy beat me in one bonus sprint and moved himself up to third. I won the second, overtaking him again. In the final sprint, I was relying on a favour from Greipel and his HTC-Columbia team – Katusha's riding had saved the race for him, so he owed us the help. Unfortunately, we all got caught out by Sky in the final sprint, and Hendy got in front of me to take third overall.

But I was fourth in the Tour Down Under, with a string of high finishes. I never finished lower than 15th in six days and had three top fours. I felt like I was back. And it felt even more like 2010 was going to be 2009, only without the shocking luck, when I went to the Tour of Mallorca again and won the first stage. I'd shown Óscar Freire – still one of the best sprinters in the world – my back wheel, but the important thing was that I'd touched 73 kilometres per hour in that sprint, on a flat road. That's something that has only happened rarely in my career. I was as good as I'd ever been.

Unfortunately, not everybody on the team agreed. I can tell managers until I'm blue in the face that, in a flat race, you take a sprinter, even if it is the plan B. But it still sometimes doesn't happen.

Parsani had big plans for Milan–San Remo. It's a very hard race to win, and it's the longest race of the season – just under 300 kilometres – but it's not like a flat stage of the Tour de

France, which ends with a sprint after 200 kilometres. However, I'm a sprinter, and if the race finishes in a sprint the team is better off with me there than with somebody else. But Parsani only wanted one plan in Milan–San Remo: Pozzato. He'd attack on the Poggio, just before the finish, and win the race. Except I'd been watching the other main sprinters during Tirreno–Adriatico. I'd seen that Petacchi, Boonen, Freire and Bennati were all climbing extremely well. I couldn't see Pozzato dropping them on the Poggio.

Guess what happened? Bunch sprint. Who knows if I'd have been able to make it over the Poggio with Freire, the winner, and the other sprinters, but if I had I could have been on the podium.

The funny thing is that Parsani needed a huge favour off me a few weeks later when Pozzato had made no impression in Milan–San Remo or the Tour of Flanders. They'd expected him to achieve great things in both, but he couldn't drop the sprinters in the first and got ill for the second. I was still the team's highest-ranked rider in the ProTour.

I knew what was coming – Parsani came to me in the team hotel at the Classics, and ummed and aahed a bit before blurting out that the team needed me to do them a favour. I had to ride Paris–Roubaix, to keep the Katusha team car up near the front of the convoy, because the convoy order depends on the highest-ranked selected rider. If I didn't ride, they'd be stuck near the back, which would compromise the team's chances if a rider had a mechanical or crash. To be fair, Pozzato did a good ride there and finished seventh.

Pozzato's a nice-enough guy, and very talented, even though he made no impression in the 2010 Milan–San Remo. He's won

Giro stages, Tour stages, Classics. But he's incredibly showy, especially when he's riding well, and a bit self-centred. In the Tour of Flanders in 2009, he shadowed Boonen, the strongest rider in the race, following his attack up the Koppenberg, and he looked like he was out for an easy training sprint. But he didn't follow through with the attack and just sat on Boonen, who refused to do all the work himself, while the bunch came back to them.

To take Tchmil as an example, when he was a rider you wouldn't see him on television until the final move went. The perfect tactician hides until the crucial moment of a race, just like a sprinter needs to hide until the final 200 or so metres.

But Pozzato follows attacks, sits on them and then doesn't carry through, which is a waste of energy. The impression I got from our teammates was that he wasn't very grateful for their work after races. And they'd be annoyed because he only ever sprinted for first place. If it was for fourth or fifth, he just wouldn't bother. It's fine to have a winner's mentality, but you can still sprint for fourth place and win a few thousand euros, which goes to your teammates. It's a nice way of thanking them for their effort, even if the win didn't work out this time.

Pozzato had a great win at the Giro in 2010, however, which I was part of. I'd not had a great race myself – crashes took me out of the first two sprints, and then I got sick after the wet and muddy stage to Montalcino, over the *strade bianche* (white gravel) roads. But I was coming round by stage 12.

The day before, there'd been a huge split between the race favourites, and a large group had got away by 12 minutes. I knew that the big riders who'd been caught behind it would want to make a show of strength on stage 12, and that it was only bad luck that had put them behind. I said to Pozzato that he should go with them on the last climb before the finish, because I was sure it was going to kick off. He could go with the leaders, while behind I could clean up in the sprint. We had a good plan A and a good plan B. All our bases were covered.

Sure enough, the favourites attacked, and Pozzato turned himself inside out to follow them. The group only hovered a few seconds ahead of my group on the run-in, but it was a bloody strong group: Italy's Ivan Basso and Vincenzo Nibali, Alexandre Vinokourov, plus Pozzato.

It was a close sprint at the front, but Pozzato held off a late surge from Thomas Voeckler to win. Ten seconds later, I won the bunch sprint. That's how a team should work.

30

The Hardest Sport in the World

HERE'S HOW HARD the Tour de France is.

After a few days, I start to wake up in the morning feeling like I've been punched all over the day before. My body just aches.

The fatigue goes right down into the marrow of my bones. The tiredness can be so deep that I wonder how I'm going to get up and get to the breakfast table. It's not the kind of tiredness that sleep can do anything about, and I'm always puffed out. Normally, I'm running a surplus on physical energy, but at the Tour I don't walk up stairs for the simple reason that it gets me out of breath. Even walking down stairs is painful.

Every day, the race forces me to squeeze everything out of my muscles. If it's a flat stage, I've got to physically hurt myself to sprint. If it's not a flat stage, I've got to physically hurt myself just to get over the climb at the same speed as everybody else. I'm stripping every ounce of glycogen out of my muscles and burning every tiny bit of fat in my body until there is none left. By halfway through the Tour, I've got veins popping out all over the place and the skin is hanging off my face. I look in the mirror and my face looks grey – it's almost as if my body, in an attempt to scrape more energy out of itself, is starting to eat the very colour out of me.

My legs ache the most. But they don't have a monopoly on the discomfort. My arms are supporting my upper-body weight for four to six hours a day, so they ache. My back aches. I'm breathing so hard for so long during a stage that the muscles between the ribs get tired. Every muscle is moving, so every muscle gets fatigued. And after fatigue comes stiffness. As soon as I stop for the day and go to sleep, everything stiffens up. The first few movements of the day actually hurt. The first pedal strokes every day hurt.

The fatigue gets so deep I start thinking that I'll never even come through it. And then, every day, after about ten kilometres, my body's warmed up and we're all going at 50 kilometres per hour again.

But when I get to the finish, click out of the pedals and try to straighten up, it's as if I am made of wood. It's difficult to stand up straight after five hours of cycling, and I can feel my back unclicking as it adjusts to verticality again.

Most riders have to compensate for all this, especially when they are off the bike, by minimising the expenditure of effort. Riders shuffle around the hotels in the evening as if there is a conference of extremely skinny sunburned geriatrics. Except freaks such as Jens Voigt, who's striding around normally because he's so strong.

Nobody's fresh after two weeks of the Tour. Fresh is relative. The leader might be fresh compared with the guy in last place, but he's not fresh by any normal understanding of the word. I've had moments, especially during the final week of the Tour, when my whole body feels so hot, achy and filthy from the sweat and road dirt that I've wanted to stop, lie down on the grass at the edge of the road and go to sleep. Helmet off. Shoes off, just to let my swollen feet relax. It would be perfect to dip my feet into one of those mountain streams, lie back in the lush grass and not have to pedal any more.

There's no comparison in real life. You could compare it to running a marathon every day for three weeks, but because cycling is a non-impact sport the fatigue goes deeper. It's indescribably tiring. And that's when I've stayed healthy and avoided injuries and crashes. If you're hurt, it's ten times worse.

It's different from the tiredness you get from going deep. The worst I ever hurt myself in a sprint was in the 1999 Tour of Holland, when I was defending the race lead for Rabobank against an attack by Jan Ullrich and Serguei Outschakov, from the Ukraine, in the final two kilometres of the last stage. Ullrich was going that hard up a false flat towards the finish that I was starting to see little pinpricks of light in my increasingly blurred vision. It was excruciating, and, just following his wheel, I could feel myself starting to black out. Then I had to sprint on top of that, for the final 200 metres. I came off Outschakov and won the stage, and I'd gone so deep I couldn't see properly. Even on the bus ten minutes after winning, my heart was going at 190 beats per minute. I'd put myself so deep that I stopped recovering after that – it essentially ended my season.

At the Tour, it's different. It's the cumulative fatigue that wears you down.

I had a good build-up to the Tour in 2010. I pulled out of the Giro about two weeks in, had a short rest, then started training again. I rode well at the Tour of Switzerland, where I got a couple of top fives and climbed well.

And then my ambition came crashing up against the forces of bad circumstances for the second year in a row. The third stage was hilly, taking us through Belgium and finishing at Spa. On one of the descents, somebody had spilled some oil – who knows how it had got there; maybe it had just leaked out of a car. It had rained lightly some time in the previous 24 hours. These two factors made the descent lethal. It was like trying to ride down a bar of soap.

There was a huge crash, and I managed to brake and slow before I got brought down. I picked my way through the bodies and bikes – it seemed like there were 100 riders down. I freewheeled through, and ahead I could see more guys going down. They weren't hitting anything, or going fast, or overcooking corners, or bringing each other down; it was as if there was a sniper somewhere, picking them off.

My rational brain was on red alert. And then, as I assessed the situation, my wheels flew sideways, picking up momentum as the weight of my body went down. I went skidding onto some really rough asphalt. It was steep and slippery, but the gravel was chewing me up at the same time – I could feel it taking chunks of meat off my body as I slid. It wasn't just the first impact – I wasn't slowing down, and I was trying to roll off the road into the grass so I could come to a halt. It was carnage. There were riders down around me and ahead of me, and more coming down as they hit more oil. Riders were coming off two, three times. A race motorbike went down. It was ridiculous – I'd never seen anything like it.

I inspected myself for damage. Nothing broken, so I got back on my bike, skidded with both feet off the pedals to the bottom of the descent and joined a chase group. The race was in chaos.

It was only when I'd been riding along for a bit that I noticed my handlebars were really slippery. I looked down and saw that there was blood everywhere, but I couldn't figure out where it was coming from. My arm hurt all over, so I squirted the blood off with my water bottle and found the source – there was a huge hole in my elbow. The blood wasn't just oozing out, it was squirting out at the same rate that my heart was beating. It was a gusher.

Another rider came up and said, 'Robbie, you're really bleeding.'

'No shit,' I replied. I went back to find the race doctor, who drives behind the bunch, but they'd all been held up treating riders at the crash site. I talked to Jean-François Pescheux, the race director, to ask for help to be sent. I could see he was really shaken by what had gone on. I told him they'd better get help to me soon, because I was losing blood and starting to feel a little bit faint. Eventually, a medic got to me, patched me up and stopped the bleeding.

For some reason, after that, the riders stopped racing. Fabian Cancellara, who was in the yellow jersey, said he'd spoken to the organisation and the race directors were neutralising the bunch. It was reported by some media as a riders' protest, but most of us weren't protesting anything. Cancellara told us there'd be no points on the line, so none of us bothered sprinting. I wasn't stupid – I still got my front wheel right up there, just in case, but the stage was effectively neutralised.

There was a minor storm afterwards. It appeared that Cancellara had told the race directors that the riders would strike and told the riders that the race directors had neutralised it. Pescheux told me later that nothing was cancelled, but nobody had sprinted, so the points would be shared equally among the entire bunch. If we'd sprinted, we'd have had the points. In the end, that cost Thor Hushovd the green jersey. But I was more concerned about my physical state.

The amount of blood I lost really buckled me. I took a blood test for the biological-passport people after the first week, and the woman who had my results asked me, 'Did you lose a lot of blood?' My blood numbers were all over the place. There's a calculation made by measuring haematocrit and reticulocytes (young red blood cells) that results in a number called an 'off score'. The average is about 90. If you have 134 or above, you'll be asked to explain yourself to the anti-doping authorities. Mine was about 45, and that was a week after the accident.

At the hospital the evening after the crash, somebody who knew nothing about cycling and the Tour de France was filling in forms and ticking boxes, and decided to give me a tetanus shot. Well, bring on the lead-heavy legs, the nausea, the headache and four days of fever, just to add to my general fatigue after the blood loss. I felt like screaming.

I'd targeted stages four, five and six before the Tour. I woke up on the morning of stage four covered in sweat. I was running a fever.

I've never liked it when riders play the percentages in a sprint. To me, winning is the point of bike racing, and I'd rather finish last, having tried to win, than finish a safe second. Sometimes, sprinters sit in other sprinters' wheels and follow them all the way to the line for second or third place, but I can't see the point.

In stage four, I was actually in the perfect position coming into the sprint, right in the eventual winner Petacchi's wheel. He'd gone for a long one and surprised Cav – it was almost presented to me on a platter. But I wasn't feeling good. If I'd stayed in his wheel, I'd have finished second, no doubt, but that wasn't why I was at the Tour de France. I had a go but wasn't strong and got passed and ran fourth. It was even worse the next day – I could hardly hang on. I still sprinted, and I came sixth.

At least the day after that – the last of the trio of sprint stages I'd hoped to do so well in – I felt better. I still ran fourth, but, more importantly, my fever had gone down. But then, as if the cruel hand of fate were grabbing my head and grinding it into the ground, a television technician jumped right out into my path about 50 metres after the finishing line, when I was still doing close on 60 kilometres per hour.

It was absolutely idiotic. There was no way I was avoiding him. I piled straight into him, did a full flip in the air and landed square on my back, where I lay, unable to move. I hadn't gone back to square one; I'd gone way past it. I sat on the floor, pain, anger and frustration coursing through me. I was in such pain that I couldn't even put on my own shoes at the team bus.

The end of a Tour stage is chaotic – the riders funnel through the finishing area and have only a short space to slow from 60 kilometres per hour through the finish line, which is about seven metres wide, past two banks of photographers on one side of the road, which halves the space, and then to a corridor of people that's about a metre and a half wide. It's surprising that accidents don't happen more often. Riders are getting pushed over by journalists; cameramen smash riders in the head as they swing around. I've seen riders throw punches, and I've seen $40,000 cameras being wrenched off people's shoulders. It's a complete fight, and rider safety appears not to be the priority.

I was taken by ambulance to the nearest hospital, 45 minutes away over bumpy roads. It had been less a Tour de France than a Tour de hospitals for me.

I got on well with the doctor, though. He said, 'You're very bruised.' I laughed and said, 'No shit!' again. The funny thing about being examined in hospitals as a racing cyclist is that doctors treat it as an anatomy lesson. I was lying there in pain, while the doctors were all saying 'Look at the size of that' about my psoas muscle, which runs down the front of the pelvis. They're always overdeveloped in cyclists. While they carried on marvelling at my muscle development, I asked if it would be okay to go now – I had recovering to do.

The team managers assumed that I wouldn't get through the Alps. I wasn't optimistic myself. I could see the look on everybody's faces at the hotel: McEwen's toast. I went to bed, pulled the covers over my head and tried to go to sleep.

I was worried about getting through the Alpine stages, but I knew that the next day, through the Vosges mountains, would be the toughest. Up and down all day, gnarly roads, and the time limit would be tight because it wasn't a full mountain stage. I was in pain all day long, but I resisted going back to the race doctor to ask for a painkiller until we were near the top of the first big climb of the day. I was hanging on and was in serious danger of popping out the back, so I tried to look comfortable and went back to the doctor. I spoke very slowly and asked him for a painkiller. No rush, doctor, I'm hanging onto the car and having a very timely and necessary rest. By the time he'd sorted me with the pill, and I'd said 'Thank you very much', I'd had 30 seconds of rest. Beauty.

And on the final climb, with eight kilometres to go, word

came back to our group that the winners were already in. We were riding at about 20 kilometres per hour, which meant three minutes per kilometre. The time limit was going to be about 23 and a half minutes, which meant we had to speed up or risk not qualifying. It got very hairy, with a lot of guys pushing very hard, over the edge of what I could sustain.

I was very grateful for a couple of colleagues, Karsten Kroon, from the Netherlands, and Jurgen Roelandts, my old Belgian Silence-Lotto teammate, both giving me pushes in that final desperate kilometre. It showed real solidarity. I'll ride right through anyone at the front of a race in order to win, but at the back of the race there's always a lot of help and support from both teammates and rivals. I'd do the same for them.

A few days later, after the Alps but still in the medium-sized mountains around Gap, I was a dead man cycling, getting dropped 15 or 20 times a day, just losing the last wheel, being distanced and having to fight my way back on. Into Gap, I was killing myself just to hang with the bunch. Then I fought over the last climb, got back to the front of the bunch and finished fourth in the bunch sprint.

Pescheux, the race director, saw me the next morning and said, 'Bravo.' He'd watched me getting dropped all day long and still trying to do my job at the finish, and he appreciated what I was going through.

Through the transition stages across to the Pyrenees, I lost count of the number of times I heard the race radios crackle into life as the organisers announced, 'Number 75, Robbie McEwen, dropped from the group.'

My Spanish teammate Joaquim Rodriguez won the stage to Mende, but my main concern, once again, was making the time limit, having been dropped early on. There was a long, horrible, draggy climb that went on for about ten kilometres, and the peloton had decided, in its collective wisdom, to ride up at 40 kilometres per hour. By halfway up, the group had split, and I was in trouble.

At points like this, survival is a question of finding allies, seeing who is useful and who is going to hold you back. Those who are capable of riding and surviving give each other nods of respect and understanding. The others get an apologetic shrug.

There was a sorry quartet of dropped riders well behind the field on the way to Mende. Me, my American sprint rival Tyler Farrar, the German rider Bert Grabsch, and Lars Boom, from the Netherlands. Farrar and Boom were having an even worse time than me, some distance behind, and I came across Grabsch after he'd crashed.

If you were picking sides for riding partners for a 120-kilometre time trial to the finish of a stage, Grabsch would probably be the first rider you'd take. He's a former world time-trial champion. But he had bent himself out of shape when he crashed, and he couldn't even hold his handlebars on the bottom, in the most aerodynamic position. I was riding faster than he was, which wasn't a good sign. I remember thinking, as we started riding together, that it was going to be an extremely long, extremely painful day.

We heard that Farrar had pulled out, and that Boom was well behind. Which made it all the more surprising when Boom appeared out of nowhere and turned up behind us. He must have recovered from whatever was wrong, because he helped us set the pace all the way to the finish. And in one of those interesting twists that are common at the Tour de France, it turned out that we made the time limit by ten minutes.

The worst was to come: the Pyrenees. And I knew which stage would cause me the most problems: stage 16, from Luchon to Pau, which went straight up the Col de Peyresourde from kilometre zero and then crossed three more of the hardest mountains in the Tour – the Aspin, Tourmalet and Aubisque. I spent the morning trying to organise as many riders as possible to take it easy at the start of the stage.

But it turned out to be a new record for me. I was dropped after 100 metres of the stage. The first attack came from the American rider Dave Zabriskie, who'd done nothing all Tour and was now deciding to make a name for himself. I had a name for him at that point, too, and it started with an 'F'.

It went absolutely nuts. Somebody chased, and I went straight out the back, about 15 seconds after the stage had started. The radio fizzed into life: '*Numéro 75 en difficulté.*' All the cars went past me, and so began the longest, loneliest day of my cycling career.

In a crisis, the people you want to surround yourself with are the organised. Nobody ever resolved a crisis by panicking, so I went straight into emergency mode. I wasn't going to be able to last long by sprinting to catch the group back up, so I settled into a tempo that I knew I could sustain up four mountains. I'd need to get back into the gruppetto by the top of the fourth climb – the Col d'Aubisque – otherwise it was going to be a very long final 60 kilometres from the top to the finish, likely resulting in elimination.

I could see groups strung out ahead of me all the way up the mountain. I could hear the race radio excitedly describing the front of the race, and it really sounded like it was kicking off.

It must have been incredibly exciting for the television viewers, but at the back of the race the sense of enjoyment is inversely proportionate to that of the fans.

While Alberto Contador, Lance Armstrong and Luxembourg's Andy Schleck were deciding the Tour and trying out their attacking tactics, I was concentrating on stripping my routine down to the absolute basics. Pedal, breathe, tempo – and don't panic.

I went over the Peyresourde about two minutes behind a small group, but the problem was that between the Peyresourde and the Aspin there are ten kilometres of slightly downhill valley. Me against a group of riders all swapping off, trying to minimise their own losses and catch another group in front? Another minute lost.

I came across my old friend and rival Jens Voigt on the valley road. He'd had a nasty crash, and they were bandaging and patching him up by the side of the road. On to the Aspin, and I got back into my pedal–breathe–tempo rhythm when I heard a voice behind me say, in a German accent, 'Oh my God, what are we going to do now?'

Jens had got back on his bike, all bandaged up, ripped shorts and a big hole in his shoe, blood oozing through his jersey. He looked exactly how I felt, but he was riding a lot faster than me. Jens is one of those annoying riders who always wants to have a conversation with you when you're riding up hills. When I'm riding uphill, I've got three conversational gambits: yes, no, and shut up and stop bothering me. Jens passed me and rode off into the distance. I remember wishing that I could ride as fast as that up mountains.

I got over the Aspin and started feeling better on the

Tourmalet, which is one of the hardest mountains in the Tour. I started getting decreasing time checks on the group in front – three minutes, two minutes 45, two minutes 30. When I passed through La Mongie, the ski-station town two-thirds of the way up, I could see the cars ahead of me. If I could close that gap, I'd be okay.

I had five kilometres left to catch them. If they got down the descent and onto the 25-kilometre valley road to the bottom of the Aubisque without me, I'd be going home. I was right on my limit, chiselling away at the gap. I felt like I was right at the point where I was bending but not quite breaking.

I told myself again and again, *Bend, don't break.* I started passing stragglers – Cav and his teammate Bernie Eisel, a couple of others – and I knew I'd be okay. I got back on over the top of the Tourmalet. Oddly, we'd only ridden 70 kilometres – possibly the 70 hardest kilometres of my life – and there were still 130 to go, but I was safe.

The back of the Tour isn't like the front through the mountains. While television shows the race favourites attacking, parrying and feinting through crowds of cheering fans, the atmosphere at the back is very different.

I formed quite a friendly relationship with one of the motorbike gendarmes who policed the back of the race – I spent most of the 2010 Tour there, so we saw each other most days. He told me one day that he'd been parked up on the Tourmalet, the day I was off the back, and a spectator had asked him if all the riders had come through.

'*Non*,' he said, pulling out his cigarette and lighter, and sparking up with a flourish. 'I wait for Robbie.'

It was nice having my own police escort, but I must have been going slowly if he had time for a cigarette break.

We came back up the Tourmalet and finished at the top the next day, and the fans had been incredible. I'd actually found it much easier than stage 16, just because there had been so many people shouting and cheering that it had helped me find extra motivation. The Basque fans were out in force, and they were fantastic – one guy gave me a huge push, running alongside me, when some French spectator, whose sense of propriety was offended by this blatant cheating, tripped him up. It almost caused me to fall off. I felt like stopping and shouting in his face. Then Dimitri Konyshev, my manager in the car behind, wound down his window and shouted '*Connard!*' at the Frenchman. It wasn't very complimentary.

But I got to the finish. From the top of the Tourmalet, visibility was about 20 metres with the fog, but I could see Paris. All that was left to do was get out of position in the sprint up the Champs-Élysées and start from way too far back. I rode up in ninth place thinking, *What an anticlimax*. Three of the hardest weeks of my life, for ninth place.

31

My Last Ever Win

ONE DAY, I'm going to win my last ever race as a professional cyclist. I don't think it's happened yet, although one can never be sure. I suppose the uncertainty makes it more fun.

Winning remains my primary motivation in cycling, and I enjoy it so much, and have won so many times, that I can't believe that one day it's not going to happen any more. The knowledge that if I toughed it out I might come round and win a late stage is what got me through the 2010 Tour. And that the training benefits of finishing would set me up for some good form later in the year. There was not a single moment during the Tour – which was probably as hard in its own way as racing with a broken back in 2004 – when I thought that my win in February, at the Trofeo Mallorca, would be my last win as a professional.

I was shattered after the Tour finished. It's a hard enough race to get through anyway, without the added physical stress of recovering from injuries. One of the tricky things about the Tour is that there are many more crashes in the first week than the last, because everybody's nervous. And if you do crash it takes about two weeks to recover properly, which means your skin has just about grown back by the time you arrive in Paris. But I wasn't recovering by the end of that race – the whole Tour had been a case of managing scant resources, and I never felt good.

I cut down on the number of post-Tour criteriums I raced in 2010. The money's always nice, but I wasn't physically capable – I'd just have run myself deeper into the ground. I needed some time away from racing, and I let my body rebuild itself while I rested up. I had my eye on the world championships, which would be in Australia for the first time ever. The course was relatively flat, with an uphill sprint at the finish – it looked perfect for me.

I took part in the Vattenfall Cyclassics for the first time since I'd won it in 2008, but I lacked racing rhythm. However, two days later I started the Eneco Tour and won the first road stage, into Rhenen, for my biggest win in two years.

When a rider comes back from injury, it's very difficult to pick up exactly where he's left off. I lost several weeks of racing when I broke my leg in 2009 and couldn't train properly for months. I completely lost the rhythm and condition of a professional cyclist. It took me a good few months of hard training to get to the point where I could race again, but that wasn't the end of the battle. Although I rode well at the Tour Down Under and won in Mallorca, I felt like it had taken those first six months of 2010, racing on a regular basis, to get back to my top level, and at the Eneco Tour I felt like myself again.

The sprint was anarchy: quite a tricky uphill, then false flat to the line. It was probably a bit harder than was ideal for me, but, on the other hand, it was chaotic, which suited me down to the ground.

Sprints have been so organised over the last ten years. First, Mario Cipollini's and Alessandro Petacchi's teams dominated the leadouts. These days, the HTC team is dominant. It's meant that riders forget how to look after themselves when it's not organised, which suits me fine because I've been looking after myself in sprints for over 15 years now.

With 500 metres to go, Edvald Boasson Hagen, from Norway, attacked, and he really went. I was in about ninth place, and I could see gaps opening all over the place. Perfect. I was sitting in the Italian rider Elia Viviani's wheel – he was supposed to be leading out his Liquigas team's sprinter and fellow countryman Francesco Chicchi, but, unbeknown to him, he was actually doing a great job for me. Just as Viviani died, Yauheni Hutarovich, from Belarus, came past me, and I jumped across to his wheel. Boasson Hagen started coming back to us, and just as Hutarovich caught him I really went for it. I was in a big gear, and I only just got it turning – I was right on the limit of stalling. But, with 50 metres to go, I knew I was going to win and I got my hands in the air. It was very important to me to do it properly. I thought, *I remember what this is like! Winning!*

Two days later, Shayne Bannan, the national coach, came and told me I wouldn't be in the world-championships team. They were going to focus the team around Allan Davis – a good sprinter, but not faster than me – plus defending champion Cadel Evans. Frustratingly, Allan had been in third place behind me in the uphill sprint I'd won in stage one.

I'd been killing myself to drop weight through the year, specifically because I knew I'd need to get over the climb on the worlds circuit. I'd got down to 64 kilos, which is a couple of kilos lighter than my normal weight. I'd shed upper-body muscle. When Bannan told me, I immediately put those two kilos back on.

I was totally shell-shocked by the decision. I'd known it was a possibility, but I think not taking me was a big mistake. To be fair, Allan did a brilliant ride, and he finished in third place behind Thor Hushovd, but just imagine if there had been two of us up there in the sprint, one leading out the other. I've done a lot for the national team since I turned professional, including winning a silver medal for them, so not to have got their confidence in 2010 really stung me.

I wish I could have been totally professional and put the non-selection behind me, but instead the decision gave me a large dose of what English-speaking riders in the peloton call the 'end-of-season CBF'. It stands for 'can't be fucked'.

I also had one of the least impressive injuries of my career in September. I took Ewan to the local BMX track, borrowed one of the BMXs there, went over a jump, slipped off the pedal as I landed and stacked it, in front of everybody. It was a very good laugh for everybody who saw it – Robbie McEwen, professional cyclist, former BMX champion, on the ground. But I fell really awkwardly on my hip, and the pedal hit me in the Achilles tendon. The next day, when I went out riding, my calf muscles were completely cramping up. I didn't tell Katusha what I'd done, because I'd probably have been fired. I pulled out of my next race and told the management that I'd had an accident while out riding. Strictly speaking, that was true. They didn't need to know that I'd been fooling around with my son at the BMX track. Ninety-nine times out of a hundred, I'd have made that jump.

I'd already decided that I wasn't going to re-sign with Katusha. Tchmil had offered me another year, which was good of him, considering I'd not raced in the second half of 2009. But I didn't feel at home at Katusha like I'd felt at home at Lotto for all those years.

Perhaps it was because Katusha signed so many new riders when they expanded at the start of 2009, or perhaps it was the language and cultural differences between us all, but the team lacked a good atmosphere. And I think it was also down to Tchmil.

Tchmil's a real authoritarian, and he loves to give big motivational speeches about the glory of the team. And for him, discipline is one of the most important aspects of life. That was what made him such a successful and tough rider – he could really make himself suffer and do what was necessary to win. And he expects a similar level of dedication from everybody around him.

I was wary of him, because I'd known him as a rider at Lotto in 2002. He was strong, but he saw other riders as just there to serve him. He roomed with the Belgian rider Marc Wauters, who is one of the nicest guys in cycling, in the 1990s when they were both on the Lotto team. The only time I ever heard of Marc losing his rag was when Tchmil was winding him up so badly that he threw him out of the bedroom. Tchmil didn't have a lot of friends in the peloton. He was respected for his riding abilities – a real hard man – but he wasn't liked.

The Russian guys on the team were all frightened of doing something wrong because they were afraid of being fired. Alexander Serov, who'd been with the team since it was a development squad in 2001, was fired in 2009, apparently for eating a portion of fries. But Tchmil's like that – he can be extremely polite and intelligent, then be an absolute dictator. If something happens that is not to his liking, he'll send an official letter threatening termination of contract. I got one myself. I'd tweeted that I hoped our teammate Kim Kirchen, from Luxembourg, who'd become seriously ill at the Tour of Switzerland, was okay, and the team felt I'd breached confidentiality.

There was always chaos about the Russian riders' programs. The team would send the rider list around to tell us who was racing where, and I'd turn up to find three different guys on the team, because of visa issues. It didn't create a settled atmosphere, and it prevented good tactical planning.

The final decision to leave came when Tchmil offered me the contract extension. One of the conditions was that I'd have to attend training camps in Europe in November and December. That, as far as I was concerned, was a deal-breaker. The only reason I've had such a long, and I believe successful, career is that I've wintered in Australia, away from the cold. It was probably an attempt by Tchmil to show me who was boss. He's got a lot of authority, but nobody's got the authority to take away my winter break.

The other reason I wanted to leave was that I'd been given an interesting offer by an old friend of mine from the Brisbane racing scene, Chris White. Chris ran Fly V, which was an Australian team racing in America. Chris wanted to expand the team into a fully fledged Australian road team racing in Europe, and he asked me if I'd like to ride with them in 2011.

I first met Chris White when I was living and racing in Brisbane. I needed to buy some tyres and saw somebody advertising some in the *Trading Post*, which was the small-ads paper.

I rang the number and arranged to pick up the tyres – and that was my first meeting with Chris.

We'd kept in touch ever since, because he stayed involved with cycling, as a racer, and then as a manager with the Fly V team. At the end of 2009, he called me up and told me that he wanted to expand the team. He said he'd love to have me on board, primarily as a rider, but longer term to work with developing younger Australian riders. As the first big name aboard, I'd also be useful for attracting other riders to join, especially Aussies.

It interested me, because I've been keen from the outset on the idea of a team of Australians. We've always been scattered all over the peloton – two riders here, a few over there – always riding against each other. But ever since I rode with the Australian national team as an amateur in 1994 and 1995, I've thought that a team should be a group of mates as well as a team of cyclists. All the Australian teams I've been part of at the world champ-ionships and Olympic Games have worked really well, and we've had a lot of fun riding together. How good would it be to have an Aussie team riding the whole season together?

In August 2010, I'd narrowed my choice of possible teams for 2011 down to Chris's team, which was going under the name Pegasus, and a couple of others, including the Vacansoleil team. My head had suggested Vacansoleil, although they blew it by signing Riccardo Riccò, a controversial and obnoxious Italian rider who'd tested positive at the 2008 Tour de France. I didn't want to ride on the same team as Riccò.

But my heart was beginning to tell me to go to Pegasus anyway. Chris had George Gillett Jnr on board to fund the pro-ject. The Gillett family own four Nascar teams in the US, the NHL Montreal Canadiens hockey team, plus Vail and Beaver

Creek ski resorts, and at the time he also co-owned Liverpool Football Club in England. He was a serious player, and he'd been looking to get into cycling because he'd seen what a fantastic advertising vehicle it is.

It's easier to build a big bike team when there's already an existing structure. Katusha, for example, was developed out of the Tinkoff team. Chris had the raw materials for a team, while Gillett wanted to put the money in. There was also the advantage that there was no other Australian team. Gillett could have picked a North American team to build on, but there were already three major teams in the US: Garmin, Columbia and BMC. A fourth would have made the market even more crowded.

It was all looking very exciting. I signed with Chris and looked forward to being part of a new project that would provide me with a fitting end to my career. Pegasus had signed some other big-name riders, such as Canada's Svein Tuft, who'd come second in the world time-trial championships in 2008, Christian Knees, the German champion, Robbie Hunter, a former Tour stage winner and the backbone of the Fly V team. Hendrik Redant was going to be a manager, and Henk was going to work with the team as well.

We went to a training camp in Noosa in Queensland, and morale was sky high. We were a group of guys who clicked immediately, and straight away it felt harmonious and right.

But there were hints that things weren't going well. I read in a newspaper that there was a conflict about the ownership of Liverpool Football Club. Gillett had been forced to sell the club for a lot less than he thought it was worth. Then I read somewhere else that one of his Nascar teams was in trouble. I thought, *Hang on, this is who's putting the money into the team.*

Chris assured me that everything would be fine, and I hoped it would be. But things that should have been sorted out dragged on. Another signal was that we didn't get our jerseys, because it was unclear who the sponsors were. In the meantime, we'd been turned down for a ProTeam licence, which meant that we wouldn't gain automatic entry to the big events. That's not necessarily a huge problem, but it meant that we'd be relying on wildcard entries to the Grand Tours and Classics, allocated by the race organisers.

Then it became official that Gillett was out, and we were suddenly left with a five-million-dollar hole in the team finances. That's a huge amount of money. I understand there were two entities involved: Pegasus Racing, which was Chris's company, and Pegasus Sports, which was 51 per cent owned by Gillett and 49 per cent owned by Chris. So, when the plug was pulled, there were no repercussions for Gillett. What was he going to do? Sue himself?

We went into panic mode, trying to find the money from somewhere. Another problem arose: to put a ProTeam application in, there needs to be a bank guarantee in place. But while we were applying for a ProContinental licence (the next level down), the guarantee wasn't there any more. We had to find a replacement bank guarantee based on a new budget, which was based on a percentage of wages. This meant that everybody had to take an immediate 50 per cent pay cut, with the hope that we could get extra sponsors later on to make up the difference.

Everybody believed so much in the project that they were prepared to take that cut, but people were already starting to ask around for other teams. In the second week of December, I told my agent to start asking around, even though December is way too late to be seeking a place on a cycling team – rosters are usually finalised by the start of November.

One thing was certain. I wasn't going to quit. I wasn't going to leave the sport in that manner.

I've had a bit of contact with Lance Armstrong over the course of my career. We've both been around for years, and we get on well, in spite of the odd run-in when we were both younger and angrier. I sent him a message just before Christmas, saying it seemed like Pegasus were going under and that I was looking for a team. When the final confirmation came that the ProContinental-licence application had been turned down, I texted him again, saying, 'Whaddya reckon?'

He immediately got back to me and said he'd get in touch with Johan Bruyneel, the RadioShack team manager, telling me to hang tough. A few minutes later, he sent another message. 'Let's do it,' it read.

Ironically, I'd be replacing my old teammate Gert Steegmans, who'd left RadioShack at the end of 2010. They were lacking a sprinter, so I filled a good gap at the team. I'd be taking a huge pay cut, and there'd be no bonuses on my salary, but there wasn't an alternative. I could have fished around a bit to try to find more, but the fact that only six of us from Pegasus had managed to find another team at all showed how late we'd left it.

In spite of the stress of Pegasus falling apart, and despite having to sign on such a small contract, I feel like I've actually ended up where I was supposed to be. I've always wanted to ride for an English-speaking team – it's just turned out to be an American one instead of an Australian one.

As I write this, I'm a RadioShack rider, possibly in my last season as a professional cyclist. I've ridden the Tour Down Under, got a couple of high placings and led the race, plus I've won a stage of the Tour of Wallonia. I might ride out this year and retire, or get a deal to ride just the Tour Down Under in 2012, or maybe even continue for the whole season. All I do know is that I'll be trying the entire time to make sure that my last win doesn't become my very last win.

32

One Way Road

MY FAVOURITE TRAINING RIDE is a 140-kilometre loop that starts from my place next to the beach on the Gold Coast. I have breakfast, meet my mates and get started early, because it's so hot. We tap out through the suburbs, chatting and laughing, then the road starts to undulate.

We climb up away from the sea, over a small hill, then further inland we hit a climb called Springbrook. It's eight kilometres long, and the gradient is about four or five per cent. Once we get to a certain height, it changes from bushland into rainforest. The bushland is full of big old trees and long grass, which is dry. But once we're in the rainforest, it's lush and moist and alive. It feels like you are breathing more oxygen, and everything is so green. I feel like I can taste the air here, it's so thick and vigorous. It's more noisy, too – I can hear the bellbirds singing as I pedal upwards.

At the top of the climb, it's bushland again. In the off-season, when I've hardly been riding my bike while I recover from the season, we take it easy up Springbrook – it takes us about 24 minutes. As we get fitter, we'll chip away time until we're going up in less than 20 minutes.

Over the top, down the other side and we're in a valley. The roads here are quiet in a way that most Europeans wouldn't understand – you can go a whole day here without seeing a car. There's a tiny village down the valley, with four houses and a general store. We'll stop for a quick snack and drink, then we're back out of the bushland onto the flat and the sugar-cane fields. There's another four-kilometre climb back over to the coast, along the river, and we follow the beach for the last 25 kilometres. It takes us about four and a half hours.

When I retire, I'm going to carry on doing that circuit, but just for fun, every now and again. The blokes I ride with are mad keen amateurs, or pros, or ex-pros. Gat still comes out from time to time. Troy Bayliss, the retired Aussie motorbike racer, has ridden with us. There are always half a dozen ring-ins who'll turn up for the ride. I've always been one of the strongest on the ride, but once I've stopped being a professional I know they're going to smash me. They'll give me a hiding, but I won't care.

In a way, it will be a relief to just enjoy riding my bike for its own sake. Every ride I've done for the last 20 years has had a purpose, and it will be nice to experience meaningless bike riding again, like real people do. During all my training rides, especially since my accident in 2009, I've been very focused on analysing my pedal stroke and making sure my entire body is balanced – it takes a lot of mental energy.

I'm not stupid. I know that I'm not at my peak any more. Cyclists are just as subject to the inevitable laws of nature as everyone else. Cycling careers follow a bell curve. I was one of the lucky ones, and I managed to keep my peak for six seasons, from 2002 to 2007. I'm not far off where I was then, but there's a small but steady downhill in physical terms. If I'd been at that 2010 Eneco Tour stage with the legs I had in 2005 and 2006, there wouldn't have been anybody else in the photograph.

People think it must be frustrating as an athlete to not to be as good as you once were. But the decline comes at the same time as the maturation and experience that make you realise it doesn't matter so much. The 25-year-old Robbie McEwen would never have accepted a decline in speed and strength, but, then again, he didn't have to. Thirty-nine-year-old Robbie McEwen, on the other hand, accepts it readily, because he's a little bit older and wiser.

I still take satisfaction in what I do. If I set my goals realistically and can still achieve them, then that's enough. When I was younger, I was winning 20 or 30 races in a year. In 2010, I won two. But they were two good wins, and with a bit of luck or different circumstances I could have won a few more.

Just as Zabel and Cipollini were starting to decline just after I hit my peak, now I'm finding myself up against fast, hungry young sprinters. I love beating them – there's life in the old dog yet – but I can't be the same sprinter I was ten years ago. It's better the decline has happened to me at 38 than 28 – I've had a good run. I was a late developer anyway. I didn't really start dominating until I was 29 or 30, and I maintained that level pretty much up to when I had my accident. I'm not as explosive as I once was, but then again, at my peak, I was the most explosive sprinter in the world. Even now, there aren't many riders who can follow me on my first jump. I'm still faster than 99 per cent of the peloton.

But I still like training. I still like racing. I still love winning. When I stop liking these things, it will be time to stop.

I recognise that nothing is going to replace the feeling I get from winning. I've never been one to get excited about a fourth place. Nobody remembers who didn't win a sprint. Retiring riders always say that they want to be equally successful in their next career, whatever it may be, but apart from having children (which I think I'm done with) I cannot imagine anything giving me the same rush and intensity as winning does.

A business deal doesn't happen in the space of 30 seconds like a sprint does. When you clinch a deal, you don't raise your arms in the air and shout 'Yeeeeeaaaaasssss!' as I have been known to do when I've won a sprint. People don't run over and hug you after a deal. You don't get journalists huddling around you ten seconds afterwards. There's nothing in life like winning.

That's why it's probably a good thing that I'm steadily winning a little less as my career heads towards its sunset. I'm weaning myself off winning gradually. For that reason, I've never under-stood people who want to go out at the top. If you win your last race, you can win another – why deny yourself the pleasure? Lance Armstrong won his last Tour in 2005 and stopped. Then he came back a few years later, because he had an itch that he couldn't scratch.

You see a lot of ex-professionals who never got over their careers, and I've got no plans whatsoever to be one of them. Other guys I've known who have retired have told me that, when the moment comes, be sure. Otherwise, you just end up talking about it a lot, pining for it, and the next thing you know you're entering triathlons.

I'm insuring myself against being the boring guy at the end

of the bar telling anyone who'll listen that it was different in my day, and that if I was still riding I'd kick the young riders' arses, by riding as long as I can while I'm still enjoying it. I hope to accept my retirement and say, 'Yes, I was bloody good in my day. But that was my day, and it was great fun, but it's over.' As I write this, I know I can still win races, but I know that the moment will come when I stop believing I can win, and I'll have to accept that it's over. But I want to be sure, because a professional cyclist is a long time retired.

I'm going to miss being physically strong, however. I know I'm going to go out riding and struggle up Springbrook, and get nostalgic about cruising up in a big gear. But that will be fine. Instead of dragging myself out of bed in the mornings and dreading flogging myself in training again, many days I won't feel like cycling. No more interval training. I'll wake up in the morning, and if I feel like going for a ride I will. But I might not be able to because I'm playing golf. Or the surf might look particularly good. Sorry, bike.

I own a coffee shop on the Gold Coast. It was my favourite coffee shop, in a great location, and when it came up for sale a few years ago I thought I should own it. At the moment, my dad is managing it, and he's doing a great job because the customers love him. I'm not going to run it as a full-time job, but I'll poke my head in and keep an eye on it. I've also got an interest in a development company erecting industrial buildings.

And, of course, I'm going to stay involved with cycling in some way. I've got a lot of knowledge, and I think it should be passed on in some capacity to younger riders who'd benefit from my experience. I'm not going to be a team manager, sitting in a team car on my fat backside for 200 days a year, but I want to stay connected to the sport. But I'm very conscious that I've got far more out of cycling than I could ever put back in.

There's nothing complicated about my life and career. I've won a lot of races through a combination of talent and hard work, but, when it comes to cycling, I've nearly used up my reserves of both. Nearly.

Major Professional Results

Overview

Over 200 career victories

Three-time green-jersey winner,
Tour de France

Winner of 12 Tour de France
stages

Winner of 12 Giro d'Italia
stages

Four-time Australian Criterium
Champion

Six-time overall winner of the
Jayco Bay Series

Winner of 113 professional
bike races

Winner of at least one race a year
from 1996 to 2011

1996 – Rabobank

NINE WINS

Tour of Murcia, stage four

Regio Tour, stage three (b)

Rheinland Pfalz Rundfahrt,
stage two

Wien–Rabenstein–Wien,
stage one

Lük Cup

Tour de l'Avenir, stage four

Herald Sun Tour, stage two

Herald Sun Tour, stage 11

Herald Sun Tour, stage 14

1997 – Rabobank

FOUR WINS
Four Days of Dunkirk, stage two
Tour of Luxembourg,
    stage three (a)
Tour of Holland, stage two
Tour of Holland, stage three

1998 – Rabobank

THREE WINS
Ruta del Sol, stage one
Tour of Holland, stage three
Tour of Holland, stage six

1999 – Rabobank

SIX WINS
Tour of Luxembourg,
    stage two
Route du Sud, stage one (a)
Tour de France, stage 20
Tour of Holland, stage two
Herald Sun Tour, stage two (b)
Herald Sun Tour, stage four

2000 – Farm Frites

TWO WINS
Tour Down Under, stage six
Trofeo Soller

OTHER MAJOR RESULTS
Runner-up, Tour de France
    green-jersey classification

2001 – Domo-Farm Frites

NINE WINS
Trofeo Palmanova
Tour of the Mediterranean,
    stage two
Circuit du Brabant Wallon
Uniqa Classic, stage two
Uniqa Classic, stage three
Tour of Wallonia, stage four
Tour of Holland, stage two
Herald Sun Tour, stage two (b)
Herald Sun Tour, stage three (a)

2002 – Lotto-Adecco

NINETEEN WINS

Australian national championships
  road race
Tour Down Under, stage one
Tour Down Under, stage three
Tour Down Under, stage four
Tour Down Under, stage six
Tour Down Under, points
  classification
Étoile de Bessèges, stage one
Étoile de Bessèges, overall
Paris–Nice, stage two
Paris–Nice, stage seven
Scheldeprijs
Giro d'Italia, stage four
Giro d'Italia, stage ten
Tour de France, stage three
Tour de France, stage 20
Tour de France, green-jersey
  classification
Delta Profronde
Paris–Brussels
Circuit Franco-Belge, stage two
Circuit Franco-Belge, stage three
Circuit Franco-Belge, overall

OTHER MAJOR RESULTS

Runner-up, world road race
  championships

2003 – Lotto-Domo

SEVEN WINS

Tour Down Under, stage three
Étoile de Bessèges, stage four
Dwars door Vlaanderen
Giro d'Italia, stage four
Giro d'Italia, stage 11
Tour of Switzerland, stage two
Circuit Franco-Belge, stage three

OTHER MAJOR RESULTS

Runner-up, Tour de France
  green-jersey classification

2004 – Lotto-Domo

EIGHT WINS

Tour Down Under, stage one
Tour Down Under,
  stage four
Tour Down Under, points
  classification
Memorial Samyn

Giro d'Italia, stage five

Tour of Switzerland, stage two

Tour of Switzerland, stage four

Tour de France, stage two

Tour de France, stage nine

Tour de France, green-jersey
classification

OTHER MAJOR RESULTS

Runner-up, Tour Down Under,
overall

Runner-up, Scheldeprijs

One day in the Tour de France
yellow jersey (race leader)

2005 – Davitamon-Lotto

SIXTEEN WINS

Australian national
championships road race

Tour Down Under, stage one

Tour Down Under, stage two

Tour Down Under, stage six

Tour Down Under, points
classification

Tour of Qatar, stage five

Niedersachsen Rundfahrt,
stage two

Giro d'Italia, stage two

Giro d'Italia, stage six

Giro d'Italia, stage ten

Tour of Switzerland,
stage four

Tour de France, stage five

Tour de France, stage seven

Tour de France, stage 13

GP Stad Geraardsbergen

Paris–Brussels

GP de Fourmies

OTHER MAJOR RESULTS

One day in the Giro d'Italia
pink jersey (race leader)

Third place, Tour de France
green-jersey classification

Fifth place, world road race
championships

2006 – Davitamon-Lotto

TWELVE WINS

GP Costa Azul, stage one

GP Costa Azul, overall

Three Days of West Flanders,
stage two

Tour of Romandy, stage one

Giro d'Italia, stage two

Giro d'Italia, stage four

Giro d'Italia, stage six

Tour de France, stage two

Tour de France, stage four

Tour de France, stage six

Tour de France, green-jersey
classification

Paris–Brussels

Herald Sun Tour, stage seven

OTHER MAJOR RESULTS

Third place, Tour Down Under,
overall

2007 – Predictor-Lotto

EIGHT WINS

Tour Down Under, stage five

Tirreno–Adriatico, stage one

Tour of Romandy, stage two

Giro d'Italia, stage two

Tour of Switzerland, stage four

Tour de France, stage one

Eneco Tour, stage three

Paris–Brussels

OTHER MAJOR RESULTS

Fourth place, Milan–San Remo

Runner-up, Scheldeprijs

2008 – Silence-Lotto

FIVE WINS

Tour of Romandy, stage two

Tour of Switzerland, stage three

Tour of Switzerland, stage four

Vattenfall Cyclassics – Hamburg

Paris–Brussels

OTHER MAJOR RESULTS

Third place, Scheldeprijs

2009 – Katusha

TWO WINS

Trofeo Cala Millor

Tour of Picardy, stage three

2010 – Katusha

TWO WINS

Trofeo Mallorca

Eneco Tour, stage one

OTHER MAJOR RESULTS

Fourth place, Tour Down Under,
overall

Runner-up, Scheldeprijs

2011 – RadioShack

ONE WIN
Tour of Wallonia, stage four

OTHER MAJOR RESULTS
Runner-up, Giro d'Italia team
   time trial

Acknowledgements

I would like to give my special thanks to the following people.

My wife, Angélique; my kids, Ewan, Elena and Claudia; my parents, Ken and Jacki; my brothers, Ross and Cameron; my parents-in-law, Walther and Frida; my friends and teammates Nick Gates, Jason Phillips, Craig Cahill, Aart Vierhouten, Hans De Clercq, Gert Steegmans, Henk Vogels, Mario Aerts, Johan Vansummeren, Bob Panter, Peter Day, Heiko Salzwedel, Brian Stephens, Christophe Brandt and Wim Vansevenant; my physio Victor Popov; my genius chiropractor Stefan Meersemann; motorpacer Etienne Sobrie; supporter-number-one Pascal Van Cauwenberghe; my surgeon Håkan Alfredson; my personal sponsors Oakley, SIDI, Jayco, ATS and BMW; all sponsors who support cycling; and, of course, all the dedicated team staff with whom I've ever had the benefit of working.

Robbie McEwen

Index

Abdoujaparov, Djamolidine 9, 40,
    47–9, 64, 121
accidents and crashes 1–2, 33,
    85–6, 98, 104–5, 112, 118,
    127–8, 144–5, 172–3, 176–81,
    232–3, 255, 266, 269–71,
    283, 288, 291, 296, 299
Acqua e Sapone 136, 198–9
adrenalin 10, 66, 86, 87, 145, 163,
    224
Aebersold, Niki 51
Aerts, Mario 5, 123, 124, 216,
    219–23, 226–7, 242, 256,
    259
Aitken, Brett 22, 31, 208
Albertville 147
alcohol 17, 22, 31, 37, 41, 46, 53,
    61, 62, 70, 93, 212, 216–17,
    226
Aldag, Rolf 130
Alfredson, Håkan 276

Alps 128, 146, 151, 170, 218, 221,
    239, 249, 292–3
altitude training 32, 36, 61
ambition 5, 44, 45, 77, 79, 167,
    210, 218, 226, 240, 253,
    262, 288
ambushes 46, 202, 241
Amstel Gold 91
Anderson, Michael 46
Anderson, Phil 191
anger and aggression 5, 47, 53–4,
    56–7, 86, 89, 119, 138, 145,
    163, 183, 213, 237, 291
Angers 178–9
anti-doping contract 264–5
Armstrong, Lance 47, 55, 79,
    127–8, 131–2, 152, 172–3,
    223, 254, 296, 308, 313
Aspin 295–7
Australian character 186–8
Australian Cycling Federation 188

Australian Institute of Sport (AIS)
26–7, 29–34, 36, 45–6, 191,
201, 208
Australian National
Championships (BMX)
15–16
Australian National
Championships (road cycling)
113, 193, 225

Bäckstedt, Magnus 160
Baguet, Serge 124, 183
Baker, Darren 68
Ballerini, Franco 63
Bannan, Shayne 301–2
Baranowski, Dariusz 42
barrage 5
Bartoli, Michele 117
Basso, Ivan 284
Bay Series 103, 113
Bayliss, Troy 311
Belgium 70–2, 102, 138, 153, 164,
167, 171, 186–7, 216, 220,
228, 232, 288–9
Bennati, Daniele 4, 121, 238, 282
Bertogliati, Rubens 123
Bettini, Paolo 19, 27, 189, 202,
226, 241, 242, 265–6
Bicicleta Vizcaya Bira 26

Big Mat team 38, 44–6
Blijlevens, Jeroen 64, 65, 77, 79,
90, 91
BMC team 306
BMX 12–17, 25, 35, 101, 127,
154, 159–60, 198, 269,
302
Boasson Hagen, Edvald 301
bodybuilding 17
Bölts, Udo 85
Boogerd, Michael 81–2, 226
Boom, Lars 294
Boonen, Tom 4, 162, 194–5, 204,
206–7, 212–13, 227, 231–2,
238–9, 240, 244, 248–9,
282, 283
Bordeaux 83, 84, 88, 151
Botcharov, Alexandre 118
Bourg d'Oisans 146
Bourg-en-Bresse 129
Braeckevelt, Jef 115, 116, 117, 133
Brakel 71–3
Brandt, Christophe 199, 220,
223, 226
breakaways 37, 41, 42, 43, 56, 68,
77, 81–3, 106, 113, 117, 123,
125, 127, 129, 140, 152–3,
164, 169, 170, 181, 182, 189,
194, 204, 217–18, 221–3,
258, 259, 266

Breschel, Matti 269

Breukink, Erik 79

Brisbane 10–11, 70

Brittany 127, 181, 183

Brown, Graeme 103, 189

Brozyna, Tomasz 42

Bruyneel, Johan 308

bunch 6, 7, 25, 49, 68, 81, 86, 127,
  145, 163, 170, 182, 200, 217,
  222, 235, 270, 283, 289
  riding the 1, 4, 5, 55, 63, 78,
    111, 136–7, 162, 194–5, 233,
    254
  sprint 48, 104, 105, 106, 126,
    137–8, 153, 160, 200, 211,
    225, 263, 282, 284

Caen 236–7

Cancellara, Fabian 55, 169, 170,
  172–4, 225, 289

Cancer Council Classic 263, 279

Canterbury 2–8, 244, 246–7, 248

Casar, Sandy 149, 150

Casper, Jimmy 231

Cavendish, Mark 9, 65, 79, 121,
  135, 225, 245–6, 255, 290,
  297

Championship of Zurich 51

Champs-Élysées 75, 84, 86, 98,

131, 132, 143, 153, 155, 163,
  184, 239, 246, 298

Chandler Velodrome 16, 18, 20

Chartres 160, 177

Chavanel, Sylvain 223–4

cheating 95–6

Chicchi, Francesco 301

Ciolek, Gerald 255

Cioni, Dario 5

Cipollini, Mario 9, 62–3, 77, 79,
  82, 119–20, 121, 144, 160,
  166, 169, 170, 194–5, 197,
  225, 242, 246, 312
  sprinting 135–42, 211, 212, 301

Cipressa 280

Classic Haribo 183

Classics 27, 77, 79, 82, 92, 108,
  139, 172, 183, 210–12, 217,
  250, 263, 265, 278, 282, 283,
  307

climbing 19, 39, 55, 68, 69, 88,
  104, 116–18, 122, 128, 129,
  146–8, 150, 151, 159, 221,
  226, 232, 240–1, 247, 249,
  252, 254, 280, 287, 292–5,
  301

coaches 23–4, 29–30, 37, 301–2

Col d'Aubisque 126–8, 295, 297

Col de la Colombière 249

Col de Peyresourde 295, 296

Col d'Izoard 147, 148

Col des Saisies 147

Col du Lautaret 146–7

Collstrop team 50

Colom, Toni 263–4

Columbia team 135, 255, 306

Commonwealth Bank Classic
37, 46

Commonwealth Games 188

competitiveness 9–10, 13, 35–6,
53–4, 67, 135–6, 142, 163,
210

constant passive movement (CPM)
machine 273

contact 57–8, 140–1, 155–6,
163–4, 168, 198, 207–8,
224, 231–2

Contador, Alberto 250, 296

convoy 5, 50, 235, 278, 282

Cooke, Baden 132, 144–5,
151–6, 163, 177, 187, 189,
251

corners 8, 55–6, 124, 152, 198,
224, 245
BMX 13–14, 159

Cottbus 40–1, 46, 48

Coucke, Marc 192, 224

Courchevel 146, 218

cow 183

Crake, Paul 193

Crédit Lyonnais lions 174

cricket 10, 22, 30

Criquielion, Claude 115, 125–6

criteriums 25, 36, 61, 103, 113,
133, 150, 152, 184, 185, 209,
239, 263, 274, 275, 279, 300

cycling 21–2, 42, 71, 111, 127,
132, 149, 163, 198, 273, 287,
310–11
Australian 187–8, 305

Da Cruz, Carlos 153–4, 222

Damiani, Roberto 258–9, 265

Davis, Allan 259, 301–2

Davitamon 192

Davitamon-Lotto team 192–3,
202–3 see also Lotto team

Day, Peter 26, 36, 37

De Clerq, Hans 124

De Rooy, Theo 70, 77, 79, 82, 84,
88–9

Dean, Julian 182, 202

deep, going 182, 218–19, 287

Dekker, Erik 26, 233

Deutschland Tour 258

di Grosseto, Marina 202

Di Luca, Danilo 247

diet 30

Discovery team 223

disqualifications 65–7, 96, 122,
    177, 208, 211, 225
Doha 194
domestiques 88, 191, 217, 218,
    254–5, 259
Domina Vacanze 136
Domo team 99–100, 104, 106–7,
    113, 117
drift 55, 66, 153, 241
dropped, being 24, 33, 42, 46, 68,
    88, 94, 95, 97, 118, 124, 128,
    129, 144, 146, 147, 150, 168,
    170, 172, 218, 219, 223, 231,
    249, 259, 266, 293–5
drugs and doping 78, 88, 252,
    264–5, 305

Eisel, Bernie 7, 297
Ekimov, Viatcheslav 79, 173
endurance 14
Eneco Tour 9, 250, 300, 312
energy 53–6, 80, 120, 138, 141,
    163, 200, 218, 232, 233,
    255–6, 259, 285–6
equipment 21, 115, 263
Étoile de Bessèges 116, 118
Evans, Cadel 5, 190, 192–3, 219,
    223, 225, 230, 252–60,
    280, 301

Fagnini, Gian Matteo 130, 137
family 11–12, 73–5, 101, 158–62
Farm Frites team 89–90, 91, 93–4,
    99, 102, 113
Farrar, Tyler 121, 294
Fassa Bortolo team 167, 202–3
fatherhood 74–5, 273, 313
fatigue 83, 110, 169, 197, 219,
    285–7, 290
Fédrigo, Pierrick 148
Ferretti, Giancarlo 145
Flecha, Juan Antonio 222
Flèche Wallonne 219
Florenico, Xavier 241
Fly V team 304–5, 306
focus 5–7, 19, 47, 53–4, 56, 57,
    59–60, 87, 112, 124, 155,
    163, 170, 311
form 39, 62, 74, 83, 89, 94, 99,
    103, 104, 105, 108–9, 113–16,
    122, 143–4, 156, 167, 177,
    196, 197, 202, 204, 213, 226,
    230–1, 240, 244, 247, 250,
    258, 267, 279, 299
Française des Jeux team 153
Fraser, Gord 65
Freire, Óscar 9, 121, 123, 231,
    232, 239, 281, 282
friendships 19, 201–2, 216
Frison, Herman 234, 257

Gap 146–8, 150–1, 293

gaps 6, 8, 56, 58, 124, 130, 136,
    163, 171, 182, 203, 207,
    214, 241, 242

Garmin team 306

Gates, Nick 38, 47, 134, 148–50,
    199–201, 259, 311

Gerolsteiner team 178, 222

Gerrans, Simon 193

Ghent 229, 248

Ghent–Wevelgem 93, 105, 108,
    271

Giant 38

Gillett, George Jnr 305–7

Giro d'Italia 38, 47, 94, 95, 115,
    119–20, 142, 144, 166–7,
    190, 196–9, 201–2, 225,
    228–9, 230, 238, 245, 247,
    248, 250, 253, 259, 261,
    267–8, 277, 283, 287
  Prologue 228, 229

goals, setting 23

Golden West Tour (Qld) 25

GP Etruschi 62–3

Grabsch, Bert 294

Grand Prix Fourmies 225

Grand Tour 74, 75, 80, 91, 95,
    109, 133, 164, 196, 197,
    204, 247–8, 250, 255, 307

green jersey 64, 68, 74–6, 97,
    122–34, 143–57, 166, 167,
    171–3, 174, 177–9, 182–4,
    190, 193, 197, 205, 208, 210,
    212, 225, 228, 232, 239,
    246, 250, 252, 258, 290

Greipel, André 15, 280–1

Grillo, Paride 203

gruppetto 95, 146, 147, 295

Guidi, Fabrizio 63, 67

Hall, Jonathan 38, 47

Hamburg 211, 258

Hamburg Classic 211

handicap races 21–2

Hanegraaf, Jacques 91–3, 97, 99

Harelbeke 93

Haselbacher, René 178–9

headwind 149, 237, 265

Henderson, Greg 280–1

Hérve, Cédric 249

Hespel, Dr Peter 103

Het Nieuwsblad *see* Het Volk

Het Volk 92, 228, 229, 250

Hinault, Bernard 183

Hincapie, George 173

hip on the handlebars trick 58,
    137–8, 140–1, 163

Holland 43, 73, 78–9, 89, 98, 219,
    228–9, 287

Horner, Chris 5, 222, 223–4, 230

Hoste, Leif 5, 6

Hotel des Pyrénées 215–16, 256

HTC-Columbia team 281, 301

Hunt, Jeremy 251

Hunter, Robbie 7, 306

Hushovd, Thor 9, 121, 169–72, 181–2, 184, 204, 225, 231, 238, 239, 290, 302

Hutarovich, Yauheni 301

illness 93–4, 99, 266–7, 290–1

injuries 3, 33, 61–2, 81–2, 98, 104–6, 153, 176–7, 182, 248–50, 269–70, 288–90, 300, 302

  fracture of transverse process 180–5, 269

  knee (2009) 270–7

inner bastard 19, 36, 53, 54, 164

International Cycling Union 229

intervals 12, 30, 47, 314

Itera 262, 263

Ivanov, Serguei 93, 268

Jalabert, Laurent 117–18, 128

Jarno, Frank 48

Jekyll and Hyde 53, 165

Jonker, Pat 82, 83

jumps

  BMX 12, 14–15, 164, 269, 302

  race tactics 8, 25, 48, 51, 59, 63, 119, 130–1, 135–7, 154, 170, 204, 207, 212, 224, 233, 236, 255, 301, 312

Kappes, Andreas 68

Katusha team 261–8, 274, 276–7, 281, 282, 302–3, 306

Kazakh team 39

kermesse race 98

King Albert (Belgium) 171

Kingston, Brisbane 11

Kirchen, Kim 304

Kirsipuu, Jaan 57, 169–70, 173, 202–4

Knees, Christian 306

Konyshev, Dimitri 69, 298

Koppenberg 283

Kroon, Karsten 293

Lampre team 4, 5, 222, 223

Lancaster, Brett 203

Landis, Floyd 127, 218, 252

leadouts 1, 77, 78, 130, 136, 137,

142, 151, 173, 192, 194, 195, 198, 202–4, 225, 231, 233, 236, 239, 248, 252–5, 263, 301

Lefevre, Patrick 99–100, 102–8, 113, 115, 192

Leipheimer, Levi 237

Leysen, Bart 271

Liquigas team 224, 301

Lombardi, Giovanni 119–20, 138, 141

Lotto team 106, 109, 112–16, 118, 123, 133, 135, 163, 171, 174, 183, 190–2, 201, 215–27, 228–9, 231, 239–40, 252–60, 265, 303

Lotto-Domo team 143, 192

Ludwig, Olaf 67–8

Lük Cup 68

Luxembourg 67, 82, 123, 231, 296, 304

Lyon 144–5, 177

Madrid 108, 225, 226, 240

Makarov, Igor 262, 263, 274

Manx team 9

Mapei team 98, 100

Marseille 151

Martin, Kelvin 38

mateship 45–7, 273, 305

Mattan, Nico 226

Mayo, Iban 173

McDonald, Damien 38

McEwen, Angélique 70–5, 87, 116, 174, 228–31, 274

McEwen, Cameron 11–12, 16

McEwen, Claudia 73, 230

McEwen, Elena 73, 229–30

McEwen, Ewan 73–5, 164, 174, 187, 228–9, 302

McEwen, Ross 11–12, 16

McGee, Brad 151, 153–4, 225

McKenzie, David 38, 42

McLachlan, Robert 193

media 84, 87–8, 107–8, 148, 168, 188, 232, 244, 257, 274–5, 289, 291, 297

memory 58, 160, 161

Mende 293–4

Merckx, Axel 107, 189

Merckx, Eddy 171

Mexico 32, 36

Mikhailov, Guennadi 130–1

Milan–San Remo 211, 250, 280, 281–2

Millar, David 242

Milram team 230, 247

Monaco 274

money 38, 51, 74, 81, 100, 101–2,

133–4, 193, 239–40, 250–1, 262, 306–8
  anti-doping fine 264–5
  bonuses 250–1, 253, 308
  post-Tour 150–1, 300
Mont Faron 116–17
Montargis 213
Montpellier 221, 225
morale 3, 5, 82–3, 95, 108–9, 145, 302, 306
Morzine 147
Motorola team 47
Museeuw, Johan 104

Napolitano, Danilo 138, 249
Nazon, Jean-Patrick 155, 173
Nelissen, Wilfried 271
nerves 13, 129, 231, 299–300
Nibali, Vincenzo 284
Norton Summit 30
Novell team 49–50

O'Grady, Stuart 22, 31, 32, 64, 65, 83, 103, 160, 169, 177, 179, 181–2, 187, 189, 193, 205, 206–14, 231, 242
  2005 Tour de France 205–8, 211–12, 224

Olympia's Tour 43
Olympic Games 188, 208
  Athens (2004) 189
  Atlanta (1996) 34, 73
  Barcelona (1992) 26
  Sydney (2000) 98–9
Omega Pharma Company 192, 244
O'Neill, Nathan 113
Ousse 215, 256
Outschakov, Serguei 287

Panaria team 203
Panasonic team 88
Panter, Bob 23–4, 26
parents 11, 158–62, 187, 314
Paris–Brussels 225, 250, 260
Paris–Nice 81, 104, 118, 133, 250, 264
Paris–Roubaix 172, 211, 218, 282
Paris–Tours 139, 160, 250
Parsani, Serge 265–7, 277, 281–2
Pau 126, 215, 256, 295
Paulinho, Sérgio 189
Peace Race (Czech Republic) 41, 42
Pegasus Racing 307
Pegasus Sports 307
Pegasus team 305–8
Peiper, Allan 163, 190–1, 193

peloton 1, 3, 6, 7, 21, 55–6, 58,
    86, 11, 117, 124, 128, 130,
    136, 137, 164, 170, 172,
    187–8, 194–5, 216, 218–19,
    223, 232, 234–5, 241, 294,
    302, 303, 305, 312
  surfing the 196–205
Peschel, Uwe 42
Pescheux, Jean-François 289, 293
Petacchi, Alessandro 58, 65, 121,
    144–5, 150, 156, 160, 166,
    167, 169, 170, 190, 199,
    202–4, 225, 230, 244,
    247–8, 282, 290
  sprinting 135–7, 138, 141, 211,
    212, 301
Pfannberger, Christian 264
pink jersey 202, 267
Planckaert, Walter 114, 133–4, 229
Plant, Mike 48
Poggio 280, 282
points 32, 122–3, 125, 128–9, 144,
    153, 156, 177, 179, 184, 278,
    289–90
Popov, Victor 176–85, 189, 248,
    273, 275–6, 279
Post, Peter 88–9
Postgirot Open 49
Pozzato, Filippo 265–7, 282–4
Predictor-Lotto team 5, 244, 248

pressure 13, 54, 71, 106, 133,
    162–3, 169, 173, 183, 213,
    233
Priem, Cees 90, 91
prizes 45, 48–9, 113, 150, 183, 193
professional cycling 40, 44–5,
    50–1, 61–2, 70–1, 74, 80, 90,
    110–13, 209, 216, 311, 313
psychology 14, 31, 53, 152–3, 172
pursuit cycling 30, 208
Pyrenees 126, 151, 153, 170,
    215–16, 221–2, 225, 239,
    256, 293, 295

Queensland Academy of Sport
    (QAS) 26, 36, 176
Queensland State Championships
    12–14, 36
Quick Step team 4, 5, 192, 212,
    223, 240

Raas, Jan 49–50, 51, 66, 68–9, 70,
    77, 80
Rabobank team 51, 55, 61–2, 70,
    76–9, 81–9, 96, 105, 113,
    146, 168–9, 192, 226, 287
RadioShack team 105, 308
rainbow jersey 139

Rasmussen, Michael 249

Rebellin, Davide 117, 247

Redant, Hendrik 106, 222, 306

Regio Tour 73

rehab 273–7, 279

Reims 124–5

Relax-Bodysol team 192

Renshaw, Mark 103, 259

Rheinland Pfalz Tour 67

Riccò, Riccardo 305

Rich, Michael 41

road cycling 37–9

    phases of a race 54–60

Rodriguez, Fred 1, 5, 192, 195,
      206–7, 223–4, 231–3, 240–3,
      245

Rodriguez, Joaquim 293

Roelandts, Jurgen 293

Rogers, Michael 189

Rogers, Pete 38, 40

Rominger, Tony 47

Route du Sud 82

routes 2–3, 245, 251, 266

routine 115–16

Russian cycling 261, 303–4

Ruta del Sol 93

Saeco team 62–3, 135–6

Salzburg 240, 242

Salzwedel, Heiko 29, 37, 40–2,
    47, 246

San Dona 198–9

Sánchez, Sammy 241

Sastre, Carlos 255–6

Scheldeprijs 65, 118, 245, 266

Schleck, Andy 296

Sercu, Christophe 109, 112,
    114, 133–4

Sergeant, Marc 190, 192

Serov, Alexander 303

Setmana Catalana 65

sewerage works track 22–3

shotgun, riding 25

Silence-Lotto team 253, 258–60,
    261, 265, 266, 293 *see also*
    Lotto team

Skil team 164

Sky team 280–1

slipstream 6, 8, 154, 155, 207, 236,
    256

Smith, Darren 18, 19–28, 29, 37

soigneur (team helper) 41, 74, 229

Sørensen, Rolf 55, 79

Springbrook 310, 314

sprinting 9, 20, 31, 39, 45, 48, 49,
    51, 52–60, 62, 68, 76–7, 79,
    94, 96, 103–4, 111, 116, 119,
    121, 130–2, 135–42, 145,
    153, 162, 170, 183–4, 207,

209–10, 238, 244, 253, 265, 267, 281, 290–1, 300–1, 312

dangerous 66–7, 138

Steegmans, Gert 'Steggles' 230, 233–40, 246, 248, 255, 263, 265, 308

Steels, Tom 9, 83, 121

storytelling 160–1

Strasbourg 119, 197, 231, 197, 231

Strazzer, Massimo 48

strength 30, 31, 38, 114, 146, 210, 283, 312

stress 89, 112, 129, 131, 133, 151, 162–3, 168–9, 171, 213, 219

SunTour 109

Surfers Paradise Cycling Club 20, 22

surfing 17, 199–201, 314

Svorada, Ján 64, 65, 77

Sweet, Jay 38

tactics 14–15, 25, 62–3, 77, 81, 89, 114, 125, 128, 135–7, 140, 159, 161, 169, 177, 193, 199, 204, 237, 241, 283, 296, 304

Tafi, Andrea 63

Tchmil, Andrei 262–5, 274, 276–7, 278, 283, 303–4

team-car order 278, 282

team harmony 192–3, 257–8, 264–5, 283

team managers 84, 88, 89, 103, 106, 114, 118, 133, 145, 163, 222, 234, 257, 258

team riding 26, 56, 77–8, 79, 82–3, 114, 119–20, 126–7, 130, 140, 194–5, 199–200, 215–21, 226–7, 254–5, 257–8, 266, 281, 283–4, 293

technology 188

Teleflex Tour 65–7

Telekom team 128, 130, 190

Teutenberg, Sven 66

Thomson, David 20–1

Three Days of West Flanders 269

Tignes 145, 249

time trials 19, 108, 125, 136, 153, 176, 174, 176, 255, 266, 267, 280

Tinkoff, Oleg 261–3

Tinkoff Credit Systems team 261, 306

Tirreno–Adriatico 94, 237, 244, 250, 270, 282

toilet stops 49–50, 159, 234–5

Tour de France 37, 39, 55, 64, 68–9, 75, 76–8, 82, 92, 106–7, 109, 115, 117, 120, 122, 167–9, 193, 196–7, 235,

244, 256, 260, 275, 282,
285–7, 297, 299–300
1991 40, 191
1996 67, 105
1997 81, 146
1998 78, 81
1999 82–7, 197
2000 97–8, 147
2001 105–7
2002 122–32, 197
2003 143–57, 163, 166, 197
2004 160, 177, 189, 197, 269
2005 197, 204, 206–14, 221–5
2006 197, 218, 228, 231–9, 243,
246, 252
2007 2, 123, 145, 240, 244,
246–7
2008 253–5
2009 265, 277
2010 287–98, 299
GC 106, 107, 168, 209, 250
mountains 82, 89, 92, 95–7, 106,
116, 122, 127, 145–9, 151,
215, 218–19, 221, 230, 249,
254, 292–3, 295–7
points 122–3, 125, 128–9, 144,
153, 156, 177, 179, 184
Prologue 169, 274
Tour de l'Avenir 44, 50
Tour Down Under 93, 94, 104,

113–14, 116, 167, 244, 263,
277, 278–81, 300, 309
Tour du Haut Var 117, 118
Tour DuPont 47, 48–9
Tour of Belgium 9, 267–8, 270,
273
Tour of California 187
Tour of Denmark 67, 73
Tour of Flanders 71, 92, 172, 282,
283
Tour of Holland 73, 78–9, 89, 98,
287
Tour of Luxembourg 82
Tour of Mallorca 93, 104, 263, 281
Tour of the Mediterranean 64, 104,
116
Tour of Murcia 64, 246
Tour of Picardy 267–8
Tour of Poland 98, 250
Tour of Qatar 194, 236
Tour of Romandy 250, 266
Tour of Sweden *see* Postgirot Open
Tour of Switzerland 106, 190, 197,
204, 230, 250, 287, 304
Tour of Taiwan 10, 39
Tour of Wallonia 107, 309
Tourmalet 295, 297–8
Tours 206, 211
track cycling 18, 29–34, 36, 51,
207, 208

training 12, 14, 15–16, 21, 29, 32, 46, 65, 92–3, 94, 99, 103, 110, 113, 115, 159, 300, 304, 306, 310

transition stages 221, 293

Trevorrow, John 171

trivia 160

Trofeo Bunyola 263

Trofeo Cala Millor 263

Trofeo Mallorca 263, 299, 300

Tuft, Svein 306

Turpin, Ludovic 222

TVM team 89–90, 91

Ullrich, Jan 37, 130, 152, 287

Uniqa Classic 107

US Postal team 127–8, 172–3

Usov, Alexandre 195

Vacansoleil team 305

Vainsteins, Romans 105–7, 108

Valverde, Alejandro 241, 280

Van Bon, Léon 77, 78, 148–50

Van Bondt, Geert 93

Van Den Broeck, Jurgen 258–9

Van Houwelingen, Adri 77, 81–2, 84–6, 88–9

Van Huffel, Wim 258–9

Van Kessel, Miquel 95, 96

Van Petegem, Peter 92–3, 118, 198, 217, 225, 226–7, 242

Van Roosbroeck, Chris 50

Van Steen, Martin 95

Vansevenant, Wim 'Sevi' 5, 215–23, 226, 256

Vansummeren, Johan 'Summie' 3–5, 216, 218–20, 223

Vattenfall Cyclassics 258, 300

Ventoso, Francisco 7

Verbrugghe, Rik 123, 124

victory salute 237–8

Vierhouten, Aart 77, 78, 124, 170–1, 191, 192, 194

Vinokourov, Alexandre 39, 117–18, 225, 284

Vitré 238, 246

Viviani, Elia 301

Voeckler, Thomas 222, 284

Vogels, Henk 38, 47, 70, 190, 191, 199–201, 203, 209, 226, 306

Voigt, Jens 41–2, 46, 286, 296

Vuelta a España 47, 89, 90, 108

Walsh, Charlie 29–34, 36

Wauters, Marc 303

Wesemann, Steffen 130

West, Shane 13–14

White, Chris 304–7

White, Matt 189, 193

Willunga 280

winning 1, 9, 35–6, 40, 46, 50, 53, 54–5, 65, 74, 78, 114, 122, 130, 148, 159, 163–4, 173, 202, 213, 220, 245, 248, 263, 290, 299, 313–14

world championships 27, 31, 61, 105, 137–9, 142, 188, 190, 201, 225, 226, 232, 242, 280, 300, 301, 305

world championships (BMX) 16–17

yellow jersey 76, 106, 168, 170–3, 174, 190, 202, 218, 222, 232, 234, 252–3, 257, 289

Zabel, Erik 77, 79, 83, 86–7, 97, 104, 137, 140–2, 144, 146, 151, 152, 169, 173, 182, 231, 238, 239, 241, 242, 312

    2002 Tour de France 121–33, 210

Zabriskie, Dave 295

Zanini, Stefano 98, 148, 149

Zberg, Beat 83

Zberg, Markus 270

Zoetemelk, Joop 68–9, 88, 105

Zolder 138, 242